D1253608

Memories of
Books and Places

BRUGES

Frontis.

Memories of Books and Places

by

J. A. HAMMERTON

With 17 original sketches by
HESKETH HUBBARD

Essay Index Reprint Series

BOOKS FOR LIBRARIES PRESS
FREEPORT, NEW YORK

First Published 1928
Reprinted 1968

LIBRARY OF CONGRESS CATALOG CARD NUMBER:
68-57318

PRINTED IN THE UNITED STATES OF AMERICA

CONTENTS

v

LIST OF ILLUSTRATIONS

I

THE BOOK AND THE PLACE

To Arthur Mee

THE book and the place, I sing. Were I a 'modernist', and had I taken the advice which E. V. Lucas and C. L. Graves so delicately tendered by implication just nineteen years ago, when you and I were busy epitomising 'The World's Great Books':

> They tackled Mr. Henry James
>   Till tears stood in their ee,
> 'Look up the trains for Colney Hatch,'
>   Said Hammerton to Mee—

had I once penetrated that haven of the bereft, the hither side of whose portals I have since so often passed, I can imagine myself—gibbering from James Joyceism and maundering from Gertrude Steinitis—continuing thus:

> The book and the place
> The place and the book
> The book in the place
> The place in the book
> The book

The hook
The plaice
The plaice and the hook
The hook in the plaice
Hook!
Plaice!

Tell me, dear Arthur, if that sounds more or less maniacal than this brief excerpt from ' Madrigal & Mardigras ' by Gertrude Stein:

Place.   In a place,
A place for everything and everything in its
    place.
In place in place of everything, in a place.
Again search for me.
She looked for me at me.
May we seat
May we be having a seat
May we be seated.
May I see
May I see
Martha
May I see Martha
May I see.

That is a sample of a modernist poet, and God knows she says some true things.   Her second line has an old familiar ring of sanity, and I could tell Miss Gertrude the place which I think most suited to her ' pome ', as that other star of the moderns, James Joyce, would call it.   But I refrain.

A few days ago you were urging me to make a serious study of this strange new literature.   But how could one hope to be serious when the subject matter runs to such stuff as nightmares are made on: this, for example, from 'Opening Pages of a Work in Progress' by James Joyce?—

His clay feet, swarded in verdigrass, stick up starck where he last fellonem, by the mund of the magazine wall, where our maggy seen all, with her sister-in shawl. While over against this belles' alliance beyind Ill Sixty, ollollowed ill! bagsides of the fort, bom, tarabom, taraarabom, lurk the ombushes, the site of the lyffing-in-wait of the upjock and hockums. Hence when the clouds roll by, jamey, a proudseye view is enjoyable of our mounding's mass, now Wallinstone national museum, with, in some greenish distance, the charmful waterloose country and they two quitewhite villagettes who hear show of themselves so gigglesomes minxt the follyages, the prettilees! Penetrators are permitted into the museomound, free. Welsh and the Paddy Patkinses, one shelenk. For her passkey supply to the janitrix, the mistress Kathe. Tip.

Or this?—

Stonewall Willingdone is an old maxy montrumeny. Lipoleums is nice hung bushellors. This is hiena hinnessy laughing alout at the Willingdone. This is lipsyg dooley krieging the funk from the hinnessy. This is the hinndoo Shimar Shin between the dooley boy and the hinnessy. Tip. This is the wixy old Willingdone picket up the half of the threefoiled hat of lipoleums fromoud of the bluddlefilth. This is the hinndoo waxing ranjymad for a bombshoob.

Or yet again such as we have here from the same threatening new work?—

How bootifull and how truetowife of her, when strengly forebidden, to steal our historic presents from the past postpropheticals so as to will make us all lordy heirs and lady-maidesses of a pretty nice kettle of fruit. She is livving in our midst of debt and laffing through all plores for us (her birth is uncontrollable), with a naperon for her mask and her sabboes kickin arias (so sair! so solly!) if yous ask me and I saack you. Hou! Hou!

I can imagine myself, after a course of Gertrude and James, and others who call themselves ' modernists ' or ' transitionists ', crouching in a dusky corner of a padded cell and gibbering:

> Book and place
> Replace book
> Rebook place
> Plays and books
> Books are played
> Plays are booked
> Gertrude says:
> ' Brown and white. The nigger and the night and
> mistaken for mean. I didn't mean to.
> I do read better there.'
> Can she mean here? Here in Colney!
> Hatch! Hatch!
> ' Hou! Hou!'

So I thank you kindly, Arthur, for the suggestion, but I had rather preserve my present modicum of sanity, and not until I am feeling superfluously strong shall I adventure farther into that weird and gloomsome jungle of modernist ' literachoor ' (*vide* Joyce) where these dread writers ' gyre and gimble in the wabe '. I might add, however, that I suspect ' Willingdone ' to be a modernist variant of ' Wellington ' and 'lipoleums' of 'Napoleon'. That this monstrous amorphous 'tosh' should be produced by a man who could strike such chords as he does in these lines:

I heard their young hearts crying
Loveward above the glancing oar
And heard the prairie grasses sighing:
No more, return no more!

and could write so great and sane a book as 'A Portrait of the Artist as a Young Man', is surely matter for mourning.

But touching the subject of books and places, just as I have rid my mind of 'mad wriggles' and their writers, I find Browning cropping up there with his

Never the time, and the place
And the loved one all together,

and I accept the challenge. For if 'the loved one' be a book, you will agree there is no such word as 'never' in the attainment of this ideal. The book-lover who sits amidst the treasures of his crowded shelves knows that the time and the place and the favourite book may, at his will, be joined, in happy union. Why, Solomon with all his concubines had a poorer chance of synchronising time, place and the loved one!

Most of our reading, I suppose, is done by our study fire-sides, or in bed. I had long been addicted to reading in bed, although doctors and other wise-acres used to warn me of the terrible consequences that might ensue. I have now forgotten what these were to be, but I know they have not yet appeared, and since that eminent surgeon, the late Sir Malcolm Morris, assured me about twenty-five years ago that most of his own reading was done in his bed, I have never listened to any contrary opinion. I must have read more than five thousand short stories in bed, and it was there that I first read through the whole of Gibbon and the twelve volumes of Frazer's ' Golden Bough '. Whenever I have taken up a large joyous task of reading, such as the Bible, Bury's ' Later Roman Empire ', Grote's ' Greece ', Hodgkin's ' Italy and her Invaders,' or any many-volumed work, it is thus I tackle it lying down, like Dr. John Brown's famous fighting dog that won all his battles lying on his back, as we are told in ' Horæ Subsecivæ '.

To become a well-read man one must first make sure of a comfortable bed with a cunningly placed light that shows a clear and unshadowed page held at the proper reading angle to the eye. Such reading hours as one may snatch in hammocks under trees, in deck chairs on verandahs, or by the ingle-neuk or at stretch on the library couch are precious and not to be despised, but give me the dozy hours when the house is quiet and nothing but the drowsy god can come between me and my bed-time book and ah! those excursions into the realms of gold.

In beds of all sorts, on land and sea, the world over—once in Mollendo, Peru, I had to use my bed-book to thin the ranks of the bed-bugs upon the wall—I have read myself to sleep or kept myself awake, for this manner of reading is curiously adaptable to either end. I can remember very clearly lying a-bed with one of the many ' Sherlock Holmes ' volumes in the Hotel de Jena at Paris in October, 1900, and reading therein ' The Speckled Band '. Nor have I forgotten how, when half-way through, I ' spotted ' the end of that story which I had heard was so ingeniously surprising. The moment that mention was made of placing a saucer— I think it was a saucer—of milk upon the top of a safe, I knew that ' the speckled band ' was a snake. For instantly there flashed into my mind a story I had read in one of Chambers's admired publications of my boyhood about an English child in India who disappeared from home every morning with a bowl of milk and was eventually found by her parents giving it to a deadly snake that came at that hour out of the undergrowth to meet her. A wonderful thing this mind of ours that stores such seemingly forgotten trifles for many years and switches the light of memory on to them at the one moment when they avail.

Again, I recall an odd experience of temper with a book written by one for whom I have a deep and grateful admiration: Eden Phillpotts. When staying in Buenos Ayres I had sent home for his newly published ' Widecombe Fair ' which had been so highly spoken of by the reviewers. He was then an established favourite of mine—' The Human Boy ', ' The Silent Woman ', ' The American Prisoner ' and many of his books I had read with enjoyment—

and had written of some with enthusiasm—including, I feel sure, ' The Good Red Earth ' which I cannot now trace to him, to say nothing of those early trifles ' Folly and Fresh Air ' and ' In Sugar Cane Land ', possibly still abiding in some of the remoter shelves of my library.   Phillpotts is not only a great writer, but he has written greatly, which some of our later and lesser geniuses do not dare to do lest they too quickly touch the lees of their talent.

Well, ' Widecombe Fair ' had to wait until I had got through some other reading I had in hand, but I remember that I started it at Antofagasta, a horrible Pacific port familiar I fancy to ' the bold bad mate of Henry Morgan ' as I am sure it is to John Masefield.   Most likely I turned to the book with its promise of intellectual joy as a relief from the deathly dullness of the place and when I took train thence to La Paz I was still fingering it hopefully; but I feel sure that it yielded me no pleasure, and I know that in the middle of the night as I still read on in my sleeping berth and felt no reaction of laughter—laughter of the mind, I mean—where the reviewers had promised me so much, I got up and, opening the window, threw ' Widecombe Fair ' as far as I could hurl it out upon the starlit desert of Atacama!   Yet I could not have my fill of ' The Farmer's Wife ' or ' Yellow Sands ', and both of these splendid comedies of Devon character exist, in essence, I am told, in ' Widecombe Fair '.   Perhaps here was a case where the time and the place and the book were not all together: the exception to prove the rule.

Yet the train is a good place for reading, and as one who has made much use of the motor car for many years I have often regretted the loss of reading hours involved, and welcomed a recent change of residence which has brought me back to many hours of undisturbed train journeys every week. But I despair of attaining the rapidity of the dear lady who once told me that she read ' The Egoist ' in a train journey between London and York. I suppose it took me about a month at least to read it in my bed-time hours. The great Victorians were lavish in their measure of words, and Meredith used close upon a quarter of a million to tell his story. Dick Turpin's ride was a poor performance by comparison with this lady's achievement on her ride to York. But there is reading *and* reading. I feel a perfect devil of a fellow when I've read ten thousand words of manuscript in an hour; and still I am only a snail to this dear lady, unless indeed she travelled at a distant date when it took twenty-five hours for the journey. She smiled so innocently when she told me of her achievement, and she was (and is still I trust) a very popular religious writer and editress.

I may be a mere faddist in this matter of associating books with places; but I derive a certain pleasure from it. Possibly I am not alone in this. A tenuous, ectoplasmic sort of pleasure it may be, but it endures, and if I gravely set my memory the task I could recall so many of these associations that I should probably end by boring you with their recital. Hence I shall hope to stay my hand in time. Yet, among bookmen, I think there is exhilaration in the exchange of experiences in these endless adventures of reading. I see myself a youth ' 'neath boughs of breathing may ' late in June or mid July (for the hawthorn flourishes later in Scotland than in the more genial south) lying on a hillside in Bute, and reading day after day through Hazlitt's ' Winterslow ', Lowell's ' My Study Windows ', and a selection of Addison's essays and Reynolds' ' Discourses on Art '. I recall no happier days than these; nor can I hope or wish for better. These were ' immortal ' days, in a double sense: one was spending the hours of adolescence with immortals, and does not Hazlitt say ' youth is immortal '? Nevertheless, if I were asked to name four books peculiarly suitable for reading ' beneath the bough ' I cannot imagine myself readily selecting these four. I suspect they were chosen by my youthful self on some quite irrational basis of selection, or just at random, and now, with forty years of reading superadded, I can suggest no better plan. I have always hated ' courses of reading ', or anything that tinges the most delightful of all human occupations with the sense of task-work.

Maeterlinck in ' The Life of the White Ant ' speculates upon the unknown, mysterious pleasures which a certain ant, the *Lasius Mixtus*, may derive from permitting two or three enormous parasitic lice to live upon its body, and the casual reader who picks up a book anywhere, peruses it and promptly

forgets all about book, place, and time, may wonder
what obscure pleasure I derive from circumstances
that appear to him hardly worthy remembering.
But I know that with you, my dear Arthur, and with
all bookish folk, I have an essential community of
interests; that in all matters of reading, be they great
or slight, we ' belong ' as the Americans say.   That
we shall agree in all things, I should be foolish to
expect and sorry if it were so.   The enduring profit
of human intercourse is born not of facile agreement,
but of discussion and the effort to reconcile differ-
ences of opinion.

If you bear me company through the nineteen
chapters of this book—for despite their superscriptions
they are addressed, of course, to you and to all who
find pleasure in talk of books just as much as this
particular chapter—you may have some new entertainment from these memories of book-reading and
bookish wanderings in many lands, although much
that is here printed you have had from me by word
of mouth in our *causeries* of more than thirty years.

The ' ports of origin ' of the different chapters
have been indicated, though they have all under-
gone later and severe revision at a desk remote, in
some instances, from that of their first writing.   The
relation of the book and the place is not always or
necessarily obvious.   Had I chosen to write only of
such associations as my reading of ' Pêcheur d'Islande '
during a stay at Paimpol, or of ' Le Tre Damme della
Kasbah ' picked up and read at Algiers, or of ' La
Montaña de las Brujas ' read amid its Andine scenes,

or of ' The Lady of the Lake ' while holidaying at
the Trossachs, or any of scores of such very obvious
collocations, I fear I should have failed of that more
natural variety which, I hope, is not absent from these
chapters that have been allowed such waywardness as
they seemed of themselves to demand.

A final word on the book and the place, of personal
application to you who have found and hold the
largest audience of young readers that any writer of
our generation could boast. A noble row of your
volumes stands on the shelves of my library devoted
to the books of my friends, and the other day, in a
house where I was visiting, I saw just such another
row, accumulated during the years of their youth by
three young people, of whom the youngest has just
passed her twenty-first year. You have been their
mentor, as you have been to scores of thousands.
Your whole immense literary product might be
labelled *Virginibus Puerisque* more happily than Stevenson's volume so christened; but it is R.L.S. who
supplies the most apt and delightful quotation touching
both book and place, for the life-work of which you
may be justly proud:

> How am I to sing your praise,
> Happy chimney-corner days,
> Sitting safe in nursery nooks,
> Reading picture story-books?

De Walden Lodge, Meads,
Eastbourne.

II

OF 'BRUGES-LA-MORTE' AND DREAMS

To R. H.

'WHEN we went a-gipsying, a long time ago ', taking the footpath-way through Belgium with bicycle and knapsack, there was no place in that land of storied towns to which our thoughts leant forward more eagerly than they did to Bruges; none that we have more often talked about in the after years. The atmosphere of drama that surrounds the old, decayed towns has always had a fascination for me, and has drawn me to places so far apart as Timgad and Tiahuanaco. Cities which, in antique or ancient days, surged with human life, and knew 'the ebb and flow of feet ', but now stand in forlorn fragments, peopled only by ghosts; these take hold of my imagination even more surely than that soaring marvel of all cities past or present which you so dislike—wonderful New York. For I delight in the actual, as well as in the imagined, and there are not many who have wandered the world that can outdo me in this inappeasable curiosity about its cities old and new.

I am turning my pen to-night to the subject of Bruges because, by the mere hazard of the bookshelf,

I have just been reading again, more than thirty years after my first reading, a story which is little known to the present generation: ' Bruges-la-Morte ', by Georges Rodenbach.   I was still under its spell in those distant days when you and I rode awheel along the Bruges and Ostend Canal in our questing youth, sensible that we were adventuring into the grey things of the past, and thrilling a little at the prospect.   And what of the re-reading?   Ah, well, it may be that I have changed, that the sentimental bent of our younger days has long ceased to influence my thoughts and emotions.   Youth is the time for sentiment: you have to be very young to feel the eye moisten at ' Love's Old Sweet Song '.   And yet another and similar experiment recently made found me re-capturing an old enthusiasm for a sentimental writer, which I had fully expected to find extinct, beyond all revival.   So it may be that the ' Bruges-la-Morte ' lacks the lasting quality which, in my less discriminating years, I seemed to find in it.

Here was the impression I had of my first reading, as I would have set it down a week ago: a strangely moving story, in which the author seeks, by a subtle and beautiful symbolism, to express, in a man's rrational love for his dead wife, the brooding yet elusive melancholy which those who come to love deeply the old city of Bruges must feel for it.   Yes, that is what I have thought of ' Bruges-la-Morte ' for thirty years and more; but . . .

In the 'nineties there was much chatter about the French and Belgian symbolists; it is a Belgian who

has survived, and that, perhaps, because he is something far better than a mere experimenter in literary
affectations. Maeterlinck, I mean. Rodenbach had
little beyond his symbolism, though had he lived
longer he might have outgrown that phase, and that
is why his name is not likely to signify anything to
most book-readers of our present generation. ' Bruges
la-Morte ', as I now perceive it to be, is only a study
of a morbid passion, and as a symbol of Bruges it
conjures up a mere ineffectual wraith instead of the
undying soul of the town. Let me tell briefly such
story as it contains.

Hugues Viane, a man of wealth and an idle sentiment-
alist, loses his wife by untimely death. We are to
picture him so devoted a widower that he saves all
her clothes, her jewellery and every object which has
any association with her. Soon after the unheard-of
tragedy of so unparalleled a loss he chooses to settle
in a fine house at Bruges because, forsooth, in that
dead city he may wallow in his grief. He lives alone
in his gloomy house with an old servant, Barbe; knows
no one; eats his sad meals in silence, and haunts the
deserted streets and the lonely banks of the grey-
green canals. Then on a day in a bye-street he is
astounded to see a woman walking before him, whose
every motion reminds him of his beloved wife. He
contrives to get a glimpse of her features; they are
those of the dead one. Imagine his perturbation:

Doubtless the woman was aware of his agitation, for on
her part she looked at him with an air of astonishment. Ah,

that look that came back to him out of the void! (*sortie du néant!*)
That look which he had believed he could never see again,
which he imagined had faded into the earth, he felt it now
upon him, calm, sweet, caressing.   A look that came from so
far away, arisen from the very grave, such, may be, as that
which Lazarus would have for Jesus.

I have translated without attempting to find in English
the delicate shades which Rodenbach contrives in the
French, but my version may pass as illustrating his
excess of statement, which, with his calculated repetition of phrase, is a characteristic fault of his school.

Having found the living image of the dear departed
—nay, having heard again that ' well-remembered
voice '—Hugues must needs pursue this weird matter
further.   Jane Scott, for such is the name of the living
replica of the dead wife, is a dancer from Lille, who
comes over two or three times a week to appear at the
theatre of Bruges (the town, you will see, was not so
' dead ' after all), and as you know, dancers, like
sailors, ' don't care '; so that Jane was soon established
in a charming old house at Bruges and the strange
wooer spent hours of each day with her there, chiefly,
we are to suppose, gazing at her and loving the dead
in the living.   I translate another passage freely:

In looking upon Jane, Hugh was dreaming of the dead,
and of her kisses and embraces, that he knew a little while
ago.   He believed he was regaining the lost in possessing this
living one.   All that he had thought ended was beginning
again.   Nor was he thus unfaithful to his wife, since it would
be her that he would love in this image, her lips that he would
be meeting when he kissed this mouth.

And so on.   Really I blush to think that this sort
of stuff ever took me in; and I now feel that the
proper place for Hugues was at the bottom of one of
the silent, deserted canals of Bruges.   But, bless you,
there would have been no story, had the proper thing
been done at the proper time.   Nor is there much
of a story as it is.   His worship of the dead in the
living induces him to make Jane dress up in
the clothes of his wife and to surround her with the
sacred belongings of the dead.   Then the dancer does
the right thing by insisting upon going to the house
of Hugues to see the procession of the Holy Blood.
Her entry there means the exit of poor old Barbe, and
a great scandal in the neighbourhood.   Besides, Jane
—and who shall blame her—had now tired of her
strange lover, and made a mock of the loved things
of the wife.   Then the slumbering fiend in Hugues
awoke and he strangled Jane there in that room where
she had profaned the souvenirs of the dead. . . .

And in the silence came the noise of the bells, all the bells
ringing at one time, to mark the return of the procession to
the sanctuary of the Holy Blood.   It was ended, that beautiful
cortége, with its solemn chanting, the resurrection of a morning
of life.   The streets were empty again.   The town was once
more withdrawing into its lone self.

And Hugh continually repeated: ' Dead . . . dead . . .
Bruges-the-Dead ' . . . in a mechanical way, and in tone-
less voice, trying to time ' Dead . . . dead . . . Bruges-
the-Dead ' with the cadence of the last of the bells, those weary,
slow sounds, like little tenuous old things, which seem to
flicker slowly down like softly falling leaves upon the town—
or was it on a tomb?

c

Frankly, I confess that I have sought in vain for the beautiful symbolism which I was once persuaded this book contained. In some mystic way Rodenbach was supposed to illustrate the spell of the antique town in the widower's love for his dead mate, but while Hugues has been the lonely one loving the dead thing, I find at the end, when he has strangled its living image—the image of the dead, as it were, becoming itself the instrument of death—we are told it was the town that was ' alone ' again. In short I have a suspicion that symbolism is a thing to take on trust and not to begin examining with any critical eye. I shall not again read Rodenbach, and I am so little in sympathy with his point of view that I shall try here to offer a picture of Bruges that is neither divorced from history nor from imagination, but is merely free from morbidity.

For seven hundred years and more, this little Flemish city has been a queen of Northern Europe. For long she ruled by right of patient skill and resilient courage, holding even the trade of England under her sway, breaking the chivalry of France, and beating down many a rival. And when at length her strength failed, she still queened it by right of loveliness. From this ancient capital of Flanders was largely derived England's mediæval system of town government. From modern Bruges has come indirectly the new school of guildsmen in Britain. In truth there is much that is alive and eloquent in Bruges to-day.

Its special charm lies in a combination of mediæval picturesqueness and homely interest. It presents, I

think, the most perfect living picture in Europe of
the externals of ordinary town life in the Middle
Ages. While it lacks entirely the air of vanished
splendour which we find in Venice, it offers an idea
of the way men lived in London in the days of
Chaucer. There were no palaces in Bruges; the finest
of the larger private houses were built by merchants
and trade corporations, but there are many amply
proportioned and picturesque houses that were the
homes of the guild-workers in their days of short
hours and splendid ease that led so surely to bank-
ruptcy and loss of independence. With the possible
exception of some churches and towers erected under
French rule, no famed architect has played a part
in the making of the magical loveliness of Bruges.
From her superb belfry to the humblest of her old
cottages, Bruges is the home of a democratic art.
I have read that the designs for her best buildings
came from a blacksmith, a lawyer, a bricklayer and
ordinary craftsmen.

Working life in this city of romance would be, at
first, something dull. Fighting was the real, if not
the only, outlet for the main energies of the seaboard
Flemings—brothers in blood to the Southern English
—who were the builders of Bruges. They smashed
the Danes of Alfred's day, broke the Normans and
French in the age of William the Conqueror, received
thousands of fugitive Englishmen, and, like the
early Lowland Scot to whom they are also related,
they remained more primitively English than the
Norman-ruled Englishmen themselves. When the

younger generation of these yeomen-freemen collected about the bridge, or ' Brugge ', by the castled
river-island of their chief, Count Baldwin, a storm-
centre had been formed in the feudal system of
Western Europe.

Little remains in Bruges of this stormy period,
during which the town was burnt and wrecked. By
the thirteenth century the working class had grown
so powerful that the wealthy master merchants called
the French King to their aid. Now, weaving, like
boot-making, conduces to brooding thought, and is a
fine soil for the spirit of revolt, even as the history
of ' Thrums ' reveals; so the Bruges weavers, who
led the guildsmen, would not submit to the French
garrison of their city, and in the spring of 1302, under
an obscure leader, Pieter de Coning, or Peter King,
they massacred the French troops. Then, alongside
the craftsmen of Ghent and sister cities, they met
the chivalry of France, the archers of Genoa, and
knights of Brabant and Hainault, by the marshes
of Courtrai. There, on July 11, 1302, in the action
called the Battle of the Spurs, working men of Bruges
and yeomen of the Flemish seaboard, with con-
tingents from every town of Flanders, may be said
to have opened the modern era of popular government in the world, with a complete victory of roughly
armed and unprotected, untrained working folk over
a superior number of well-horsed knights in armour,
and professional bowmen.

Inspired by the example of Bruges, the Swiss
mountaineers broke the chivalry of Austria, and

later the Scottish farmers at Bannockburn and the
English peasant archers at Crecy completed the
lesson of the Battle of the Spurs. Thus you will
see that all who value our democratic institutions
should be familiar with the history of this antique
Flemish town.

It was now that, having harvested thus suddenly
the fruit of centuries of skilled labour and social
experiment, Bruges flowered into the miracle of
quiet loveliness that makes her still the jewel of
Northern Europe. Her rich merchants, having sold
themselves to defeated France, were stripped of
power. The guild of weavers ruled, sharing the
conduct of affairs with smiths, carpenters, butchers,
fishmongers, bakers and cobblers, leatherworkers and
lesser craftsmen. The wholesale importers and
exporters and men living on their means were allowed
but one-ninth share in the government; but they
could always sway the assembly when they spoke
as experts on some problem of foreign trade, on the
right solution of which the livelihood of half the
working-folk depended. Yet, this old oligarchy,
while paying heavy taxes, and silently provoking
all the trouble they could, generously contributed
to the beautifying of their fairylike city, so strong
was the corporate spirit of the place. Nor were the
triumphant working folk lacking in artistic enthusiasm, as their homes and the art of the period
proclaim.

Bruges owes nothing to her natural surroundings.
Alike from a business standpoint and an artistic

point of view, the surrounding country is among the worst in Europe. It is a sunken marshland of thin, hungry, sodden soil, subject to devastating tidal floods, yet with no natural waterway for commerce to the sea. Nevertheless, the folk of Bruges made their city a little Venice. Unlike Ravenna, whose canals were made into streets, the streets of Bruges were turned into canals. They built their palace-like warehouses over vaulted little docks, so that goods could be lifted up and down into barges. The main canal system ran into the Zwyn river in Zeeland, by the port of Sluys, which was part of Bruges territory. In this fashion Bruges dug her way to the North Sea, and became the richest, busiest seaport and manufacturing and distributing centre of Western Europe.

What appeals to me as the strangest thing about her is that she is an inland city, rising from the water like Stockholm and Venice; and though the water element is vastly less, it is canal water, not the tidal salt sea, without which neither Stockholm nor Venice could have remained habitable. Out of a small brook and a bog, Bruges made, in a roadless age of packhorse traffic along muddy bridle paths, a network of canals as the main instrument of her empire of commerce, and spread her waterways down her chief trade routes. Again, in later times, many of her canals were changed into roads and streets, since wheeled vehicles and good highways came into general use, but sufficient of these ancient waterways wind in and around the city to mirror and enhance the charm of the towered, turreted, many-tinted shapes of brickwork. Under a glowing sunset, Bruges puts on robes of enchantment, and if, while the level golden radiance streams upon her, a breeze touches the waters on which she sits, something happens that neither paint nor words can depict. The old brick-built working-class town trembles into liquid iridescences of a romantic witchery such as no city of marble glories can surpass.

Bruges has also her great monuments, that strike the eye and imagination with immediate power. Her world-famed belfry, which has been, in its time, citadel, watch-tower, treasure-house, and marketing place, was enlarged and adorned after the victory, and is the finest souvenir of the great days of the guilds. I still recall the eerie feeling which came upon me as we climbed to the top and found strange, little, gnome-like men employed upon the intricate machinery of the bells. Her town hall, raised in the age of victory and afterwards graced by the work of Jan van Eyck, the Hospital of St. John, with its exquisite Memlings, the offices of the guilds, the lovely brick-built churches and mansions of noblemen and foreign merchants, are all joyously beautiful things to contemplate.

Yet these form only the lesser part of Bruges. It is in the narrow byways, the lonely reaches of green water, fringed with trees, lily-strewn, perhaps, shadowed by wonderful walls and lightened by white

swans, bred from the Middle Ages as an ornament
of the canals, that we find best reflected the spirit
of the old city of the guild craftsmen. An apparent
infinity of little homes in rose, apricot, dim gold
and silvery grey brick, ranged in harmonious masses
and heightened at intervals by some building of
peculiar picturesqueness, tells of the joy with which
these craftsmen worked. When they were not contending with feudal kings and lords or the men of
Ghent, they might have been accounted among
the happiest folk in the world. All had been
arranged that they might labour in comfort and
enjoy good leisure. No man was allowed to extend
his business. He could not work longer than his
fellows; nor could he trade with money obtained by
inheritance or marriage; he could not attract new
customers, nor invent or use a new tool. Appren-
tices succeeded to journeymen, journeymen to
masters, the numbers of the craftsmen being
restricted to the needs of the city. Strangest thing
of all: a true feeling of brotherly love prevailed
among the craftsmen.

It was an alluring dream that lasted for some
years. Bruges was really an aristocracy of some ten
thousand working men of all round ability, who,
either in their labour or in their leisure, were artists.
On every unaltered old house may still be seen the
iron ring from which hung the festoons of flowers
and foliage that brightened both sides of the street.
The statues in the niches of house-fronts were painted
so cunningly that even fine artists did not despise

the work. The many-coloured tapestries hung from
the windows were, in a way, a lesson from craftsmen
to the professional artists. At first it was the custom
for the Flemish painters to provide colour designs
for the weavers, as Raphael did in later days when
Flanders was decadent. But, in spite of inventiveness
being forbidden by guild law, the tapestry weavers
were so brimming with inventive genius that they
needed no more than a black and white design. Out
of their tinted wools, they could compose colour
effects that painters could not equal. They were, if
I may hazard the suggestion, forerunners of the
modern impressionists, who can so skilfully place
their harsh, raw dabs of colour that they blend in a
lively, yet harmonious whole.

Friendly lords jousted in the Grand'Place, where
the belfry soars aloft with a grace that appeals to me
as not greatly inferior to that of the supreme miracle
of airy grace, the Torre del Mangia at Siena. English
knights went to these festivals in considerable numbers,
for Edward III of England proposed to the Flemish
communes an alliance that would have freed them
from French interference. Owing, however, to
domestic feuds, Bruges and her sister cities fell into
the power of the Duke of Burgundy, and lost strength
and freedom. Yet the city derived new glories from
her new master, who was then the richest sovereign
in Europe, with the most splendid court. Indeed,
it was he and his descendants who garbed old Bruges
in fresh beauty; but it was a withering body that he
tricked out in the attire of youth. For the dream of

her guildsmen had faded for ever.   Its end, I believe,
has been variously attributed to misfortunes in war,
to the silting of the Zwyn that closed the passage to
the sea, to the feud with Ghent, and to the refusal of
the English alliance.

All these things were but symptoms of weakness,
the root cause of which has only recently appeared
to the investigators of history.   England, who for a
time had been tending towards the system of the
Bruges guildsmen, evolved the capitalist system, and
in an adventurous, inventive, strong-handed way,
created free village industries and free town manu-
factures, weaving her own wool at competitive prices
into yarn and cloth.   Here was the sealing of the
downfall of Bruges.   Many of the best weavers there
migrated to England, while the best Bruges merchants
settled in Antwerp, and there saved Flanders by
adopting the English system of free village industries
that attracted the journeymen from the old communes.
So at least historians, better versed in these matters
than I am, tell me, and I am in no case to contradict
them.

Most probably the journeymen left the guilds of
Bruges because the communal rule had hardened
into the inevitable, unfair tyranny, producing a new
hereditary ruling caste, as communism always will.
The little working masters, who should have acted
as disinterested foremen, and let their best journey-
man succeed them, kept their positions open for
their own heirs, and concerted together to this end.
The religious inspiration in guild socialism would

die away as the Church grew more worldly. Frank self-interest had full play, and by the close of the sixteenth century Bruges, with her small tradesmen and artisans still maintaining a pretence of guild socialism, was dwindling into a penurious village. Religious houses of monks and nuns took the places of the once thriving industrial guilds, and they have outlasted all else, to characterise latter-day Bruges as the city of *béguinages* and cloistered women, whose dim lives are lightened by hopes of a city not made with hands.

One great thing Bruges has gained by her failure. Peace. England's ' world-revolution '—her industrial system—has spread ugliness even into far Japan. Bruges has her lilied canals and sleepy streets instead of roaring factories. But she is not ' dead ', nor does she love this peace; rather is she quickening with hope that her improved canal system may enable her to renew the old struggle for mercantile power with Antwerp and Ghent. Moreover, she is giving of her unspoiled beauty inspiration to English artists and architects, and has even shown how a factory that is beautiful may be designed with little or no cost for the beauty.

No, I do not think that Bruges is dead, and I am persuaded that she never resembled the vague complex of morbid passions rending a dying body that Georges Rodenbach has symbolised for us in ' Bruges-la-Morte '.

Meads,
  Eastbourne.

III

RAVENNA AND THE ROMANCE OF HISTORY

To W. Romaine Paterson

HERE in this ultimate city of the Cæsars, long-established in my mind as the home of many things romantic—a Venice ages before Venice ' arose from out the wave ', the death-bed of the Western Empire, the scene of Galla Placidia's imperial power and eerie entombment, of Theodoric's oriental pomp, of Dante's ending years, of Byron's philandering with the Countess Guiccioli, and many another happening great or small, I am impressed, my dear Paterson, mainly with the futility of things, the littleness of what we deem great. But for a certain serenity that seems to exhale from the tomb of Dante, where a wounded veteran of the Arditi acts as custodian and recited to me some sonorous stanzas from ' Inferno ', this dusty, yet damp, unbeautiful town does cry aloud that all is vanity.

It was you, I believe, who first, and many a year ago, recommended to me Thomas Hodgkin's ' Italy and Her Invaders ' as a rich mine of information on a period of the declining Empire in which I was deeply interested. And much have I profited by that famous work—like many another masterpiece the by-product of a banker's leisure. Indeed, it is mainly due to Hodgkin that I am writing this in what I had pictured as the most interesting city of Italy after Rome, and find to be a shabby casket that holds some priceless gems.

In my portfolio I have brought the notes I made on the reading of Hodgkin's fascinating book some twelve years, back and they restore to me, with singular freshness, the points of that work which most caught my imagination at the time; for I am one who believes that the best way either to read or to write history is with the aid of the imagination. Once I asked a celebrated authority on ancient history to write for a work that I was planning, a chapter ' giving an imaginative description ' of one of the mighty cities of antiquity. ' I am a historian ', he replied rather tartly, ' and deal in facts, not imagination; so that I cannot do what you ask of me '. But I persuaded him, after some argument, that facts touched with imagination remained not the less facts, and were probably more true to actuality, and he wrote a most lively and truthful description of the life of that ancient city for me. It is nonsense to suggest that the historian is only a fact-monger. Unless he is a person of imagination his work must be mere building material for better men to shape into forms of life.

Hodgkin had imagination; he had knowledge; and he had, alas, a literary style that was deplorably slovenly, with the true amateur's weakness for quoting hackneyed tags of verse. I find that at the time of reading him I made this note: ' Impressed with the sheer weight of the material he has worked over, although it is shovelled out in a formless and unattractive manner '. From a literary point of view his book is quite undistinguished, from the historical it is a study of first importance. Withal, ' Italy and Her Invaders ' is a book to be read and one that will be enjoyed by all who like to rebuild in imagination the vanished palaces and cities of the past from the vestiges that still survive. The edition, in two ponderous volumes, which I read, had a further evidence of the amateur, in that it was peppered with printers' errors. But, if careless alike of style and orthography, Hodgkin was meticulous in all matters of fact, and he had dug out of obscure quarries an immense amount of illuminating information about Goth, Hun, and Vandal unknown to Gibbon, whom, in certain details, he corrects; though for that matter, I had rather be misled by Gibbon than corrected by Hodgkin. I certainly had much profit of Hodgkin's pages, and transcribed a number of passages.

Here, for example, is a finely imaginative piece on the death of Attila, wherein the persuasive story of the facts loses nothing of the dramatic value which attached to the legend that Ildico did the deed as Meredith describes in his majestic poem

' The Nuptials of Attila ', with its haunting refrains
' Attila, my Attila! ' and ' Make the bed for Attila! '—

It was in the year 453, the year that followed his Italian
campaign, that Attila took to himself, in addition to all his
other wives (and, as we have seen, his harem was an extensive
one), the very beautiful damsel, Ildico. At the wedding
feast he relaxed his usual saturnine demeanour, drank copiously,
and gave way to abundant merriment. Then when the guests
were departed, he mounted the flight of steps that led up to
his couch, placed high in the banqueting hall, and there lay
down to sleep the heavy sleep of a reveller. He had long
been subject to fits of violent bleeding at the nose, and this
night he was attacked by one of them. But lying as he was
upon his back in his deep and drunken slumber, the blood
could not find its usual exit, but passed down his throat and
choked him. The day dawned, the sun rose high in the
heavens, the afternoon was far spent, and no sign was made
from the nuptial chamber of the king. Then at length his
servants, suspecting something wrong, after uttering loud
shouts, battered in the door and entered. They found him
lying dead, with no sign of a wound upon his body, the blood
streaming from his mouth, and Ildico, with downcast face,
silently weeping behind her veil. Such a death would, of
course, excite some suspicion—suspicion which one of the
Eastern chroniclers expanded into certainty—of the guilt of
Ildico, who was probably regarded as the Jael by whose hand
this new and more terrible Sisera had fallen. It is more probable, however, that the cause assigned by Jordanes, apparently
on the authority of Priscus, is the true one, and that the mighty
king died, as he says, a drunkard's death.

That is a good, vigorous passage, in which the
dramatic and historic are properly fused. And
there is real imagination in the ensuing quotation

where Hodgkin tells us how all the glories of
Venice sprang from the terror of Attila, which drove
the Italians of the north-east to shelter among the
islets of the lagoons where they laid the foundations
of the future queen city of the Adriatic:

There, then, engaged in their humble beaver-like labours,
we leave for the present the Venetian refugees from the rage
of Attila.   But even while protesting, it is impossible not to
let into our minds some thought of what those desolate fishing
villages will one day become.   The dim religious light, half-
revealing the slowly-gathered glories of St. Mark's; the Ducal
Palace—that history in stone; the Rialto, with its babble of
many languages; the Piazza, with its flocks of fearless pigeons;
the Brazen Horses; the Winged Lion; the Bucentaur; all that
the artists of Venice did to make her beautiful, her ambassadors
to make her wise, her secret tribunals to make her terrible;
memories of these things must come thronging upon the mind
at the mere mention of her spell-like name.   Now, with these
pictures glowing vividly before you, wrench the mind away
with sudden effort to the dreary plains of Pannonia.   Think
of the moody Tartar, sitting in his log-hut, surrounded by his
barbarous guests, of Zercon gabbling his uncouth mixture of
Hunnish and Latin, of the bath-man of Onegesh, and the
wool-work of Kreka, and the reed-candles in the village of
Bleda's widow; and say if cause and effect were ever more
strangely mated in history than the rude and brutal might of
Attila with the stately and gorgeous and subtle Republic of
Venice.

Assuredly it is an arresting thought, that all that
exquisite beauty which is Venice, the true wonder
city of all time—whence I have come but yesterday from another spell of joy in it—was produced
by the irritation of a barbaric conqueror working

facing p. 32

CHURCH OF ST FRANCIS
PIAZZA BYRON, RAVENNA

upon a superior culture, as we owe the beauty of the pearl to an irritant in the oyster. A devil in this way might be as creative as a god. Nay, I am sure that Hodgkin would readily have agreed, had the point been put to him, that Attila was expressly created by an all-wise Providence to set in motion the obscure forces that were to create Venice with all its brimming loveliness. Read this and judge ye:

The present writer belongs to the old-fashioned school, which still dares and delights to speak of God in Nature and of God in History. To declare, as we venture to do, with all reverence and confession of our dim-sightedness, that we believe we can trace the finger of the Creator and Lord of the world in events like the Rise and Fall of the Roman Empire, is by no means to assert that we can explain the ways of Providence in all the occurrences either of the present or of the past; it by no means commits us to the proposition that ' all things have happened for the best in the best of all possible worlds'. For one who believes in the God of whom the Christian Revelation speaks, or even in the God whom Socrates felt after and found, neither optimism nor pessimism would seem to be the rational frame of mind. We look back over our own lives; we see faults and blunders in them past counting. Assuredly it would have been better for our little fragment of the world that these should not have been committed— so much the pessimist truly urges. But then, we can also see, as we think—but here each individual of the race must speak for himself—traces of a higher Power contending with us in our blindness, sometimes bringing good out of our follies and mistakes, always seeking to educate and to raise us

> ' On stepping-stones
> Of our dead selves to higher things.'

In all this we do but ratify the statement of one who had
meditated on human nature at least as deeply as any modern
sociologist:

> ' There's a divinity that shapes our ends
> Rough-hew them as we will. '

So much the optimist may claim. Why the divinity has not
shaped the whole world's career to nought but a good end is
confessedly inexplicable, and will perhaps be for ever unintel-
ligible to us. Meantime, therefore, we hold the two unrecon-
ciled beliefs, in the Almightiness of God, and in the existence
of evil which is His enemy. To discard either of these beliefs,
or to harmonise them, we find equally impossible, and therefore we desist from the attempt, and let both grow together
till the harvest.

Just when I was having a fear that I might appear
a little less than just to him, and was looking for his
best points, he lets slip this damaging avowal, which
is about as pitiful in an interpreter of history as
Mr. Hilaire Belloc's slogan, ' Man, a fixed type ',
is in a critic of biogeny. You will note also the
familiar ring of the poetical quotations.

Hodgkin is a good example of the author whose
matter, as a whole, is so valuable, whose common
sense so seldom fails him, that his sympathetic
reader resents his occasional lapses and his careless
style, just as we are apt to be unduly, almost irra-
tionally, annoyed with friends whom we esteem if
we detect in them little evidences of slovenliness.
There is no doubt about the interestingness of
Hodgkin, and there would be no end to quotation
from his pages until his two hefty volumes were

'gutted', if to string such extracts together were my only object—and to you, my dear Paterson, familiar before I was with Hodgkin's pages, steeped in Italian history, and more familiar with its scenes than with your native Scotland, that would be a vain performance. But, touching this matter of Ravenna and Romance, there are still some passages that I must borrow, and also one of general application for which I am especially indebted to the honest Hodgkin. He found the following in a life of St. Exuperantius (whoever he was) concerning some bishops of whom the obscure chronicler wished to give some record but lacked the necessary data:

> Where I have not found any History of any of these bishops, and have not been able by conversation with aged men, or inspection of the monuments, or from any other authentic source to obtain information concerning them, in such a case, that there might not be a break in the series, I have composed the life myself, with the help of God and the prayers of the brethren.

How many lives of the saints have the same substantial foundation for their sweet miracles!

One of the most curious of the many notes I made from Hodgkin brings me back to this city of Ravenna, whence I have tended a little to stray. It is a sentence from a letter of the famous Apollinarius Sidonius, liveliest of the scholars of the fifth century. In 467 he wrote: 'It is hard to say whether the old city of Ravenna is separated from the new harbour or joined to it by the Via Cæsaria

which lies between them.'   Now, you will remember
that in 'Tartarin of Tarascon' Daudet tells us it
was a pleasantry among the fellow citizens of the
great Tartarin, who looked across the river to Beaucaire with a none-too-friendly eye, to observe that
'the two towns were separated by the bridge across
the Rhone'.   It is odd to think that 1400 years
before the days of Tartarin, Sidonius, himself a
countryman of his, was cracking a very similar joke
about Ravenna after one of his trips from Clermont-
Ferrand, where he lived in princely state.

But of all the stories in 'Italy and Her Invaders'
I confess, not without some shyness, since my concern in it is so removed from all that touches the
graver and scientific side of history, that Hodgkin's
'truthful anecdote of the year 1577' most stirred
my imagination.   The Empress Placidia, mother of
the dissolute Valentinian II, died in Rome in her
sixtieth year, on the 27th of November, 450, after
a life more charged with adventure than any other
regal lady ever knew.   Her body was brought to
Ravenna, whence the Imperial court had removed to
Rome only a year before, and in the mausoleum
of the church of St. Nazarius she was entombed:

For eleven centuries the embalmed body of the Augusta
remained undisturbed in its tomb, sitting upright in a chair
of cypress wood and arrayed in royal robes.   It was one of
the sights of Ravenna to peep through a little hole in the back
and see this changeless queen, but unhappily, 300 years ago
some careless or mischievous children, determined to have a
thoroughly good look at the stately lady, thrust a lighted taper

through the hole. Crowding and pushing, and each one bent on getting the best view possible, they at length brought the light too near to the corpse; at once royal robes and royal flesh and cypress wood chair were all wrapped in flames. In a few minutes the work of cremation was accomplished and the daughter of Theodosius was reduced to ashes as effectually as any daughter of the pagan Cæsars.

That story has long appealed to me as one of the curiosities of history, and I had rather Gibbon, who was not in possession of the details, had told it than Hodgkin. But having to-day spent some time in Placidia's Mausoleum, I am less able to visualise the circumstances of her long deferred incineration than I was before coming to Ravenna. If we are to understand that throughout these eleven hundred years the empress sat in her cypress-wood chair inside her massy sarcophagus—an immense and crudely shaped receptacle of white marble, whose ponderous top must weigh a ton or two and nowhere to my scrutiny revealed a peep-hole large enough to offer a view of the contents, except, indeed, the whole interior were lighted from within—if so, then I find myself a little sceptical of this ' truthful anecdote '.

If it had been better for my belief in the story not to have seen the sarcophagus, I am richly rewarded for the toil of travel thither in the enduring beauty of Ravenna's mosaic treasures from the fifth and sixth centuries of our era, which give such enduring distinction to the churches of St. Vitale, St. Apollinare Nuovo, and to St. Apollinare in

Classe some three miles outside the town, as well as to the Mausoleum of Placidia. But I do not propose to continue this lengthening sketch (thanks to the rain that keeps me indoors to-day) by attempting a disquisition on early Christian art; rather shall I endeavour to recall something of the long vanished splendour of a city that was the virtual capital of Italy for 350 years, as I have imagined it from much reading of books, and now can picture it from the few but splendid remnants of its wonderful past that have been preserved through fifteen centuries of change.

Nature did little for Ravenna, except to make her unapproachable. She was a city built in the sea, by the labour of five hundred and fifty years. Augustus began the work on the great, black, boggy marsh, south of the Po River, by taking the lagoons, mudbanks and islands as a breakwater, and constructing behind them a naval harbour, Classis, to shelter 250 of his warships, and linking the port by a three-mile causeway, Cæsarea, to the mournful marshland village of Ravenna. The watery spot was long notorious for malaria, foul smells, and for lack of drinking water, a fact brought back to my mind on asking the maid at the hotel to bring me a glass of drinking water. After nigh on two thousand years, Ravenna is still lacking in this primal need, although from Trajan's day to the Gothic kingdom an aqueduct gave an ample supply, except for a disturbed period when it was broken. Ravenna's lack of water was, as you may remember, a favourite

target for the jests of Juvenal, who says that, at a
Ravenna inn, he ordered a drink of wine and water,
but the cheating tavern-keeper gave him neat wine.
It seems a fact that wine was cheaper here than
good drinking water, though a branch of the Po
was turned into the town and combined with the
currents of two local streams to cleanse the extraordinary network of canals veining the rows of pile-
built houses.

Contrary to common slander, the Goths were
barbaric only in energy and in personal appearance.
In monumental art, at least, they were able quickly
to cultivate as fine a taste as any Roman or Greek of
their age, and, seized in Italy as well as in Spain
with a passion for grandiose works, they made both
Ravenna and Seville lasting monuments of a con-
structive genius comparable with that of the
Normans—their Viking successors in the art of
absorbing civilisation.

Let Ravenna of the year 520 speak to the eye and
imagination concerning the directing power of the
much-maligned Goth.   He was a man of nomad habit,
hating town life.   He had come to Ravenna on horseback, shepherding the vast herds of cattle and sheep
on which he lived, and convoying many thousands of
wagons, containing his women and children.   He
cleansed the city of disease by flushing the canals
once more with the strong flood waters of the Po,
and by rebuilding the aqueduct obtained an abundant supply of drinking water.   The great land
ramparts of the capital, falling in places into the

oozes on which they had been built, were made
strong, and the battlemented sea wall of Classis,
with its towered water gate and lighthouse, was
repaired.

Armies of native labourers were engaged to cleanse
immense stretches of marshland of malaria by means
of draining dykes, and make the soil fruitful.
Alpine timber was rafted down to the arsenal and
building yards of the port for making warships
and merchantmen. Consequently, with good food
supplies and energetic industry, the native population
was able contentedly to support sufficient taxation
for a great scheme of building. Theodoric himself
was undoubtedly the mind and soul of all the
political and artistic work of reconstruction. As
hostage for the good conduct of the wandering Goths,
he had spent ten years in the imperial palace of
Constantinople, and though the handsome young
barbarian had not there taken the trouble to learn
to write, his capacious intellect was stored with
practical learning. To the end of his life he could
not sign his name, except by means of a stencil with
the letters cut out of it, so as to guide his pen, but
' Thiudraeiks ', or ' people-ruler ', as his own folk
continued to call him, was one of the masters of
wisdom.

By sheer magnificence of person and gorgeous
surroundings, he dazzled his own Goths. Taking
a large part of the eastern side of Ravenna, he constructed a palace of Oriental splendour. It was
made in two storeys, with a grand triple entrance

of four Corinthian columns, surmounted by a
sparkling mosaic of gold, and smaller pillars forming
an encircling colonnade to the mass of halls, chambers
and apartments. Above the arcades were mosaics
of winged victories, graceful figures carrying gar-
lands; between the long ranges of pillars and the
columns of the main portals hung rich embroidered
purple cloths, like those veiling the sublime majesty of
the King of Kings of Persia. Within, behind the
mighty-limbed Gothic guardsmen in glittering mail,
armed with the old broadsword of the tribe, were
all the luxuries of ornament, furniture and display
that sword could win, wealth acquire and groups
of artists provide.

In Ravenna there was little clash between the
Goths and the Italians. In fact, except for the
strong Gothic garrison, and a few Gothic orders
of highly-trusted officials immediately concerned in
the safety of the realm and the redress of dangerous
abuses, captains of thousands visiting the army
commander, and the annual stream of soldiers coming
for their pay, the capital was usually peopled and
run by Italians. The civil administration was in
the hands of Roman officials, and Roman nobles
composed the formal court of the great Goth.
His design was to infuse Gothic vigour into the
Italian race, while disciplining, by Roman law and
civility, his own lawless nation. With large domains
whose prosperity he revived and populations notably
increasing in numbers, he lavished art on Ravenna
so that she might eclipse Constantinople.

His craftsmen and artists were mainly Roman.
The fine work they had done in Ravenna, even before
any Byzantine masterpiece such as St. Sophia was
erected, prove they were among the leaders of the
new movement.   In decorative art particularly, they
had qualities of Asiatic intensity, speaking something
of Babylon, somewhat of Susa, and presumed to
have been transmitted to Italy by the Greeks of
Antioch, in union with the old Hellenic tradition
of proportion and grace.   Their large pictorial
mosaics, with colours more glowing and more peren-
nially fresh than any pictures, were already the pride
of the churches built by the romantic Galla Placidia,
who was first Queen of the Goths of Spain and then
Empress Regent of the Western Empire.   Her
work was continued by her Gothic successor to
imperial rule.   He adorned the great gate of Ravenna
with the golden mosaic.   Above the highest pinnacle
of his many-coloured palace he set a colossal portrait
of himself that could be seen by sailors far out on
the Adriatic.   Formed of pieces of stained glass,
with a gemlike depth of hue and deep metallic
lustre, it depicted Theodoric sitting on a brazen
horse, clad in coat of mail, holding shield and spear,
while the armed genius of Rome guarded him, and
the genius of Ravenna, with one foot resting on
land and the other passing over the sea, glided
forward with a welcome.

In those grand days, mosaic workers must have
thronged in Ravenna and doubtless there was great
argument about colour and design among them.   An

almost intact specimen of their work for Theodoric
is seen in the basilica now bearing the name of St.
Apollinare Nuovo. When built by the Goth it
was known as St. Martin's church, and famous
for an exquisite gold-inlaid roof. Its changed
exterior is not now remarkable, but within, above
the northern colonnade, a line of virgin martyrs is
making a procession from the port of Classis, and
above the southern colonnade a procession of
martyred men moves from Theodoric's palace towards the judgement seat of Christ. Between the
windows, on a background of gold, are figures of
saints, prophets and apostles; on high, runs a line
of little pictures of the miracles and Passion of
Christ. The dazzling beauty of the whole is difficult to describe. Here are none of the defects,
moral and artistic, of the Byzantine school. Save
for the stiffness of design natural to mosaic, the
spirit of the work is classic. The girl martyrs,
Agnes and Eulalia, Lucia and Agatha, and others,
are fresh, lovely and smiling, and attired like
daughters of a king. Something about them stirs
one's memories of the frieze of the Parthenon.
This, perhaps the best surviving example of the
quality of the art that the great Goth of Ravenna
fostered, indicates what Christendom lost when the
arms of reactionary Constantinople, under Justinian,
triumphed over the reviving genius of Gothic Italy.

A great evolution of art can be traced between
the mosaics done for Galla Placidia and those done
about half a century later for Theodoric. An

equally remarkable degradation in art is visible in
the mosaics done in the fanes of Ravenna at the
order of Justinian, the supreme Byzantine, a few
years after the death of the Goth. It took the
genius of the Italian race nearly nine hundred years
to escape completely from the trammels reimposed
by the Byzantine reactionaries. But in the early
part of the fourteenth century, probably about 1317,
Dante and Giotto settled in Ravenna. There Dante
finished the last stanzas of his 'Divine Comedy'
and died, while Giotto finely displayed the renewed
genius of his race in painting by a series of frescoes.
His work, fading into colourlessness, is but a ghost
of his achievement. The best extant work of Theodoric's craftsmen, where not barbarously destroyed
by command of Justinian, keeps yet its primal,
blending hues like coloured fires.

In spite of their supremacy in early Christian
art, the folk of Ravenna were neither saints nor
æsthetes. Rather the contrary. Much of the fine
work was done just for the joy of it and a living wage,
and perhaps at times there was a strain of lighthearted
pagan feeling in designing maiden martyrs as lovely
smiling girls in rich raiment, and adorning the
Emperor's palace with winged victories. A considerable section of the old Roman nobility was
still stubbornly pagan. Larger yet was the sect
of quiet Anti-Christians of the philosophic school,
who held to a vague theism, and were headed by the
most famous man of letters in Theodoric's court,
Boethius. Theodoric and his Goths were, in their

barbaric way, men of a somewhat similar frame of mind. As ignorant Arian heretics, they were usually, in practice, rough deists of an uncertain Christian tint. Had they accepted the doctrine of the Trinity and championed the cause of the native Church of Rome against the Greek church, the way of empire would have been smoothed for them. Theodoric might have been lifted to the position afterwards occupied by Charlemagne.

But the Goths of Ravenna proved obstinate and slow-minded. While they hesitated, in both Italy and Spain, over a religious as well as a political amalgamation with the natives of the Western Empire of old Rome, quicker-witted Clovis, of France, agreed to be baptised, and became the swordsman of Rome, breaking Arian nations in Southern Gaul and Burgundy. Meanwhile the free-living eastern Goth, while erecting Arian churches of marvellous beauty, was more attracted by the amphitheatre of Ravenna and by the circus. It was the chariot races and the wild beast fights in the capital that brought Theodoric's barbarians and his civilised subjects into friendly relationships. During the games, Ravenna did seem to be peopled by Goths, as well as Italians.

Long as was his reign (493–526), Theodoric was not able, without the aid of the Church, to lay the foundations of a new, strengthened Italy. His own ambitious daughter began to betray the country, and in the year 540 the Byzantines resumed possession of Ravenna. The Emperor Justinian took

over several fine buildings in course of erection,
among them being the Church of St. Vitale, with
a dome boldly set on a polygonal base, in a manner
anticipating the architectural scheme of St. Sophia
in Constantinople. The intricate, strong, novel
design was carried out at the expense of a banker
of Ravenna, and it was his master-mason, a genius
of the Syrian Greek school, though perhaps of
Italian stock, who forestalled, and educated in
audacity the Byzantine architects. Many mosaics,
however, were carried out by Byzantine craftsmen,
with special Byzantine materials. They include portraits of Justinian, and his notorious wife, Theodora,
the courtesan empress, and gazing up at these in
the lunettes of the dome, in all their sparkling
immortality of colour, one enters more closely, I
think, into the joy of the artist than into the joy of
even the great sculptor, for there is a subtle community of feeling in colour as distinct from form.
I had always imagined these mosaics as intolerably
stiff and crude of form, but, regarding them with
critical eye in St. Vitale and the other churches, I
was mainly impressed with their lustrous loveliness,
their vivid sense of life.

Much of what the jealous Byzantine allowed to
remain in the city as memorials of Theodoric was
afterwards pillaged by Charlemagne. The Frankish
barbarian stripped the palace of the great Goth,
in order to embellish with the spoil his own residence at Aix-la-Chapelle. He also took away a
statue of Theodoric on horseback, reckoned the best

work of its kind in western Christendom. This happened about the year 801. Ravenna had then become part of the Papal domain, and was falling into decay, the black, river-borne loam of Lombardy smudging out canals, lagoons, seaward passages, mouldering houses and fallen walls.

Of the Augustan war-port of Classis (Classe) little remains save the church of St. Apollinarius, wonderfully preserved, and where once stood the seaport of Cæsarea, with its long causeway linking Classis to Ravenna through the swamps, flat lands stretch to distant horizons. The ancient highway was being macadamised as a track for motor-car racing the day I passed along. Ages ago the advancing mud had reached the shore, and connected islands and mainlands, till the last lagoons became rice swamps, described by Dante, and on the chief natural breakwater grew a pinewood,

> Rooted where once the Adrian wave flowed o'er
> To where the last Cæsarean fortress stood,

as Byron sang. Only from the church spires can the withdrawn waters of the Adriatic now be seen, but the city, with maize fields and vineyards flourishing where the fleets of Augustus and Theodoric sailed, is again connected with the sea by a little northing canal. And the trade in eels is very brisk. The poorest Neapolitan will, it is said, sell his shirt, if he has one, rather than miss his Ravenna eel on Christmas eve.

Ravenna.

IV

OF SIR WALTER AND SOME OTHERS

To Cranstoun Metcalfe

I HAVE left my room with the turret window that overlooked the bustling Plaza Matriz, in this pleasant town of Montevideo. It was perfectly planned for the meditative life, and but for the vileness of man and the supineness of the municipal authorities, one could have passed some months there tolerably, looking out upon the panorama of Montevidean life and setting one's thoughts on paper when the mood came. But the men who drive motor cars in this far land are the worst of the breed. The plaza is filled with luxurious cars that ply for hire, each handled by an engaging rascal who is little better than a highwayman by day and a rowdy by night. The law of the town prohibits the use of the 'cut out', or opening of the exhaust pipe of the motor, but no one respects the law, and it is the custom for the demons who drive these cars to keep one foot all the time on the pedal that opens the exhaust. The consequent noise is so appalling that the main streets of Montevideo have become a veritable pandemonium.

Thus bad begins, but worse continues when the hour has passed midnight. The endless stream of electric ' trams ' with hideous clanging of super-fluously clamorous bells goes on till two, mingled with every variety of motor noise; then between two and four the motorists delight to ' test ' their engines, running round the plaza with open exhausts. Sleep is impossible, especially when you add a temperature anywhere between 80 and 90, and mosquitoes buzzing through your room athirst for blood.

So we are no longer tenants of ' the room with a view '. After some weeks of suffering bravely borne, we have fled the hotel and are now living seaward in the Calle Sarandí, where there is no view by day and few motors by night, and where the noise of the ' electricos ' keeps one awake only until two in the morning.

It is a poor heart that cannot extract some joy from conditions that seem framed for misery. In my case this new need to keep awake until the last of the long procession of clattering cars has been absorbed into the dreadful night has not been with-out profit. What reams of reading I am getting through!

The professional literary man, who has so often to occupy his days with tasks that others make their pastimes, has in his hours of ease to turn for sheer change to other pursuits than ' reading for pleasure '. I, at least, have often longed to pass some evenings in reading, just as a clerk of bookish tastes might

E

pass his evenings.   How difficult this is of attainment only the hard-wrought editor, with everlasting
piles of manuscripts on his study desk, or the reviewer with rows of books that *must* be read waiting
on his shelves, or the biographer, with his gathered
piles of notes and references at his elbow, can
adequately realise.   As I have been all three in turn,
and in truth at once, I have often been oppressed
with the hopelessness of sharing that rare delight of
the amateur who can sit him down by the hour and
enjoy ' a quiet read ', with no drooping eye on a
column to be written about what he is reading.

In my exile, however, I have recaptured this
rare and lost delight of my youth—for I began to
write for my living ere I had said good-bye to my
'teens.   Without the slightest compunction I find
myself reading at random all sorts of books, good
and bad, in English, French, and Spanish, and I
had flattered myself that I had even succeeded in
ridding myself of the critical mood and slipping
into that of ' the average reader ' in these midnight
hours of aimless reading.   But, alas! once a critic,
always a critic, and these notes, which I have begun
at one in the morning, are evidence that a man of
letters cannot be content merely to enjoy, but must
analyse his literary sensations and record them—
this, no doubt, as much for his own entertainment
as for that of others.   More, perchance.

My excuse in the present case is an enthusiasm.
I have just finished reading a novel which, first read
in my youth and later re-read when I had occasion

to write an editorial introduction to it, has for the
last three nights held me spell-bound in a way that
I had not thought possible. For I am by no means
sure that it is near the front of its author's achievement. What I said about it a few years back when
editing the ' Fine Art Scott ' I do not now recall
even dimly, and so far as my present mood is concerned I do not greatly care. But I am certain
that never have I been more acutely stirred to admiration of the matchless romancer than at this midnight
hour in Montevideo. For hours the horrid trams
have been rolling past my windows all unheard:
the Wizard has had me transported, almost bodily,
to Ellangowan and thereawa'.

I started on ' Guy Mannering ' purely for pleasure,
and have had three nights of unstinted happiness.
But, when I turned the last page to-night, I felt as
puny and powerless under the spell of the Wizard
as when, a boy in Glasgow, I used to gaze in awe
and wonder at the effigy of Sir Walter which tops
the high and massy column in the centre of George
Square. The confidence of the writing man, however, is strong enough within me to warrant my
attempting some consideration of what I have been
reading.

The edition of the book is an old Tauchnitz,
printed at Leipzig eighty years ago, and worthy
to be exhibited to English publishers as a model of
craftsmanship. The paper remains as freshly white
as when it left the mill; the impression is faultless,
as densely black and clear as beautiful type and

good ink, combined with a true printer's loving
use of his machine, could make it. How many
of the books that are being printed in England
to-day will endure for eighty years?

I came upon the book by chance among a scratch
collection of French and German volumes in a
corner of my room. The German books were
sealed to me, but I had wasted some hours among
the French, which were chiefly trashy novels by
'Willy'—much too well printed and illustrated for
the stuff they contained—before I thought of reading
'Guy Mannering'. Meanwhile I had been plough-
ing my way with an energy worthy of a better cause
through the first series of the 'Episodios Nacionales'
of that great Spanish novelist, Pérez Galdos. To
this last fact I attribute something of the exaltation
I have experienced these three nights in the hands
of Sir Walter.

The first of the novels in the series mentioned
is 'Trafalgar', and my critical sense has seldom
had greater content in reading any book. Compared
with such romances as 'Kenilworth' or 'Ivanhoe',
it is no more than a longish short story—if I may
so describe it. But regarded as an episode, it touches
perfection. The battle of Trafalgar at once took
a new and vividly defined place in my imagination,
set there for the rest of my days by an artist of meticulous care who lacks personal power and magnetism.
As I read, I was charmed by the careful and graphic
phrasing, and mentally noted the man of letters at
work, in contrast with the mighty but careless giant

who threw the Waverley series from his pen with as little concern as a Newfoundland shakes himself on emerging from the water. The literary sense thus encouraged me through the rest of the ' Primera Serie ' of the ' Episodios Nacionales ' with a gradual sinking of my resolution, until it was reaching zero in ' La Batalla de los Arapiles ', as stupid a string of *tonterias* as any real artist ever constructed, relieved only by the magnificent description of the battle which gives this unduly long novel its title.

In this novel appears one of the absurdest characters in historical romance: a certain Miss Fly, daughter of Lord Fly, Count of Chichester. (Ye gods!) She is never for one breathing moment real. I think of her and of Meg Merrilees, whose stories lie side by side at this moment on my reading table. Oceans divide them, and the waste of seas. One overlooks such assertions as that the Highlanders in the Peninsular War wore kilts made of red and black cloth chess-board design, or that all the English officers could gabble Spanish, or that the hero Gabriel Araceli should have been placed in command of a Highland regiment at the critical moment of the final assault on the Arapil Grande, and was able to shout his commands in English, which language he had never spoken before and never spoke again! All these absurdities would be forgiven if Miss Fly—who curiously reminds me of that ludicrous Englishman of Jules Verne's invention, Phineas Fogg—or, indeed, any of the other imaginary characters, ever spoke or acted for a second as human beings. But they never do, and all the while one is conscious that their chronicler is still a literary artist.

Now, in reading 'Guy Mannering' one is never conscious of the literary artist. Truth to say, if the critical mood assert itself, there is occasion for sharing Stevenson's strictures on the slovenliness of Sir Walter's style. For instance, in the first fifty pages of 'Guy Mannering' (including the author's introduction of 1829), one is reminded of the *Daily Telegraph's* late Victorian 'style'. There is much talk of the stars, yet only once is the word 'stars' boldly written. They are described frequently as 'the heavenly bodies', as 'constellations', and in other phrases of pure journalese. Nor is this because the author is careful to distinguish between stars, planets, and constellations. There is no need for such distinction. He has simply been reeling off his words in splendid carelessness, and such a phrase as 'the heavenly bodies' has slid from his pen in tune with the sweeping movement of his narrative. Sir Walter, unlike Stevenson, never worried about *le mot juste*, but we all know which was the greater man and the better teller of tales.

Scott is so much more than a literary artist, so eminently above all puling criticism, that if we give ourselves up to the enchantment of his story we shall never greatly care whether he could write as good a sentence as R. L. S., or even if he split his infinitives or sinned with Thackeray in his 'and whiches'. Did not Meredith commit 'different to '? I know many pretentious pedants who could correct Sir Walter's English, but with a fairly wide acquaintance in the literary world of to-day I should be at a loss to name you anyone who could have written ' Guy Mannering '.

And I am far from saying that this is Scott at his best. There are at least eight of the Waverley Novels that I would place before it, yet not one of them has given me pleasure greater than that I have revelled in these last three nights. I seem to have passed from the study of a clever writer into the boundless world of romance the moment I laid down ' La Batalla de los Arapiles ' and took up ' Guy Mannering '. I am almost ready to aver that, when I was reading the story by Galdos, all the time I was conscious of the clatter of the tramways in the Calle Sarandí, as I am again while I write; but no nerveless demon of a tram-driver batters his bell in the realms of Romance. (There is, by the way, fine use of a weird bell in Stevenson's ' Black Arrow ', where it serves to warn the approach of a leper.)

From the moment that Guy Mannering arrives at Ellangowan on that dark and fateful night we are caught up on the wings of romance, and such inter- ludes of pure comic characterisation as are supplied by the appearances of Dandie Dinmont and Mr. Pleydell, or by the funeral of Mrs. Margaret Bertram (one of the most characteristically Scott chapters in all the Waverleys), jar on the romantic no more than the grave-diggers jar on the tragic in ' Hamlet '. The brooding spirit of Fate is over all, and co-

ordinates the other elements.   The comic is as much
a part of Fate as the tragic, and there is ' laughter
of gods ' in ' Guy Mannering '.

If the novelist himself had not pointed out the
change in his design, whereby his novel, begun as
' The Astrologer ', was soon deflected from its
original lines, as he grew conscious of the danger
of devoting the whole to the theme of a discredited
science and the influence of the stars on poor
humanity, he would have been a sharp critic who
had noted this, or he would certainly not have been
giving himself to the whole-hearted enjoyment of
the story.   It would be easy, of course, to pick
holes in it, dissecting the novel like a dead body;
but is there a more futile occupation?   When one
thinks of the extraordinary group of personages
who have trooped out of the author's inexhaustible
imagination into its pages—of Meg Merrilees, of
Dominie Sampson, Dandie Dinmont, Glossin, of
Dirk Hatteraick, Mr. Pleydell, Miss Mannering,
Miss Bertram, young Hazlewood, Harry Bertram,
and Guy Mannering himself, to say nothing of a
score of minor characters, any of whom were a
feather in the cap of some of our ' popular ' novelists
of to-day—one is ashamed to have read a tale of
such brimming interest only thrice.

And yet my book-seller friends in London will
tell me ' there is no great demand for Scott now-a-
days.'   He certainly cuts a poor figure as a ' best
seller ' alongside of my friend, the late Charles
Garvice.   Even in these lands of South America

the paper-covered ' sixpennies ' of Mr. Garvice are strewn with prodigal hand. Unlike the tales of ' Sherlock Holmes ', the South American's favourite reading, which exist in countless editions and varying degrees of bad translations—Sherlock Holmes has even given his name to an Argentine native weekly magazine of the ' penny blood ' variety— Mr. Garvice's stories are seldom if ever seen here in translations; but the demand for them among the exiled English must be enormous. Garvice has at least this in common with Sir Walter: he does not trouble much about ' style '—he is no Stevensonian—and he tells a forthright story.

If that story varies but slightly in each of his multitudinous books, it is because the great British public likes ' the mixture as before.'

But is it really true that we British are so far weakened in our national intellect, so atrophied in our imaginative faculties, that the virile, full-blooded tales of Sir Walter have to make way for pappy ' love stories ' such as fill the pages of the home weeklies and the fiction magazines? This I do not believe, nor do I despair that those who read Miss Annie S. Swan and Mr. Silas Hocking to-day may read Scott to-morrow. In all seriousness, I say that the two novelists I have just named have more in common with Sir Walter than the brilliant author of ' Trafalgar '. They are born storytellers, whereas Pérez Galdos is a literary artist turned novelist against his will, just as it is certain Meredith would never have written a novel had not the literary taste of his day urged him to adopt that vehicle.

For, after all, it is the business of the story-teller to tell us a story, to ' take us out of ourselves ', and to the extent that he enchants us and furnishes our minds with enduring and beautiful memories is he great or little. Among those in our land who have sought to perform this most humane of services to their fellows Sir Walter Scott is surely so immeasurably greater than any other that, until mechanism has completely brutalised the brain, destroyed imagination and sensibility, there will be many ready to submit themselves again and again to the spell of the Master Magician.

.   .   .   .   .

The last of the trams has long since passed, and the strange horseman, armed with the long pole, who clatters under my window every night between twelve and one to turn off the street lights, must have gone by unnoticed hours ago, for even in this town of restless night there is now no sound save the long-drawn and faint whistle of a far policeman. And I must to bed, breaking for once Sir Walter's rule of never writing up to bed-time, but leaving an interval for reading before ' turning in '.

Calle Sarandi,
    Montevideo.

V

A STEVENSON PILGRIMAGE

To A. MacCallum Scott

LIKE all true Scots—among whom how can I pretend to be numbered, with a father from Lancashire?—you are a blade-bright Stevensonian. You, too, are a writer of travel-books, ranging among scenes near and far, from those of our native Clydesdale to beyond the Baltic and the coasts of Barbary. And travel, as you know, my dear Scott, together with ancient history and biography, engages the main affections of my bookman's heart. That is why I find myself, when the mood for a companionable book comes over me, so often taking down a volume of travels from my shelves. There are not many that stand there unread, and there would be none were it not that a favourite one has so often beguiled me again, that the time which would have brought a newcomer into my already long list of ' books read ' has gone to another reading of one that I have read several times before. In this irrational fashion does one's taste constrain, at times, to further companionship with a familiar friend when new adventures in reading are waiting at arm's reach.

And, touching friends and companionship, I am sure you will agree with me that not the least reward of the literary life is the companionship it brings. Perhaps I should call it rather the journalistic life, since a man may write books and win fame without making any sort of contact with other writing folk: the journalist is essentially gregarious. I think of such authors as Philip James Bailey, J. H. Shorthouse, and R. D. Blackmore, all famous in their day, whose ways of life never debouched upon our highway of letters, that street of adventure which is called Fleet. Yes, it is the journalistic life that brings us those vagrom intellectual companionships which we cherish more than any material reward that may attend our efforts of the pen. American journalism is richer in this Bohemian character than our own, and with the alarming increase of respectability in British journalism I foresee a day when the newspaper office will be as tame an establishment as an insurance office or a bank.

' Wyoming Kit ', who came unknown out of the wildest West into Detroit, wrote some brilliant humorous verse and prose in the old *Detroit Free Press* and after a few weeks ' silently stole away '; Ambrose Bierce, another vagabond journalist who contrived to vanish into the unknown after producing a series of short stories unrivalled for dramatic power—do not such figures attract you more than, let us say, the great Delane of the *Times*, or the prosperous and honoured Robinson of the *Daily News*? I know they do, my dear Scott, from many a gossip we have had through a long tale of years. Journalism brings us strange companions, but, so they have character, all are welcome, as our main concern is the study of human nature. I know also that you share with me the opinion that Robert Louis Stevenson, himself a queer creature, and prince of all his contemporaries in the art of studying character, is nowhere more true to himself than in his first two books of vagabondage, which austere criticism will not allow to be other than pieces of imitative writing.

There is no more barren pursuit of criticism than the hunting of derivative traces. What though 'An Inland Voyage' and 'Travels with a Donkey' may have been inspired by 'A Sentimental Journey', and though both may be in style a trifle self-conscious, a little artificial, still are they two of the author's most characteristic works. A Stevensonian told me the other day that he reads each book of R. L. S. once every year, except these two, and these he reads at least twice. 'The world is so full of a number of things' to absorb my brief leisure, that I lack the time for such commendable devotion; but if I had the time I should not think it ill-spent if I used it in the same way.

To me there is a dewy freshness of youth in 'An Inland Voyage' and 'Travels with a Donkey', there is a brave and delicate humour, a gay sobriety of thought, a charm of personality, that has never staled at any of a dozen re-readings in thirty years. They are true companionable books, and I hope Professor Gordon, who has recently been lecturing and writing on that subject, has included them in his list. For a Merton professor of English literature to condescend upon a topic so humanly interesting is a sign of progress, and I feel sure he cannot have overlooked those two books, which are of the very essence of companionship.   Anyone who could omit them would be capable of including Kelly's London Directory. That they were published originally without attracting attention is properly in tune with the history of many another charming piece of literature: not until their author 'got away with it' in the vulgar field of fiction did any of his earlier work begin to draw the *quidnuncs*. Of 'An Inland Voyage', the first of the two, and the lesser in literary worth, I write in another essay; here I would ask you to let me ramble on about 'Travels with a Donkey', and my own travels with a bicycle a quarter of a century later on the trail of the 'green donkey-driver'.

I am not greatly exercised over the literary qualities of 'Travels with a Donkey': you must not be too inquisitorial with a companionable book, just as with your best friend of all (if you are wise) you will

> Be to her virtues very kind;
> Be to her faults a little blind.

This one argues that because Stevenson, in these earlier writings, was more intent upon the thoughts and emotions of R.L.S. than upon the objective world around him, they rank much below his maturer

work, while that one complains that in all his travels
Stevenson was but examining himself afresh against
a changing background. Can you tell me why the
subjective method need be held inferior to the
objective (to use the modern jargon of criticism)
in its literary issue? I doubt if you can, and if you
could I should still proclaim my delight in these
two books of sentimental travel. They throw open
the door to their writer's heart with an unmistakable
gesture of welcome that is nowhere attained in
fictional narrative even of the ' self-revealing ' kind.
It has been suggested, and with a good show of
plausibility, that woven into the fabric of ' Travels
with a Donkey ', something, I shall suppose, like
those bright silken strands that enliven a woollen cloth,
or it may be hidden in the best Baconian cypher
style within the text, is many a message of love and
admiration to the remarkable woman who, within two
years, was to become his partner for the remainder
of his life. I do not doubt it; but to seek for these
' hidden meanings ' has never seemed to me worth
while: the searcher is too ready to find more than the
author has concealed. In his dedication R.L.S. writes:

Every book is, in an intimate sense, a circular letter to the
friends of him who writes it. They alone take his meaning;
they find private messages, assurances of love, and expressions
of gratitude, dropped for them in every corner. The public
is but a generous patron who defrays the postage.

This is wisely stated and, mark you, he speaks
not of ' Travels with a Donkey ' but of *every book*.

Why may we not leave it at that? I think I have sufficient resolution to do so.

In the reading of travel-books there is a heightening of the pleasure if the reader can be beguiled into imagining himself the traveller. With myself, at least, this is so, and Hazlitt may be authority enough for supposing that my experience is not singular. To me the chief charm in a book of travel is this fanciful assumption of the rôle of the traveller; so far, indeed, does it condition my reading, that my readiest appetite is for a story of wayfaring in a region where I may reasonably hope to look some day upon the scenes that have first engaged my mind's eye. The adventures of a Sven Hedin in Tibet, or a Stanley in innermost Africa, attract me less than the narrative of a journey such as Elihu Burritt's famous walk from London to John o' Groats, or Hilaire Belloc on ' The Path to Rome '. That is yet another of my reasons for delighting in ' Travels with a Donkey in the Cevennes ', and it had long been a dream of mine to track the path of R. L. S. through that romantic region of old France in the pilgrim spirit of love for him who

> Here passed one day, nor came again—
> A prince among the tribes of men.

I might have suspected that many of the places with which I was romantically familiar through Tusitala's witchery of words would be drab and dull enough in reality: sufficient for me that here, in his pilgrim

facing p. 64

ST MICHEL, LE PUY

way, that 'blithe and rare spirit' had rested for a little while.

A quarter of a century has been added to the scroll of time since I translated this dream into reality; but I find that every detail of my pilgrimage is enamelled with astonishing clearness in my mind to-day. As my plan was to strike the trail of R. L. S. after some wanderings awheel northward of Clermont-Ferrand, I approached the Cevennes from Le Puy, which so excellent a judge as Joseph Pennell considered 'the most picturesque town in Europe'. Stevenson himself had often wandered its quaint, unusual streets, while preparing for his journey with immortal Modestine. 'I decided on a sleeping sack,' says he; 'and after repeated visits to Le Puy, and a deal of high living for myself and my advisers, a sleeping sack was designed, constructed, and triumphantly brought home.' The wanderer's brief 'home' in these parts was in the mountain town of Le Monastier, some fifteen miles south-east of Le Puy, where, in the autumn of 1878, he spent 'about a month of fine days', variously occupied in completing his 'New Arabian Nights' and 'Picturesque Notes on Edinburgh', and conducting, with no little personal and general entertainment, the preliminaries of the journey that was to provide so much pleasure for generations of readers.

In all his travels Stevenson, I fancy, was less moved by the aspects of nature, or by the purely picturesque qualities of landscape, than by the hazard of human encounter. The adventures that he went

F

to seek were those that lay beyond the bend of the road, across the hill: he was ever on his way to Serendip. That he had the seeing eye for the hills and dales through which his way zig-zagged his pages bear abundant witness, but he is seldom occupied with the scene to the exclusion of the actors, however humble these may be; nay, his curtest passages are those that set his stage for the commerce of his characters, real or imagined. Not in all his romantic life did he ever look upon a town of more surprising aspect than this same Le Puy, set in a landscape that suggests an Atlantic storm staged at its most tempestuous moment, its mountain waves magically changed into everlasting hills of green. Yet, he makes no attempt to convey the impression which the place must have made upon him. Perhaps he felt that it defied description, and the only art that could express it was that of Joseph Pennell, whose pencil never tired of picturing the pinnacled marvels of Le Puy.

Though I shall not rush in where R. L. S. did not care to tread, I would recall my intercourse with one of whom I have often thought since my own brief sojourn there in the summer of 1903: the sacristan of the cathedral. He was a merry rogue, and as I spent much of three or four rainy days in the cathedral, at a time, remember, when English visitors during a whole year were numbered on the fingers of one hand, we were quickly friends. It may have been the coal-black virgin of the great altar that fascinated me. She wore a crown of gold and precious stones, while from the bosom of her rich silken robe, stiff with brocade, a smaller piccanniny head, also with a golden crown, peeped out, the ensemble giving a most grotesque suggestion of a marsupial deity such as the Australian ' black fellow ' might have attained to had he advanced a step or two in the evolution of the divine idea.

Of so amiable a disposition did I find the sacristan that during the office of Mass, when attending the celebrant, he would nod familiarly on recognising me among the congregation. One morning in the sacristy he opened a great oaken cupboard and produced first a brass monstrance, containing, behind the little glass disc, a tiny morsel of white feather sewn to a bit of cloth.

' This,' he said, ' is a piece of the wing of the angel who visited Joan of Arc '.

' Indeed,' I said, suitably surprised, ' and who got hold of the feather first ? '

' The mother of Joan,' he replied, as though he were giving the name of his tailor. ' It is, M'sieu, an object of the greatest veneration, and has attracted pilgrims from far parts of France. It has cured the most terrible diseases; it has brought riches to those who were poor; it has brought children to barren women '—and many other wonders that I have forgotten did that little bit of feather achieve.

In a very similar setting he showed me a tiny thorn. ' This, M'sieu, is a thorn from the crown that Jesus wore on the Cross,' and while I was still gazing upon the sacred relic he produced a small box sealed with red wax and having a glass lid, behind which was preserved a good six inches of ' the true Cross '. Finally he thrust his hand into a cotton bag, and fished out a Turkish slipper, worn and battered, but probably no more than fifty years old. Without a quiver of an eyelid he said, ' *Voici, le soulier de la Sainte Vierge.*' The shoe of the holy Virgin! He drew attention to the pure Oriental workmanship of the sacred slipper, but I declare frankly that it was not until the Protestant pastor of the town mentioned it next day that I realised the shoe was ' a No. 9 '.

When the weather cleared I set out awheel together with a companion of the road for the little mountain town of Le Monastier, which in those days seemed for ever safe from tourist intrusion, but may now be a busy motoring centre for all I know. The town, seen at a distance, was a mere huddle of grey houses stuck on the side of a bleak, treeless upland, and at close quarters it presented few allurements to the traveller. Stevenson thought it ' notable for the making of lace, for drunkenness, for freedom of language, and for unparalleled political dissension '. Certainly it was not notable for the comfort of its hostelries, but I have never regretted my brief stay at the Hotel de Chabrier.

Lame of a leg, his feet shod with the tattered fragments of slippers, a pair of unclean heels peeping out of his stockings, mine host was the living advertisement of his frowsy and dilapidated inn, the ground

facing p. 68

IN THE MARKET PLACE
AT LE MONASTIER

floor of which, still bearing the legend *Café*, had been turned into a stable for oxen, and lay open to the highway. But withal, if one turned a shut eye on the kitchen, the cooking was good, and M. Chabrier assured us that he was renowned for game patties, which he exported to 'all parts of Europe'. His frank satisfaction with himself and his hotel, betrayed at every turn, would have rejoiced the heart of R. L. S., and the chances are that in that month of fine days, five-and-twenty years before, Stevenson may have gossiped with M. Chabrier, who was then, as at my passing, making his guests welcome and baking his inimitable patties.

Did he know Stevenson? ' *Oui, oui, oui, M'sieu!* ' Stevenson was a writer of books who had spent some time there years ago. ' *Oui, oui, parfaitement, M'sieu Stevenzong.* ' What a memory the man had, and how blithely he recalled the distant past!

' Then, of course, you must have known the noted village character, Father Adam, who sold his donkey to this Scottish traveller? '

' *Père Adam—oui, oui, oui—ah, non, non, je ne le connais pas* ', thus shuffling when asked for some further details.

M. Chabrier, who read the duty of an inn-keeper to be the humouring of his guests, could clearly supply me with the most surprising details of him whose footsteps I was tracing; so, to test his evidence at the outset, I asked how many years had passed since he of whom we spoke had rested at Le Monastier. He scratched his head and thought hard:

this Scotsman—oh, he was sure he was a Scotsman
—had stayed in that very hotel, and occupied bedroom number three, just four years back.

A bad shot clearly, and his cheerful avowal that
he was 'a partisan of no religion', did not increase
my faith in him. There were few Protestants in
Le Monastier, he said; but as I knew from the pastor
of Le Puy that the postmaster here was of the
reformed faith, and might be supposed a man of
some reading, I hoped there to find some knowledge
of Stevenson. Alas, '*J'n' sais pas*' was all the
postmaster could contribute.

In the evil-smelling by-ways of Le Monastier,
noting the ancient crones at every other door busy
with their lace-making pillows, the grizzled wood-
choppers at work in open spaces, one felt that many
of these same folk must have been mightily interested
in the strange figure, 'slight unspeakably', that
moved among them a quarter of a century before;
but to find one that could recall him were a hopeless
task; and to identify the *auberge*, in the billiard room
of which 'at the witching hour of dawn' he con-
cluded the purchase of the donkey and administered
brandy to its disconsolate seller, proved no simpler
matter. The market-place where Father Adam and
his donkey were first encountered was the only parcel
of sure ground. So, with the stench of the church,
whose interior seemed to enclose the common sewer
of the town, still lingering in our nostrils, we resumed
our journey southward across the little river Gazeille,
and headed uphill in the direction of St. Martin de

Frugères, lingering for a little as we mounted on the other side of the valley by the straggling lane down which Modestine, laden with that wonderful sleeping sack and the paraphernalia of the quaintest of travellers, 'tripped along upon her four small hoofs with a sober daintiness of gait' to the ford across the river.

I still remember the agreeable surprise with which, as we went upon our way, I discovered the identical patches of rock and pine, and notably the romantic ruins of Château Neuf, with the little village clustered at their roots, which had furnished subjects for Stevenson's block and pencil. Reproductions of these drawings I had seen five years before in the *Studio* magazine, and the vivid truth of their amateurish lines flashed them back into my mind as I beheld the actual scenes. Among these efforts of the amateur limner there had also been published a sketch of his that gives a fine impression of the far-reaching panorama of volcanic mountain masses westward of Le Monastier, a scene of wild and austere aspect.

As we advanced the road grew wilder towards St. Martin de Frugères, to which village the sentimental traveller came, upon a Sabbath, and wrote of the 'home feeling' the scene at the church aroused in him—a sentiment difficult to share as we wandered the filth-sodden streets and examined the ugly little church, white-washed within and stuffed with crude symbols of a worship that is anathema to all descendants of the Shorter-Catechists. Here was a bleak

and cheerless countryside, a little reminiscent of the
Scottish highlands westward of Tomintoul, though
the silvery Loire far below in the valley had promise
of fairer scenes as we descended to the neighbourhood
of Goudet.

There at the Café Rivet we found the first of the
Stevenson landmarks, and living folk who had entertained an angel unawares. It was one of the usual
small plastered buildings, destitute of any quaintness,
but cleaner than most, and sporting a large wooden
tobacco pipe, crudely fashioned, by way of a sign.
The old people who kept it were good Cevennol
types, the woman wearing the curious head-gear of
the peasant folk that resembles the tiny burlesque
hats worn by musical clowns, and the man in every
trait of dress and feature capable of passing for a
country Scot. The couple were engagingly ignorant,
and had never heard of Scotland, so it was no surprise
to learn that they knew nothing of its famous son
who had once ' hurried over his midday meal ' in
the dining-room where I was endeavouring to
instruct Madame Rivet in the art of brewing tea.
The Rivets had been four years in possession of
the inn at the time of Stevenson's visit, and I should
judge that the place had changed in no essential
feature, though I missed the portrait of the host's
nephew, Regis Senac, ' Professor of Fencing and
Champion of the Two Americas ', that had amused
the donkey-driver.

The highway from Goudet to Ussel is one of
the most beautiful on the whole route, lying in a

facing p. 72

CHATEAU BEAUFORT
NEAR GOUDET

wide and deep glen, similar to many that exist in the Scottish Highlands, but again unlike all these in its innumerable terraces that carry little fields of vines or wheat.

It was along this road, where on our right the terraces climbed upward to the naked basalt, and on the other side of the valley, now flooded with a pale yellow sunset that picked out vividly children at play tending a scanty herd of cattle on the hillside, that our donkey-driver of old had some of his bitterest experiences with that thrawn jade Modestine. Fortunate in our more docile mounts, we made good progress to Ussel, after faring some two miles on foot. And when we arrived at Costaros, a town drab and dismal beyond words, the evening was wearing out under a leaden sky, promising the stragglers from the market good use for their bulky umbrellas, while eight kilometres of rough country roads still lay between us and the Lake of Bouchet, where we hoped to find a lodging for the night.

Stevenson, in his heart-breaking struggles with the wayward ass, must have crossed the highway in the dark some little distance south of Costaros, to have arrived at the village of Bouchet St. Nicolas, two miles beyond the lake; and, pressing forward in the rain, which now fell pitilessly and turned the darkling mountains into phantom masses smoking with mist, one could measure the satisfaction with which he abandoned his quest of the lake and spent his first night snug at the inn of Bouchet. We learned at Cayres that the chalet on the shore of the lake had opened for the season, and in our dripping state we pressed thither uphill, feeling that two miles more in the rain could not worsen our condition.   It was a weird and moving experience —the ghostly woods on the hillside, the tuneless tinkle of bells on unseen sheep, the hissing noise of our wheels on the moist earth—and our delight was great when at length we heard the lapse of water on our left, and knew we had reached the lake.

'I had been told,' says R. L. S., 'that the neighbourhood of the lake was uninhabited except by trout.'   He travelled in the days before the *Syndicat d'Initiative du Velay*, which I shall ever bless for its chalet by the Lac du Bouchet, whose lighted windows two weary pilgrims descried that night with joy unspeakable.   Our arrival was the cause of no small commotion to the good folk who kept this two-storeyed wooden hostel. We were their first visitors of the season, and they hailed us with delight, despite the lateness of the hour.

Next morning the whole countryside was sweet with the incense of faggot fires burning on many a cottage hearth. The road south of Costaros even on a bright summer day must appear bleak and cheerless, but that morning of scudding cloud and eager air our chief desire was to move along it as quickly as we could. By the time we had reached the hamlet of La Sauvetat, however, the sun was showing fitfully, and on our right it suddenly flooded with amber light a meadow, yellow with marigolds, where cows were pasturing, attended by a small

girl who was playing at skipping-rope. Here we
had again joined the track of R. L. S., where, now
armed with a goad, he drove his donkey. ' The
perverse little devil, since she would not be taken
with kindness, must even go with pricking.' His
recorded treatment of Modestine here and later
would not have qualified him for membership
of the R.S.P.C.A. I fear. But not until one has
had a turn at donkey-driving can one speak with
understanding.

The slattern town of Pradelles perched at an
altitude of 3,800 feet above sea-level, where we had
now come, wore an unmistakable ' foreign ' appearance, and we walked its streets with a sense of moving
cautiously along the sloping roof of a house. The
interior of the church was quaint enough to make
me sorry that Stevenson had not yielded to the urging
of the landlady of the inn to visit Our Lady of Pradelles, ' who performed many miracles, although she
was of wood ', for his impressions of the church
could not have failed to be illuminating. The
miraculous image of the virgin is a wooden doll,
dressed in lace and set on the high altar. Pilgrims
come in large numbers to its shrine every fifteenth
of August; and one of the spirited paintings on the
wall depicts the rescue of the idol from a burning
of the church, probably about the time of the Revolution. The rescuers of Our Lady were not prepared,
it would seem, to submit her to the crucial test her
ebonised sister image at Le Puy survived—' burning
for thirty-six hours without being consumed '.

While footing it along an unridable path on the road to Langogne, a young woman on a terrace by the wayside came forward to greet us, tripping unexpectedly over the tether of a goat, and landing softly and naturally on the ground, where, after her moment's surprise, she smilingly asked, ' *Où allez vous promener ?* ' more usually our bucolic greeting than ' *D'où'st-ce-que vous venez ?* ' the ' sacramental phrase ', on which Stevenson remarked. The bridge across the Allier at Langogne, where he met the ' lassie of some seven or eight ' who demanded whence he came, had become a crazy ruin, and a serviceable modern structure spanned the river some little distance to the west.

His track now lay somewhat to the west of the Allier, as he made for the little village of Cheylard l'Evêque, on the borders of the Forest of Mercoire, and in this stage of his journey he was more than usually faithful to his ideal of travel: ' For my part, I travel not to go anywhere, but to go. I travel for travel's sake. The great affair is to move; to feel the needs and hitches of our life more nearly; to come down off this feather-bed of civilization, and find the globe granite underfoot and strewn with cutting flints.'

There was no need for his quitting the highway, since his further objective lay due south through the pleasant valley of the Allier. But his diversion among the by-ways was rich in adventure, and furnished him with his best chapter, ' A Camp in the Dark '. He had the good fortune to lose his

way after nightfall, and to be forced to camp in a
wood of pines in happy ignorance of his whereabouts.
Here was just the sort of adventure he had hoped
for when he set out from Le Monastier. When,
he did reach Cheylard next morning he was fain
to confess that 'it seemed little worthy of all this
searching'.

'Why anyone should desire to visit either Luc
or Cheylard is more than my much inventing spirit
can suppose', our vagabond goes on. But, journeying at a more genial season of the year, I found the
neighbourhood of Luc not devoid of beauty. The
valley of the Allier is here broken into wide and
picturesque gorges, and in many ways the scenery
is reminiscent of Glen Coe, where Alan Breck and
David Balfour dodged the redcoats. But late in
September it would bear a very different aspect,
and Stevenson admits that 'a more unsightly prospect
at this season of the year it would be hard to fancy.
Shelving hills rose round it on all sides, here dabbled
with wood and fields, there rising to peaks alter-
nately naked and hairy with pines. The colour
throughout was black or ashen, and came to a point
in the ruins of the castle of Luc, which pricked up
impudently from below my feet, carrying on a
pinnacle a tall white statue of Our Lady'. There
is now a railway station at Luc, the line running
near the road all the way to La Bastide. As we
continued southward that sunny June day, it was
only the shrilling of the crickets and the unusual
quilt work of the diligently husbanded hillsides that

told us we were not looking upon a Perthshire landscape.

At La Bastide, he tells us, ' I was directed to leave the river, and follow a road that mounted on the left among the hills of Vivarais, the modern Ardèche; for I was now come within a little way of my strange destination, the Trappist monastery of Our Lady of the Snows'. And there I have reached one of the ' emotional moments ' in the story of my pilgrimage. ' Our Lady of the Snows ' is a name endeared to every Stevensonian by wistful memories of that pilgrim of genius who sought for admission at the monastery gate just half a century ago. Surely the porter never looked through his wicket at a stranger pair than the gaunt young man and his little donkey that stood without.

Stevenson's stay at Our Lady of the Snows provided him with the richest experience of his journey, and not only informed the most important section of his book, but inspired one of the best of his earlier poems: the twenty-third of ' Underwoods '. You, I am sure, do not need to have it recalled, but I repeat the opening verses for the pleasure of transcribing them:

> Out of the sun, out of the blast,
> Out of the world, alone I passed
> Across the moor and through the wood
> To where the monastery stood.
> There neither lute nor breathing fife,
> Nor rumour of the world of life,
> Nor confidences low and dear,
> Shall strike the meditative ear.

Aloof, unhelpful, and unkind,
The prisoners of the iron mind,
Where nothing speaks except the bell
The unfraternal brothers dwell.

The poem is really a restatement in fine, dignified
verse of the impression made upon its author by
the suffocating existence of these silentious shirkers
of life's battle, and already conveyed in the finely
polished prose of his ' Travels ':

O to be up and doing, O
Unfearing and unshamed to go
In all the uproar and the press
About my human business!

This he had expressed in concluding his chapter
on ' The Monks ': ' And I blessed God that I was
free to wander, free to hope, and free to love.'

As I observed the monks dully occupied with
their various holy offices during our stay, which
extended through a day and night, and saw how,
in the passages twixt chapel and cell, they strove to
avoid the slightest brotherly contact, my heart leapt
up to the donkey-driver in an eager communion of
sentiment. Often in later years I have tried to
imagine the terror of the dreadful night that came
to Our Lady of the Snows some nine years after
my visit when the fine quadrangle of buildings was
gutted by fire. How were the vows of silence
observed then? The monastery, I have heard, was
rebuilt in another site, and only a sorry ruin marks

the scene of that which once had been Stevenson's
' strange destination '.

Making a swift descent to La Bastide, and by
way of Chasseradès, where Stevenson slept in the
common bedroom of the inn, we reached Le Bleymard late in the afternoon, passing through a country
of bare hills and poor villages clustered in gusty
hollows or hanging like swallows' nests on craggy
slopes.   The valley of the Lot, rich and beautiful
westward to Mende, possesses no elements of charm
in the neighbourhood of Bleymard, and we found
that town so mean and featureless that we had no
wish to pass the evening there.   But fire had
recently erased another landmark here, for the Hotel
du Lot at La Remise, where we might have lodged
with some measure of comfort, stood a charred and
dismal ruin, and we were fain to make shift with
the hospitality of a temporary tavern, a real ' hedge
inn ' near-by, as it was now after sundown, and there
lay between us and Pont de Montvert a mountain
higher than Ben Nevis.

Next day the countryside was blotted out in rain,
not a glimpse of the *massif* of the Lozère showed
for a moment, and not until late in the second morning of our most unwilling stay could we venture
forth upon the risky mountain journey.   For some
miles we had to plod upward on foot in a wild and
rocky gorge, with the merest trickle of water below.
Yet every corner where a few square feet of clover
could be coaxed into life had been cultivated by the
dogged peasants, and patches were growing at

OUR LADY OF THE SNOWS

facing p. 81

heights where one would have thought it difficult to climb without the tackle of an Alpinist. The tiny hamlet of Malavieille, about halfway up the mountain side, was the highest point permanently inhabited. Here the upland fields were densely spread with violets, narcissi and hyacinths, and a few dun cows were browsing contentedly on this fragrant fare, while a boy who attended them stood on his head, kicking his heels merrily in the sunshine. He came up as we passed, staring at us stolidly; and when we asked if the snakes, of which we had just encountered two about three feet long, were dangerous, he answered ' *Pas bien* ', and more than that we could not get him to say, though he walked beside us for a time eyeing curiously our bicycles.

On coming within sight of the Baraque de Secours, we had reached a narrow table-land stretching east and west for some miles. Eastward lay the pine woods where our vagabond spent one of his most tranquil nights as described in his chapter, ' A Night Among the Pines '. It was there that, awakening in the morning, he beheld the daybreak along the mountain-tops of Vivarais—' a solemn glee possessed my mind at this gradual and lovely coming in of day '. And it was there, too, that out of thankfulness for his night's rest he laid on the turf, as he went along, pieces of money, ' until I had left enough for my night's lodging '.

A plain two-storeyed building, with a rough stone wall and porch enclosing a muddy yard, is the brief but adequate description of the baraque. It stands

G

at a height of over five thousand feet, being thus
fully five hundred feet higher than Ben Nevis.   To the
west, a great treeless waste, the Lozère swells upward
another six hundred feet, to its highest point, the
Pic de Finiels; while a splendid mass of volcanic
origin uprears its craggy head some little distance
to the south-east. 'The view, back upon the northern Gévaudan,' says Stevenson, writing of what he
saw as he passed near this point, 'extended with
every step; scarce a tree, scarce a house, appeared
upon the fields of wild hill that ran north, east, and
west, all blue and gold in the haze and sunlight of
the morning.'   And then in a little, when he began
the descent towards the valley of the Tarn, he says:

> A step that seemed no way more decisive than many other
> steps that had preceded it—and, 'like stout Cortez when with
> eagle eyes he stared on the Pacific,' I took possession, in my
> own name, of a new quarter of the world.   For behold, instead
> of the gross turf rampart I had been mounting for so long,
> a view into the hazy air of heaven, and a land of intricate blue
> hills below my feet.

As he makes no mention of the baraque, we may
assume that it had not then been built, for one so
eager of new experience would not have missed the
opportunity of resting on his way at this high-set
house of shelter for the storm-stayed or the weary.
In the winter-time all the uplands around would lie
deep in snow, the roads impassable. The baraque
itself could be kept open only from the beginning of
June to the end of September, when its keepers

retired downhill again to Malavieille. As R. L. S. crossed the mountain on the second last day in September, the snows would soon be thick upon his track.

After a good meal and some laboured conversation in the dialect of Languedoc we went forward into the country of the Camisards along a well-made road which gangs of labourers were leisurely repairing. So good are these mountain roads, and so diligently tended, that one is inclined to think they are used chiefly for the transit of stones to keep them in repair. That on which we travelled had been made since Modestine and her driver footed it through this same valley. Doubtless it is in the summer days of these later years dusty with the passing of many motors; and the muddy yard of the baraque may be a parking place for cars. *Eheu fugaces.* . . . In less than a mile the road begins to sweep swiftly downward. Stevenson describes his descent in a very charming passage:

A sort of track appeared and began to go down a break-neck slope, turning like a corkscrew as it went. It led into a valley through falling hills, stubbly with rocks like a reaped field of corn, and floored farther down with green meadows. I followed the track with precipitation; the steepness of the slope, the continual agile turning of the line of descent, and the old unwearied hope of finding something new in a new country, all conspired to lend me wings. Yet a little lower and a stream began, collecting itself together out of many fountains, and soon making a glad noise among the hills. Sometimes it would cross the track in a bit of water fall, with a pool, in which Modestine refreshed her feet. The whole descent is like a dream to me, so rapidly was it accomplished. I had scarcely left the summit ere the valley closed round my path, and the sun beat upon me, walking in a stagnant lowland atmosphere.

The road brought us at length to Pont de Montvert 'of bloody memory', lying in a green and rocky hollow among the hills. To Stevenson 'the place, with its houses, its lanes, its glaring river-bed, wore an indescribable air of the south'. Why so, he was unable to say; as he justly observes, it would be difficult to tell in what particulars it differed from Monastier or Langogne or even Bleymard. One of the first buildings that the traveller encounters is the little Protestant temple perched on the rocky bank of the river, and perhaps it was again the Protestant education of R. L. S. that led him to note a higher degree of intelligence among the inhabitants than he had found in the purely Catholic villages. For my part, with the best will to mark the difference, I found little to choose between the Catholic and Camisard townships, unless it were a more obvious effort after cleanliness in some of the latter.

Pont de Montvert is memorable as the place where the Covenanters of France struck the first blow against their Romish persecutors; here they 'slew their Archbishop Sharpe'. The Protestant pastor, a fresh-faced man about sixty, with a short white beard, and wearing no outward symbol of office, but dressed in an ordinary jacket suit and cloth cap, I found in his home near the bridge. Directly across the rock-strewn river-bed was the Hotel des Cevennes, where Stevenson sat at the 'roaring table d'hôte', and was pleased to find three of the women passably good-looking, that being more than an average for any town in the Highlands of France.

In the parson I also found a Frenchman who had long taken a lively interest in Stevenson's travels; an interest with which he seemed to have infected his wife and golden-haired daughter, who both joined heartily in our conversation. He knew all about Modestine and the driver who urged her forward with 'Proot' and so many thwackings: the year, the day, the hour of their quaint and curious visit! He was himself but two years established in his charge at the time. And Clarisse! I knew, of course, what Stevenson had said of her? And should I care to see her photograph? She was now married, and settled in another town with a considerable family growing up. One felt that after a quarter of a century, and with a family thrown in, the romantic Stevenson would have resolutely refused to look on the counterfeit presentment of Clarisse. But I did not hesitate to accept a copy of her portrait which the pastor offered me. It shows the table-maid of the hotel as still possessing some of the featural charms so minutely and faithfully noted by our author:

What shall I say of Clarisse? She waited the table with a heavy placable nonchalance, like a performing cow; her great grey eyes were steeped in amorous languor; her features, although fleshy, were of an original and accurate design; her mouth had a curl; her nostrils spoke of dainty pride; her cheek fell into strange and interesting lines. It was a face capable of strong emotion, and with training it offered the promise of delicate sentiment. . . . Before I left I assured Clarisse of my hearty admiration. She took it like milk, without embarrassment or wonder, merely looking at me steadily with her great eyes; and I own the result upon myself was some confusion. If Clarisse could read English, I should not dare to add that her figure was unworthy of her face. Hers was a case for stays; but that may perhaps grow better as she gets up in years.

When I look again at the photograph, I fear that even this hope for her who was ' left to country admirers and a country way of thought ', had not been fulfilled.

In no respect had the road from Pont de Montvert to Florac changed since Stevenson wrote of it; not even the coming of the motor-car is likely to have altered it. The slopes of the valley have been terraced almost to the sky-line, not for baby-fields of wheat, but to furnish ground for chestnut trees, that clothe the hills with rich and sombre foliage, and give forth ' a faint, sweet perfume ' which tinctures the air with balsamic breath. It was on a terrace and under one of these trees that Stevenson camped for the night, having to scramble up some sixty feet above the place he had selected for himself, which was as high as that from the road, before he could find another terrace with space enough for his donkey. You may remember that he was awakened in the morning by peasants coming to prune the trees, and after going down to the river for his morning toilet—' To wash in one of God's rivers in the open air seems to me a sort of cheerful solemnity or semi-pagan act of worship '—he went on his way ' with a light and peaceful heart, and sang psalms to the spiritual ear as I advanced '. And then there is that pretty picture of the donkey-driver and the old man who had asked him if he knew the Lord, ' talking like Christian and Faithful by the way ' as they came down into that humble place, La Vernède, beyond which the country grew richer and more fruitful as we approached Florac, passing on our way the old castle of Miral.

The influence of a country on its people suggested to R. L. S. an interesting comparison as he journeyed through ' this landscape, smiling although wild ':

Those who took to the hills for conscience sake in Scotland had all gloomy and bedevilled thoughts; for once that they received God's comfort, they would be twice engaged with Satan; but the Camisards had only bright and supporting visions. . . . With a light conscience, they pursued their life in these rough times and circumstances. The soul of Séguier, let us not forget, was like a garden. They knew they were on God's side, with a knowledge that has no parallel among the Scots; for the Scots, although they might be certain of the cause, could never rest confident of the person.

Now, this is a singularly inapposite comparison. It was not in pleasant valleys such as these, nor in cosy little towns like Pont de Montvert, that the Camisards fought out their war with ' His Most Christian Majesty Louis, King of France and Brittany ', but on the bare and rocky plateaux westward of the Cevennes, and on such mountain-tops as the Lozère. Stevenson had never traversed the Causse Méjan or the Causse du Larzac, to the southward of the region through which he travelled, or he would have realised that their conditions were even less likely to foster 'bright and supporting visions' in the Camisards than those of the mountain-hunted Scots, though much better from a strategic point of view.

My French guide-book frankly stated that Florac is a place 'of few attractions', but R. L. S. makes the most of these in a sentence or two, describing the town as possessing 'an old castle, an alley of planes, many quaint street-corners, and a live fountain welling from the hill'. The old castle was quite without interest, being indeed the local prison, while the alley of planes, called the Esplanade, we found a dusty open space, the grey, featureless Protestant Temple at its southern end.

Along the valley of the Mimente, which branches eastward a little south of Florac, and penetrates a country very similar to that traversed since the Lozère, we still pursued the pilgrim path. A few miles from Florac our hero spent his last night *à la belle étoile* in the valley of this little river, his last resting place in the journey being at St. Germain de Calberte, where he slept at the inn, and when next afternoon he had accomplished the eight remaining miles through the waterless valley of the Gardon to St. Jean du Gard—'fifteen miles and a stiff hill in little beyond six hours'—his romantic enterprise was safely achieved and, as you will remember, he shed a tear at parting with that ' thrawn jade ' Modestine.

In taking leave of a favourite theme and concluding these memories of one of my happiest experiences, I need not remind you that I wrote at greater length, if with less reflection, upon my pilgrimage just twenty years ago in that now forgotten book of mine ' In the Track of Stevenson ', wherein were reproduced many ' snapshots ' of the places mentioned; for I was an industrious, though never an adept camera-clicker in those days. Since then many another has gone on the same pilgrimage, and I have heard of several written accounts of their experiences though none has come under my eye. It pleases me to think that I may have been in a way responsible for suggesting the idea to energetic Stevensonians casting about for new holiday ground. The bicycle seemed to me a not unworthy means of movement, involving as it did a considerable amount of actual tramping which retained at least a suggestion of the original; but now that a motor-car will take one from Le Puy to Allais in the course of one day —yes, and back again, if need be—I fear it may be difficult on the actual road to recapture anything of that real spirit of vagabondage to which the companionship of Modestine helped R. L. S. and which the old ' push-bicycle ' did not altogether abolish from later wayfaring.

Meads,
   Eastbourne.

VI

OF THE ROMANTIC AND SOME BYRON
PLACES

To H. Greenhough Smith

I SHOULD suspect you for a romantic, my dear Greenhough Smith, did I know no more of you than that, apart from your unique editorial achievement, you had written 'The Romance of History' and 'Castle Sombras', a title that recalls Walpole and the eighteenth century movement. But from our many years of talk together on most aspects of life and letters, I know the bent of your mind, and how in the supreme affair of Illusion, wherewith man has made his life more tolerable, our tastes most often agree, though on many matters of common fact we are apt to wax acrimonious in argument. Hence the inscription to you of these memories of some Byron places.

During my journalistic days in Birmingham—*fin de siècle* days in the literal sense of their being the closing three years of the nineteenth and the opening one of the twentieth century—it was my good fortune to know some of the remarkable men who had made the history of that great city. Of these perhaps

the most picturesque and certainly the most venerable
was Samuel Timmins: 'the king-maker of Birmingham', as Thackray Bunce, that splendid editor
of the old school to whom I owed so much in counsel
and friendship, used to call him with a twinkle in
his eye. In my mind's eye I see Timmins now,
with hoar head and ample beard quaintly suggestive
of the 'Ancient of Days' in one of Blake's drawings,
telling me that he was going to spend the afternoon
with Bunce (who at seventy was Timmins' junior by
a good ten years) and had bought a little 'surprise'
for him; whereupon he took from his pocket one
of these rolled paper tubes which shoot out stiffly
when blown through a squeaking mouthpiece. He
blew it with glee, and was happy in the thought
of introducing his old friend to a new toy.

In addition to many endearing qualities which
I found in this gentle old man who had once been
so virile a leader of men with both pen and tongue,
was the common ground of an enthusiasm for Byron
and his poetry. Timmins' chief memorial in Birmingham is the fine Shakespeare library which he
gathered together, and, in his later life, presented
to the city. But though he was a good Shakespearean
he held to the end an unfading admiration of all
things Byronic. Not 'all things', perhaps, if that
included the Cordy Jeafferson, the Beecher Stowe,
and many another's harvest of the muck-rake; but
rather a properly romantic affection for a hero of
romance. Only a boy at the time of Byron's death,
he was caught in his youth with the glamour of the

poet, and it was his agreeable hobby as a man to gather every available souvenir, literary or personal, of his venerated poet. In days when travel was less facile than it is now, Timmins had visited every scene of Byron's wanderings. It had been his intention to write a book—*the* book it was to be— about the poet's life and his poetry; but Timmins, for all the energy of his prime, ' lived a life of going to do ', and, from the literary point of view at least, he ' died with nothing done '. His great unwritten book about Byron was an ' enchanted cigarette ' whose fragrance he enjoyed for more than half a century. Indeed, I doubt if he ever wrote a magazine article about his Byron pilgrimages; but how he talked!

On my way home from Ravenna a few weeks ago I fell to thinking of Timmins and of the places touched with Byron memories that I myself had visited. I was astonished to find how the inconsiderate hand of chance had brought me to so many; for seldom had I gone to them in the pilgrim spirit or note-book in pocket. I was never moved to essay that book which Timmins dreamed about: for all I know someone else has written it in the meanwhile, as books on Byron have been issued a-plenty in the thirty years since I used to chat with the old man of Birmingham. From the Brig o' Balgownie, by way of Aberdeen, Nottingham, Newstead and Annesley, Harrow and Trinity, Geneva, Chillon, Pisa, Venice and Ravenna, to the grave at Hucknall Torkard, and many another spot that I might name,

I would seem to have been tracing the footsteps of
the Pilgrim of Eternity. But seldom was conscious
purpose directing my steps, and the last enterprise
that I should care to face would be one so beyond
the measure of my knowledge as an interpretation
of Byron in the spirit of place. More than mere
enthusiasm is demanded for that, and, given the
more, a massive volume would be needed to express
it. I do not doubt that even in our unromantic days
a numerous public would welcome it. Though realism
is too much with us late and soon, the hankering for
romance is always active, and at no time so surely as
when the externals of life give it least to feed upon.

It is because I am myself sufficiently romantic
not to care for the objective methods of realism
being applied to the consideration of romance that
I had rather preserve the picture of the poet that
disengages itself from his own utterance than look
upon the truth as presented in such a work as ' The
Real Lord Byron '. There is but one Lord Byron
that matters, and that is the poet whose image takes
shape in our mind as we read ' Childe Harold ' or
' Don Juan '. I have no wish to be reminded by
Cordy Jeafferson when I look upon the Palazzo
Mocenigo, on the Grand Canal, that here came
many a little tradesman's wife unfaithful to her
husband, dazzled by the English lord and libertine.
I would have no one whisper, as I read his ' Ode
to Immortality ', that Wordsworth was the father
of a daughter whose mother was not Mrs. Wordsworth, or ask me, when I am hot-foot with Alan Breck

Stewart among the bracken, if I know that the author of ' Kidnapped ' was the father of a son when himself a very young man.

Nay, I go further in this deliberate extrusion of the things that do not matter when the mind would rove amid romantic scenes—and the background of romance, its ' landscape ', is vital to the soul of the thing—I avoid the actual lest it jar upon the imagined. For this reason, when I came, in my recent travels, to Ravenna, and found that the ' palace ' which Byron hired when he went thither to pursue his hours of dalliance with the youthful Countess Teresa Gamba Guiccioli was now the Byron Hotel, I had no wish to go in. I had rather imagine him in a true setting of romance; and no modern hotel, though occupying his identical rooms, could, at least for me, be other than destructive to my mental picture. The outside of the hotel, the commonplace, unbeautiful street, the prevailing lack of the picturesque throughout the whole town, made me feel that if Byron so loved Ravenna that he could willingly pass two years of his life there, it must since have suffered some catastrophic change, or it must have appeared transformed magically to the poet when Teresa was enchanting him with her voluptuous youth: the fate-like figure of the elderly baron fitfully showing in the background.

At Venice, on the other hand, the exterior of the Palazzo Mocenigo remains, in all its richness and mellowed beauty, as it stood when Byron was composing the first cantos of ' Don Juan ' and other

famous poems at the writing-table still preserved
within, and here, where all else in sight is glamorous
with romance, where the lovely art of the palace
builders has created a veritable 'romantic landscape,'
enduring, yet dream-like, it is easy to let one's
emotions be touched by the 'grey Gothic things'
out of which romance is shaped.

Of all the stories told by Byron and his way of
life in Venice, I think I prefer that about his manner
of going home at two of the morning from the
receptions of the famous Contessa Maria Benzon,
to the Mocenigo Palace, barely a quarter of a mile
distant on the same side of the Grand Canal. His
servant would arrive, we are told, with a lantern
and a board, and Byron, going downstairs, would
undress and give his clothes to the man; then,
placing the lantern on the board he would swim
home with it! This fits better into my picture of
romance—the deep indigo sky luminous with its
clear stars, the massy shadows of the great palaces
athwart the sluggish water of the canal, the calls
of the gondoliers, the tinkle of the guitars, and the
author of 'Don Juan' swimming by the light of
his lantern—all this goes badly with the whisperings
of 'sot', 'glutton', or 'libertine', think you not?
This is the Byron picture which the selective process
of the mind most often recalls for me in Venice,
and there is no other I would care to substitute for
it.

What I have written thus far touches chiefly on
Byron landmarks that I have come upon more by

accident than design. In another paper I have
endeavoured to recall the circumstance of a little
journey to Newstead Abbey, and it was about that
time—in the 'nineties—that Clement Shorter, who
so often, through near a score of years, shared those
Savage Club gossips of ours, set me to the writing
of a series of articles on Byron's Nottinghamshire
days, to which pleasant and profitable task I now
look back with something of the wistfulness that
even the least emotional must feel when they contemplate the souvenirs of their lost youth.

Moore in the ' Life ' refers to the fondness that
Byron always showed for his early home in ' Aberdeen awa' ', and to the warmth of feeling with which
the people of Aberdeen returned this affection,
being proud to consider Byron as almost their fellow
townsman. ' The various houses where he resided
in his youth,' says Moore, ' are pointed out to the
traveller; to have seen him but once is a recollection
boasted of with pride; and the Brig of Don, beautiful
in itself, is invested, by his mere mention of it, with
an additional charm.'   What was true of Aberdeen's
reverence for the memory of Byron in 1829 is true
to-day; Aberdonians did not wait until the softening
veil of years was spread between Byron and their
vision before they might venture to express their
admiration for the greatest poetic genius of the
nineteenth century; they hailed the poet, and they
forgave the man.

Not so in Nottingham, with which town and
district Byron's name is quite as closely associated

THE MOCENIGO PALACE,
BYRON'S HOME IN VENICE

as it is with Aberdeen. A parochial prejudice, which does not mar the literary affections of the Scots, long served to make Byron an ·unhonoured prophet in the locality where a most interesting period of his life was spent. Newstead and Hucknall Torkard when I knew them were visited mainly by Americans; the scene of his first and purest love affair, the inspiration of much of his poetry at Annesley, the home of his 'Mary', few, indeed, of the local dwellers knew to be so intimately identified with the poet; and at Southwell and Newark there are other early associations, while the Nottingham of my time possessed memorials for which a visitor might then have searched in vain.

When William Winter, the famous dramatic critic of the New York *Tribune*, visited Nottingham in 1884, and endeavoured to unearth some reminiscences of Byron, he found, as many another has discovered before and since, that the local folk were deplorably ignorant of all that concerned the genius who once lived in their midst. 'It is difficult,' he writes, 'even to find prints or photographs of the Byron localities in the shops of Nottingham. One dealer, from whom I bought all the pictures that he possessed, was kind enough to explain the situation in one expressive sentence: " Much more ought to be done here as to Lord Byron's memory, that is the truth; but the fact is, the first families of the county don't approve of him." ' This was ever the way of ' the best people '; but they were not alone in their prejudice; it was shared by the

H

commonalty, for at Hucknall, when the question
of commemorating Victoria's Diamond Jubilee was
under discussion, a project to erect a statue to the
poet was abandoned in favour of setting up a
memorial to a local quack who had earned the
reputation of effecting some wonderful cures on
ignorant country folk.

In Nottingham itself, as I remember, there was
less of this prejudice, but still too much of it, as
an attempt to secure the erection of a Byron memorial
was snuffed out by the weight of local bigotry, and
in the correspondence in the local papers one grey-
beard wrote: ' Your correspondents are probably
too young to remember the discussion that took
place some years ago in the public Press on the
subject of Lord Byron's character. Otherwise they
would, I think, be content to let sleeping dogs lie.'

It was in the summer of 1798 that Byron, in his
eleventh year, arrived at Newstead, with his mother
and nurse, to enter for the first time his ancestral
home. But the dilapidated condition of the Abbey
and Mrs. Byron's lack of means made it an unattractive
place of residence; and there was the young lord's
misshapen foot to see to while yet there might be
some chance of having it made straight, so that,
soon after their arrival from Scotland, Mrs. Byron
went to reside in Nottingham, that her son might
be attended by a person named Lavender, who
professed to be able to cure him of his lameness.
This Lavender, who has been described as an
ignorant quack, was, so I gathered from a local

directory of the time, 'truss-maker to the general hospital', and may not have been so contemptible a fellow as the biographers have represented. It is clear, however, that he subjected the young lad to the most purposeless tortures, which, on the testimony of Rogers, the Nottingham schoolmaster with whom the little sufferer read Virgil and Cicero during his 'treatment', he bore with a quiet heroism. It may be worthy of record that this early tutor of Byron is mentioned in the directory just referred to as 'Dummer Rogers, Teacher of French, English, Latin, and Mathematicks', his residence being given as Hen Cross, which was within a stone-throw of the house where Byron then resided.

While staying in Nottingham to receive the benefit of the truss-maker's wisdom, the Byrons occupied a mansion that stood only a few yards from the place which, in later years, another literary genius was to identify with his name. I refer to the old *Journal* office and J. M. Barrie. At the higher end of Pelham Street, leading east from the Market Place, was the site of the house in question, and the immediate neighbourhood, known as Carlton Street, was then called 'Swine Green'. With this name and this locality Byron's first attempt at rhyme is associated.

A neighbour who used to visit Mrs. Byron during this stay in Nottingham was an elderly lady of somewhat peculiar temperament, who entertained remarkable delusions about being transported to the moon after she had finished her earthly pilgrimage. On

one occasion she greatly offended the high-spirited
boy by some ill-judged reference to his infirmity,
and after that he never could bear the sight of her.
His opinion of her is expressed in the lines quoted
by Moore:

> In Nottingham county there lives at Swan Green
> As curst an old lady as ever was seen,
> And when she does die, which I hope will be soon,
> She firmly believes she will go to the moon.

'Swan' Green is a mistake for Swine Green, or
Moore may have preferred the more pleasing word
in transcribing.

There is a dubious story that during this period
of the poet's early life he attended a Dame school
which formerly stood on the site now occupied by
a bank.   More authentic is the evidence of an old
tradesman, who informed a gentleman, well known
to me in 1897, but who must be 'dead these twenty
years' and more, that the poet had attended a school
in a house at 30 Lower Parliament Street, which
was demolished a few years before the time of which
I write, and said that he had 'often seen the lame
boy Byron carried from the carriage to the school'.
But there is no reason to doubt that Byron lived for
a time in a house then, and possibly still, standing
almost within hail of the Castle, and close by the
spot where, on August 25, 1634, Charles I raised his
standard.   Byron resided here with his mother
during the vacation at Dr. Glennie's Dulwich
Academy, in 1799, Newstead being then, and for

some years subsequently, let to another tenant.
Willoughby's 'Directory of Nottingham' for 1799
contains at page six the entry: 'Byron, Right Hon.
Lord, at Mr. Gill's, St. James's Lane'. It is said
that the son of this Mr. Gill, when walking with
Byron to Newstead, quarrelled with the poet—or,
perhaps, it were more correct to reverse the order
—they had a severe fight on the road, and were
close friends ever after.

The house in St. James's Street (the 'lane' having
risen to that titular dignity, though it had lost its
ancient prestige as a high-class residential quarter)
had been only slightly altered since Byron lived in
it. The old doorway was blocked up, the passage
space having been added to one of the rooms, and
a new entrance made higher up the street. The
building, overgrown with ivy, was a good specimen
of the old town-houses which the county gentry
maintained before the railways made London the
one great social centre, and it was still called Newstead
House.

After 1799 Mrs. Byron does not appear to have
been in residence in Nottingham for any length of
time until 1803, when, returning from Bath, Moore
tells us that she went into 'lodgings' in the town;
but the probability is that she returned to the old
mansion-house on Swine Green. Byron, now at
Harrow, spent the vacation of this year with his
mother in Nottingham. It was at this time that he
became friendly with Lord Grey de Ruthyn, then
occupying the Abbey, who gave him every facility

for enjoying the attractions of Newstead. It was also in 1803 that frequent visits to Annesley Hall, in the vicinity, gave birth to his affection for Mary Chaworth, the ' Mary ' of ' The Dream ', an episode that coloured much of his poetry. By 1804 Mrs. Byron had removed to Southwell, and Byron never resided in the county town again.

' Had I married Miss Chaworth, perhaps the whole tenor of my life would have been different '; and so it might have been; but we may doubt whether Mary would have exercised the restraining influence his turbulent spirit required, a need which Byron himself realised. Deeply though he was in love with Mary Chaworth, and greatly though she, as a beautiful young woman, could inspire affection in the breast of the young poet, it was only a boy's love for a girl. Mary, as his lost love, a pure and enduring passion of youth, had probably more power over him than if she had become his bride. It would be nearer the truth, I fancy, to say that such refining and purifying influence as Byron ever received from womankind, save only the sympathy of Augusta, came from the purified memory of his early love, and the fact that his youthful ideal of Mary Chaworth had never been impaired by the crucial intimacy of conjugal relationship.

It was early in 1803 that Byron, then studying at Harrow, met Miss Chaworth in London, and, during the summer. vacation of that year, as we have seen, he resided with his mother in Nottingham. Lord Grey de Ruthyn was very indulgent to the lad, and, knowing his great love for the old Abbey, had placed an apartment at Byron's disposal. Some three miles south-west of Newstead lies Annesley Hall, embowered in trees itself, though its farther surroundings may be truly described in Byron's lines:

> Hills of Annesley! bleak and barren.

Annesley Hall was the property of Mary Chaworth—

> Herself the solitary scion left
> Of a time-honour'd race.

Like her lover, she was a ward in Chancery. The Chaworths and the Byrons had long been the principal landowners in Nottinghamshire, and the Chaworth who was killed by 'the wicked Lord' being cousin to Mary's father, the love of Byron for Miss Chaworth had in it something of the love of Romeo for Juliet, surely an ideal start for a romantic affair. He refers to this in one of his memorandum-books:

> Our union would have healed feuds in which blood had been shed by our fathers; it would have joined lands broad and rich; it would have joined at least one heart, two persons not ill-matched in years (she is two years my elder), and—and—and—*what* has been the result?

During the vacation of 1803, Mrs. Byron, at Nottingham, saw little of her son, and Nottingham saw less. He took full advantage of Lord Grey's invitation to occupy a chamber at Newstead, not so much, we may suppose, to be in the atmosphere

of his forefathers as to be within easy distance of
Annesley and his Mary. He tramped from the
Abbey to the Hall day after day to enjoy the society
of one who cared for him but slightly, always returning at night to Newstead, and alleging as his reason
for not sleeping at Annesley that he was afraid of
the family pictures of the Chaworths: he fancied
they had taken a grudge to him on account of the
duel, and would come down from their frames at
night to haunt him. But one night he imagined he
saw a ' bogle ' on his way to Newstead, and after that
he nightly braved the family pictures at Annesley,
sleeping there during the remainder of the ' six
short summer weeks ' spent in the company of Miss
Chaworth.

Byron's time at Annesley was mostly passed in
riding with Mary and her cousin, sitting in ' idle
reverie ', or in firing with a pistol at a door which
opens from the terrace, and upon which the shot-
marks may still be seen. But his greatest delight
was to sit in the drawing-room listening to Miss
Chaworth playing, the Welsh air ' Mary Anne '
(the Christian names of his adored one) being his
favourite piece. And all the time he knew that:

> Her sighs were not for him; to her he was
> Even as a brother—but no more.

Nor, as Moore points out, was it at all probable, in
the event of her affections having been disengaged,
that she would have selected Byron as the object of
them. She seems always to have regarded him as

a mere lad; her two years' seniority taking her into the verge of womanhood, whence she looked on Byron as only a school-boy. Nor are we greatly impressed with the young lady's charity, since we know that a chance remark of hers—'Do you think that I could care anything for that lame boy?'— overheard by Byron, wounded him to the soul, and sent him hot-foot to Newstead, though the hour was late, heedless of all bogles and terrors that fly by night.

A year had gone before they met again, and on the hill at Annesley—the spot is pointed out to this day—the last interview, so beautifully recorded in 'The Dream', the chief souvenir of his first romance, took place:

> I saw two beings in the hues of youth
> Standing upon a hill, a gentle hill,
> Green, and of mild declivity, the last
> As 'twere the cape of a long ridge of such,
> Save that there was no sea to lave its base,
> But a most living landscape, and the wave
> Of woods and cornfields.
>
> .   .   .   .   .
>
> And both were young, and one was beautiful:
> And both were young—yet not alike in youth.
> As the sweet moon on the horizon's verge,
> The maid was on the verge of womanhood;
> The boy had fewer summers, but his heart
> Had far outgrown his years, and to his eye
> There was but one beloved face on earth,
> And that was shining on him; he had look'd
> Upon it till it could not pass away.

' The next time I see you,' said Byron in parting
with Miss Chaworth, ' I suppose you will be Mrs.
Musters? '; and she answered, ' I hope so.'

> He pass'd
> From out the massy gate of that old Hall,
> And mounting on his steed he went away;
> And ne'er repassed that hoary threshold more.

The statement that the lover never again repassed
the ' hoary threshold ' is something more than poetic
licence.   Miss Chaworth gave her hand and heart
to John Musters in 1805; but, while accepting
these, he surrendered only his hand in return.   Their
marriage joined the estates of Annesley and Wiverton
to that of Colwick, Musters adding the historic
name of Chaworth to his own.   The union was
not a happy one, the husband having a cold, un-
sympathetic nature, although, like most of his family,
he was a man of considerable personal attraction.

It was not till the end of 1808 that Byron saw
his Mary again, and for the last time.   Shortly
before his departure from England he was invited
to dine at Annesley, and there he went to meet Mr.
and Mrs. Musters, the latter now a mother.   The
sight of their little daughter was a trial to the poet's
sensitive nature, and the bitter-sweet sensations of the
moment are recorded for us in the tender stanzas:

> Well! thou art happy, and I feel
>   That I should thus be happy too;
> For still my heart regards thy weal
>   Warmly, as it was wont to do.

Thy husband's blest—and 'twill impart
  Some pains to view his happier lot:
But let them pass—Oh! how my heart
  Would hate him if he loved thee not!

When late I saw thy favourite child,
  I thought my jealous heart would break:
But when th' unconscious infant smiled,
  I kiss'd it for its mother's sake.

Mrs. Musters was at Colwick Hall in the winter
of 1831, when the great Reform Riots took place,
and the fright which she received when the mob
looted the Hall, together with the shock to her
delicate system occasioned by hiding in the shrubbery
from the violence of the rioters, most probably
hastened her end, the fair object of Byron's early
and purest love dying in February, 1832. But
she had been out of her mind before the poet's fiery
spirit went home in that thunderstorm at Missolonghi
eight years earlier, for the last sad lines of ' The
Dream ' close an ' ower true tale ':

My dream was past; it had no further change.
It was of a strange order, that the doom
Of these two creatures should be thus traced out
Almost like a reality—the one
To end in madness—both in misery.

Memory-haunted Annesley Hall when I saw it
was still much as it had been when Byron went there
tormented by his hopeless love for its young owner;
the room in which Mary used to beguile him

with her music, and most of the other apartments
containing many interesting relics of the poet and
his beloved. Chief among the treasures was the
pencilled original of the following lines written by
Byron after the marriage of Miss Chaworth:

> Hills of Annesley! bleak and barren,
> Where my thoughtless childhood strayed,
> How the northern tempests warring,
> Howl above thy tufted shade!
> Now no more the hours beguiling,
> Former favourite haunts I see;
> Now no more my Mary smiling,
> Makes ye seem a heaven to me.

It was not until July 16, 1824, that Nottingham
was again to be prominently associated with the
name of the immortal bard, and on that day, as a
local historian records, ' the town was agitated by
the funeral of a famous man, who, though not born
within its precincts, was very familiar to its inhabitants.
The hearse conveying the remains of Lord Byron
was met by thousands of people at the south end of
the town, and followed in silence to the Blackamoor's
Head, Pelham Street, where it remained for the
night. The coffin was placed in the room at the
north-west corner of the yard, and wax candles put
around it. The public were then admitted, about
twenty at a time, to walk round and out again, and
such was the pressure and anxiety to see the spectacle
that a very large body of constables was necessary to
clear the way and to keep anything like a clear

ingress and egress. When the procession left on the following morning, the Mayor and Corporation attended, and most of the townspeople were attired in mourning '. Thus the poet's body lay in state about a hundred yards from the house in which he had resided a quarter of a century before, and where he had written those juvenile lines about the old lady of Swine Green. Thirty years ago I knew two persons alive in Nottingham who witnessed Byron's lying-in-state there three and-seventy years before, and one of these was himself a poet of genius: Philip James Bailey, author of 'Festus '.

For many years Puritan America sent most of the pilgrims who came to Byron's shrine at Hucknall: a sympathetic interest in the wayward genius was manifested across the Atlantic while his countrymen's attitude was still one of indifference or hostility, and possibly the large influx of Continental Europeans into America may, in some measure, have accounted for this, as Byron has always stood higher in Continental appreciation than he has yet attained to in the good opinion of the British people. When I made my pilgrimage to his grave it was not a common thing to do, but it was long before the day of the charabanc, and I should not be surprised to learn that the mass transport of these vast cars, so aggressively exclusive with their flaunting notices of ' Private ', which now thunder along our highways and by-ways, may now have ' popularised ' such shrines as that at Hucknall Torkard.

I recollect the place, which is about seven miles north of Nottingham, as a town of mean streets, and social life at its crudest: the passers-by agape at any visitor. When you have traversed the main street and arrived at the market-square on which it debouches, you stand before the church of St. Mary Magdalen and the burial-place of Lord Byron. The church is a good example of old Norman architecture so much ' restored ' that only a small portion of the original structure remains, though the spirit of it has been fairly well preserved. As it sits there, in the midst of a rudely ordered graveyard, the church is certainly a pleasant sight; but on a market-day the stalls of the travelling hucksters were spread right up to its railings, and the place reeked of fried fish and chipped potatoes.

The Byron vault is under the chancel, to the left of the pulpit, and a few paces in front of the altar. There is not much to see: a plain marble slab, on which the solitary name BYRON is inlaid in brass, together with the dates of his birth and death, surrounded by the wreath of leaves in brass sent by the King of Greece. This marks the spot where the poet's body lies; for old John Brown, the former sexton, in his seventy-fifth year at the time of my visit, was able to indicate the exact place when the tablet was sent to be inserted, as he had lowered the coffin of the Countess of Lovelace—Ada, ' sole daughter of my house and heart '—when she was buried there in 1852, Byron lying with his mother on his right and his daughter on his left. Farther

along the chancel, and on the right, there are two
mural tablets, the lower of which bears these words :

In the vault beneath,
Where many of his ancestors and his
mother are buried,
Lie the remains of
GEORGE GORDON NOEL BYRON,
Lord Byron of Rochdale in the
County of Lancaster,
The Author of ' Childe Harold's Pilgrim-
age.'
He was born in London on the
22nd of January, 1788,
And died at Missolonghi, in Western
Greece, on the
19th of April, 1824,
Engaged in the glorious attempt to restore
that
Country to her ancient freedom and
renown.
His sister, the Honourable
Augusta Mary Leigh,
Placed this tablet to his memory.

These were the only outward signs of the dust of
genius that lies beneath; but in a little vestry opening
off the chancel hung a relic of Byron's funeral: a small
piece of silk on which the arms of the Byron family
were embroidered. It is understood to have been
part of the trappings of the poet's coffin on its journey
to Hucknall Torkard, and had been kept in the church
for many years, though with no particular care; but
a time came when a new rector was shocked that the

relic should have been preserved—his thoughts at
having to preach in such propinquity to the dust
of the poet are not recorded—and he ordered the
sexton to have it burned! The sexton, worthy man,
did nothing of the kind, but took the relic home,
and had it more carefully preserved than before; and
when the hostile rector was succeeded by one less
bigoted, this interesting souvenir of Byron was
brought back to the church and placed in a frame
provided by a lady. Beside it hung two small
wreaths: one of artificial forget-me-nots, left some
months before by a party of American admirers, the
other of decayed laurels. The cleaner did not know
where the latter came from; and I fancy it may have
been one of two which were mouldering here when
William Winter visited the church thirteen years
before. They had been brought, the one by the
Bishop of Norwich and the other by the American
poet, Joaquin Miller; but which it was that had
survived I could not guess.

By an odd twist of fate the remains of one whose
imagination painted some of the most sensuously
beautiful pictures that poetry contains, one who sang
romance and lived it, moulder in this little church
in this most unromantic town. And yet, as I stood
in the flood of sunshine that streamed through the
chancel windows and fell with a softened radiance
on the memorial stone, it did not seem that Byron's
last resting-place was unworthy of him. When he
died and a censorious Dean refused to inter his poor
dust in Westminster Abbey, it was only the culmina-

ST MARY MAGDALEN, HUCKNALL:
BYRON'S BURIAL PLACE

facing p. 113

tion of the events that had separated him from his countrymen during his few years of crowded life and now brought his body to the tomb of his fathers. And there, in his solitary state, in this little country church, where storied urn and animated bust are not, the name of Byron within its kingly wreath shines with even a greater glory than the crowded Abbey could give it.

The register of the visitors to the grave showed that in the early years it was a pilgrimage more often made than in later times. The actual register of the first ten years was stolen, but a copy had been preserved, from which it was seen that the original had contained many an historic signature, and not a few poetic tributes of some interest. The following I thought worth copying, as a fair sample of such impromptu rhyme, but I have no clue to its writer:

Not in that palace where the dead repose
In splendid holiness, where Time has spread
His sombre shadows, and a halo glows
Around the ashes of the mighty dead,
Life's weary pilgrim rests his aching head.
This is his resting place, and save his own,
No light, no glory, round his grave is shed;
But memory journeys to his shrine alone
To mark how sound he sleeps, beneath yon simple stone.
Ah, say, art thou ambitious? thy young breast—
Oh, does it pant for honours? dost thou chase
The phantom Fame, in fairy colours drest,
Expecting all the while to win the race?
Oh, does the flush of youth adorn thy face,

I

> And dost thou deem it lasting? dost thou crave
> The hero's wreath, the poet's meed of praise?
> Learn that of this, these, all, not one can save
> From the chill hand of death.   Behold
>   Childe Harold's grave!

That is not great verse, but whoever wrote it could turn a phrase, and had not studied his Byron in vain. And it is true.   What a climax to the life romantic— after years of passionate adventure, the outpouring of genius, clamorous fame, and the dramatic passing, this coffin-room under the flagstones of a negligible church in a dirty little mining town! And yet again, if we will look at it through the eyes of romance, it is all as it should have been, and that censorious Dean was but one of the fates, lacking whom how could life-drama move? Save that Byron sleeps among his kith and kin—with whom he had no kinship of the soul—he lies in a lonely grave and his dust is better there than placed in crowded competition with the occupants of Poets' Corner, Westminster, more in harmony with the poet's mood of his closing days:

> The fire that on my bosom preys
>   Is lone as some volcanic isle;
> No torch is kindled at its blaze—
>   A funeral pile!

Here I interpolate a paragraph to record the fact that a week ago I met a distinguished Harrovian, who assured me that Byron was buried in Harrow churchyard.   This, on the strength of ' Byron's

tombstone ', long one of the noted monuments there.
His error, which may be a common one, arose from
the fact that young Byron when at Harrow School
used to sit for hours upon the tombstone of an unknown Peachey contemplating the beautiful view
from that point of the churchyard. ' This was my
favourite spot', he wrote in 1822 to John Murray,
and it became so popular a shrine in after years that
it had to be protected with iron bars. The aforesaid
Harrovian was quite open to argue that I was in
error, but I hope I persuaded him where the error
lay, and deem the matter worth mention in case
others may have fallen into the same mistake.

And now, after all those ramblings of my pen, I find,
my dear Greenhough Smith, that I have written
scarcely a line in appreciation of Byron's poetry.
Heaven knows there is no need to write a line about
a subject on which a library in a babel of tongues
already exists, but a brief statement of one's critical
opinion would seem to be in place, and in two paragraphs from a study which I have published other-
where, I take leave of a subject in which I am sure
your interest is not less wakeful than my own.

At heart most men are romantics: even pork
butchers. Every young woman, be she of the leisured
workers or of the busy rich, dramatises her own
emotions and her knowledge of events to suit her
day dreams. To all such Byron in his sheer picturesqueness must have an irresistible appeal. He is a
figure of romance. His poetry is interfused with
his personality. We cannot conceive Byron as a

successful bank manager or chief of a great engineering works. He lived and moved in an atmosphere for ever electrical with presage of storm, joyous intervals of sunniest beauty alternating with others of sombre melancholy. In this he was intensely human: he was exceptional only in being able to give to all his moods a romantic glamour which made even his melancholy a thing of tenderness and human pity.

His hatred of shams, his passionate love of freedom, his sorrow for all afflicted: these certainly are qualities to endear him to the common people, who have not read enough of him, but hardly less to the other classes of the community who have been chiefly attracted by the sensuous beauty of so much of his descriptive poetry. Of all our great poets, he is the most subjective: he found all his emotional material within himself. In everything that he wrote it is himself that clamours for expression: the personages of his poems are but varying aspects of the poet. His poetry is really an extraordinarily brilliant and fascinating autobiography.

Highgate,
    London.

VII

PETRA : ROSE-RED OR RUSTY BROWN?

To F. Britten Austin

FROM a seaward window of my study I can look across the Pevensey marshes and the most historic bay in England to the East Cliff at Hastings, whence a little inland you and other literary friends of mine have made your pleasant dwelling places. I have been sitting there to-night, my dear Austin, thinking of our talk a week ago, when I crossed these marshes to your home at Guestling. We were speaking, as you will remember, of the advantage to an imaginative writer of not knowing too much about the matter he had chosen to present to others in a picturesque way. This was *à propos* of those brilliant tales of the ancient world—Carthage, especially—which you have been lately publishing with such marked success in America's leading magazine.

Well, here at this seaward window I have had confirmed once more my own misquotation of Pope's much misquoted aphorism. I use it as a warning to 'expert' contributors: A lot of knowledge is a deadening thing. How often have I wasted hundreds of pounds of my publishers' money by getting 'the world's most famous expert' to write on his life's study! Too often these great men prove incapable of withdrawing so little as a tankard from the brimming vats of their knowledge: they can only deal in wholesale measures. The late Lord Salisbury, who started life as a journalist, used to say that if you would learn something of a subject that was new to you, go, write an article on it. I have done it many a time and had I known more about the matter I could not have written so good an article.

This is leading up to a confession. At that seaward window I have been studying a book upon my table: a book too big to hold in the hand. It is a large quarto, superbly produced as to printing, photography, and binding, and extraordinarily valueless. It is entitled 'Petra: Its History and Monuments'. The author is Sir Alexander Kennedy, an aged professor of engineering. Printed on the title page is the too familiar quatrain from Omar beginning 'They say the Lion and the Lizard sleep', and having the third line about 'Bahrám, that great Hunter' correctly punctuated. These are the only lines in the massy and beautiful volume that thrill the mind. It is as though an expert producer of engineering catalogues had set himself to do an illustrated edition of 'A Midsummer Night's Dream'.

Now, knowing little of the place, never having been within five hundred miles of it, I once published a description of Petra, and it may be that my few pages will send more people there than Sir Alexander's

noble quarto. Presently, when I have explained,
you will not account this to me for mere vanity. Of
this I am thankful: that I had not read Sir Alexander's monumental tome until to-day. I bought it
as it came fresh from the press in 1925 chiefly for
its 211 photogravures, and now that I have been
through it, I can never write about Petra again. I
cannot see the place in my mind's eye for the con-
fusing mass of needless details thrust upon me by
this most uninspired ' survey '. I cannot see the
monuments for stones. What with ' air-plane ' views,
' obliques ', and multitudinous reproductions of bits
of rocky ground, and learned long-lined pages—the
text is criminally wide, measuring fully seven inches!
—about geology, architecture, and history, the Petra
that I had imagined has been blurred out of all
recognition. He has given me a sad superfluity of
photographs, not one of which can be compared
with any of those by Mr. Donald McLeish which
I published in ' Wonders of the Past ' and to accompany which my sketchy little contribution was hastily
' vamped up '. He has robbed me of my ' rose-red
city '. I'm told it's only ' rusty-brown '. But I
need not warn you, my dear Austin, that when you
are minded to tell a story of any ancient place you
must not let an engineer be your spiritual guide
thereto.

My own interest in the desert stronghold of the
Nabatæans was first awakened by the drawings of
it made a hundred years ago by David Roberts, R.A.,
and published in his collection ' The Holy Land,

Syria', etc., which I plundered many years back when illustrating a certain work of history. The one famous line of Burgon's from his Newdigate Prize poem of 1845:

A rose-red city half as old as Time,

which is all of his forty-five literary works known to me, has floated about in my mind since the days of youth; and when, soon after the close of the War, the American journalist, Lowell Thomas, quoted that line in his lecture 'With Allenby in Palestine', and showed us some motion pictures of Petra, I could have been off next day for the Hijaz Railway and the rocky land of Edom! Alas, there was a desk in London city that chained me and chains me, not unwillingly, still. So when it chanced that an old plan of mine to illustrate and describe the marvels of the vanished civilisations came to fulfilment, and text was needed to accompany that fine series of Petra photographs by Mr. McLeish, I sent to the London Library for various books that dealt incidentally with Petra—I remember my surprise that Doughty had so little to say of it in his 'Arabia Deserta'—and with the aid of a clever assistant I was presently in possession of just enough information to serve my instant purpose. No more, mark you; for when I had 'dressed it up' the reader knew as much as I did. This is known as 'journalism', and I am content that it should be so. The journalist is the best teacher of his time, and if he but tells to-morrow what he learns to-day, is he not better

IN THE GORGE AT PETRA

than the too common type of 'expert' who has absorbed so much both to-day and yesterday that he has become like unto an 'egg-bound' hen?

You will remember the dictionary description of a crab—'A small, red animal, that walks backward' —which was said to be an admirable definition, except that the crab was not red, was not an animal, and did not walk backward. Well, the same would seem to be true, according to the pedants, of Burgon's picture of Petra: it is not a city, it is not rose-red, and it is not half as old as Time. Does that matter? I think not; for though what interests us are the rock-hewn tombs and temples, the mud-built houses and palaces of the city having utterly vanished, it is no great licence thus to describe these tombs and temples, since they are so numerous and outwardly so imposing that they give the impression of a city far greater and more populous than it is probable ever flourished in this strange romantic corner of Arabia. Again, it is grudgingly admitted by the learned that when the red sun goes down upon it, or tinctures it with the level rays of morning, the rusty brown sandstone of the enfolding hills, in which these wondrous tombs are cut, becomes 'rose-red'. What more does the poet ask? And as for 'half as old as Time'—was not the world made in the year 4004 B.C.? To which, if we add 1927 we have 5931, the half thereof being less than 3000 and Nabatæan Petra goes back at least to 400 B.C., giving us roughly 2300 years, a fair approximation to the half of time, which Dean Burgon and any other

believer in Bible chronology ought to stand for.   A
plague on these scientific fellows; ' me for the Dean '
as our new culturists of America might say.   Anyway,
here is what I published in ' Wonders of the Past '
and now, slightly reduced in length, timidly reprint
in order to illustrate my argument:

Coming in from the desert, if towards sundown, the traveller
fronted a fantastic maze of many-hued peaks and crags, surging,
like a frozen sea of tempestuous colour, against the dusty grey
uplands of Northern Arabia.   As the caravan from the Orient
arrived, laden with scent, pearls, spice, and rare fabrics, there
seemed no path by which the weary camels and horsemen
could cross the mountain border to Palestine and Egypt.   But
there was a way, though neither Beduin on the desert side nor
Jew on the seaward side dared to take it.

For hundreds of years vague tales had been told, along the
Mediterranean, Red Sea, and Indian Ocean, of a strange gorge
in the Arabian wilderness, leading to a marvellous City of
Rock.   All that men definitely knew, however, was that most
of the trade between the Western and Eastern worlds passed
through the strong hands of a mysterious race that held the
mountains between the Dead Sea and the Red Sea.

Persians, Macedonians, and Romans tried in turn to break
the secret desert kingdom.   Some of these expeditions reached
the City of Rock, and finding the fables true, took wonderful
spoil; but the men of the mountains managed to maintain their
dominion for centuries after these raids, and took toll on the
growing commerce between the Mediterranean and the Indian
Ocean.   As the mystery of their seat of power deepened, the
marvels of their Rock increased.   Around them empires and
religions flourished and faded; but as they had refused entrance
to the disciples of Zoroaster, so they kept away the followers
of Christ, and became so hostile to the Jews that they helped
the Romans in the last attack upon Jerusalem.

Night and day a score or two of tall, lean, hawk-faced men watched the great gorge, while outposts peered and listened above all the lesser ravines.   Occasionally some foreign crafts-man was invited to adorn the City of Rock in the last period of its triumphant pride.   After a long, fatiguing, roundabout desert journey with his guides, he would enter a narrow cleft in a wall of rock.   This was the gorge of the river Mûsâ, so called because the Arabs believe it was made by the rod of Moses.   The stream that now flows through it was then diverted in flood time through a tunnel into a neighbouring ravine.   Close to the entrance was a decorative arch across the ravine, at a height of about fifty feet, forming the Grand Portal, with statues and altar niches below.   The air, still as pond water on a windless day, would be stifling, the heat hard to bear.   Oleanders in flower half curtained the passage, but greenery and blossom grew rarer as the sky narrowed into a distant thread of brightest azure, and the gorgeous colourings of the rock dimmed in a gathering twilight.   Down to a depth of twelve hundred feet the tortuous paved way sank and shrank in width, until a man could touch with outstretched arms the two dark red walls.   What with the stagnant air and the eye-straining dimness and immensity of the rocky defile, the soul of a strange visitor, even under friendly guidance, was over-borne by a feeling of superstitious terror.   Never had any fortress possessed so impregnable and sublime an entrance as this great winding gorge of the secret city.   It was a natural trap for invaders coming in strength, or for lonely spies.

Suddenly, light and beauty touched the traveller with a relieving sense of joy.   A great sideways gash in the mountain enlarged the sunken way, making a pool of gleaming sunshine, and in the radiance shone a temple carven in the rose and golden rock of the eastern precipice.   It was the rosy marvel now known as El-Khaznah or 'the Treasury,' but then a temple of Isis.   Some horses and camels might be tethered on the worn grass, and a priest in white linen thanking the riders for their offering; for here every man of the city stopped and prayed for protection when he set out for the desert, and gave thanks when he safely returned. But the Egyptian-like priest and the Arab-like worshippers would not count—the temple, a lovely thing possibly of Greek art, would enrapture the sight with its richly sculptured capitals and cornices, its graceful Corinthian columns, its sphinxes and its statue of the goddess Isis, to whom it was dedicated, all hewn with incredible labour and loving skill out of the living rock and glowing rosy in the bright sunshine and clear air.

Beyond this travellers' temple the gorge narrowed again, and then widened, revealing the mystery of Arabia. All the mountains had fallen back, leaving an oval space a little more than a mile long and about three-quarters of a mile wide. Here, out of the steep sides of the many-coloured sandstone heights, a great city of roseate glory had been hewn. Where they lived, the hillfolk had been buried. By the hundred, their carven tombs were ranged in close tiers on the iridescent mountain flanks. These rock-hewn tombs are the wonder of Petra to-day, and will remain for ages to come one of the greatest monuments of antiquity.

Some of the majestic burial caves were as large as temples, and probably two were used as Christian churches in a later age. There were other tombs sculptured from the rock in the style of imperial palaces, with two or three storeys of richly-wrought pillars. In them were laid the bodies of the kings and queens, whose successors lived in proud splendour in the palaces that once stood among gardens on the valley floor, and worshipped, with strange rites, in the grandiose temples of the living city. The hillside region of the dead was a reflection of the valley floor region of the living. Small, plain-faced tomb caves of working folk were modelled on the style of their small square cottages, and the houses of middle-class men and mansions of rich merchants were represented in the style of their family tombs.

There were tombs with exterior heights ranging to about sixty-five feet, with large, finely-carved porches, windows, and

EL-KAZNAH, PETRA

outside altars on which offerings were made to the spirits.
The inside walls were unadorned, and the family mummies
were placed in hollows along the sides and in graves in houses,
and temples extended down a triumphal way, and along a westward ravine that climbed the rocky height of Ed-Dair (the
Convent).   And here, at a distance of an hour's march from
the capital, was another wonder of the wilderness.   By the
mountain top a colossal temple was hewn from the high rock
in a solemn, classic style.   Overpowering in strength and
majesty, it seemed a work that would endure as long as the
mountain tops about it.   Stark in its grandeur, it embodied
better than anything else the energy of soul that made the
Rockmen lords of the desert.

The origin of the extraordinary cult of the dead in Petra,
that led the mountaineers to encircle their city with tiers of
tombs until death reigned above life, may possibly be found in
ancient Arab superstition.   In their view a mortal had several
souls, and one remained by a well-preserved corpse, like a kind
of guardian spirit.   As it could revenge wrongs done to its
body, it was presumed to have sufficient tribal feeling left to
help in guarding the store place for tribal plunder.   This the
shadowy army of the dead was supposed to have done in the
first Macedonian and Roman invasions, and, encouraged by
such achievements of their ghostly forbears, the Rockmen
settled permanently under their protection, and very cheerfully
lived with the spirits of their dead.

The Rockmen, known abroad as Nabatæans, began as a
robber clan of nomad Arabs.   They won and ranged over the
grey limestone upland of Edom and the red heights between
Sinai and the Dead Sea, and held up the caravan traffic along
the desert marches of Arabia and Egypt.   While living in
shifting camps of black tents, they used the Petra basin as a
secret storing-place for plunder.   After interrupting the commerce of the Eastern and Western civilizations, they found that
a combination of honesty, monopoly, and hard bargaining was
far more profitable than brigandage that frightened caravans

from the old routes, and piracy that led to the Persian and Persian-Egyptian governments increasing their naval forces in the Red Sea. So as honest brokers they reorganized the caravan routes and started to police the desert. Still they did not settle in Petra, but buried and warehoused there. A strong line of kings, with sustained ability in war and commerce, gave them strength, riches, national organization, and wider dominion. Definitely they housed themselves in Petra in the fourth century before the birth of Christ, and for a century before our era they were, with large numbers of slaves, cultivating the arts of civilization.

The air of romantic mystery which they maintained regarding their Rock City and hidden villages in Arabia was a matter of shrewd, practical business. The less aliens knew regarding the details of their mountain stronghold and the intricate organization of their trade routes, the safer the Rockmen were against invasion and competition. They took the iron, bronze, and purple dye of Mediterranean races, and, at usurious rates, traded these goods for myrrh, gold, silver, pearls, and other fine Orient produce. On the desert side they kept the Beduin in order by subsidies based on transit insurances for their caravans, and when subsidies failed to overcome the nomads' love of plunder they used methods of extermination. Rumours that have not faded from the Beduin mind, and which were collected by Lord Kitchener in his adventurous, scientific exploration of the Petra region, speak of still larger secret cities lying in lime-stone hollows by the Red Sea coastland, and witnessing to the might and mysterious ways of the fighting merchant princes of Petra.

As they would stroll in family groups from the great theatre to the stream-fed valley and glowing ring of rose-red heights, hey would look what they were—men of a lean, lithe, sunhardened, desert-hammered stock. In flowing robes of Tyrian colour and headdresses of far-brought silk, with weapons by their hand, they moved with an air of graceful strength by palmgrove and scented garden to their splendid warehouses, where trains of slaves tended them.

Above their city rose a terrible hill, inaccessible except on
the south side, where a great stairway had been cut.   It was
the Great Place of Sacrifice, to which the priests, king, and
elders climbed in procession towards the blood basin and the
altar where the throats of victims were cut and the bodies burnt
to the glory of Duchara, the divine lord of the kingdom of
Aretas, chief of the Nabatæans, who, in Egyptian fashion, took
to wife his own sister.

In the struggle of Mark Antony and Augustus, it was the
Nabatæans who completed the overthrow of Cleopatra, by
destroying the Egyptian Red Sea fleet.   This enormously
increased their trade, strength, and influence.

At last the Emperor Trajan, in A.D. 106, could not resist
the lure of the Nabatæans' wealth, and reduced Petra to the
rank of a Roman province.   For many years the Orient trade
continued, much to the profit of Rome, but the best Nabatæans
vanished, and secretly diverted the desert traffic to Palmyra.
The Beduin swept over the weakened frontier, and Petra, when
rediscovered in 1807, was a ruin-ringed waste held by Arab
robbers.

During his now historic campaign which has given
to English literature a new classic in his ' Revolt
in the Desert ', Colonel T. E. Lawrence made occasional use of Petra as a store-place, but it is perhaps
not surprising to find that, like Doughty himself,
he has other matters than these rock-hewn tombs
and temples to engage him and says nothing, where
he might have said so much, and none better than
he, about the romance of the place.   Its romance
I hope will withstand the assaults of American touring parties; for now that the Hijaz Railway has
constructed a branch line from Anaiza to within some
six or seven miles of the City of Rock, many hundreds

of 'world-tourists' from Milwaukee, Oshkosh, Pottsville and other centres of western culture will be scrambling each recurring season over the rocks of Petra and scratching their names, perchance, on the immemorial walls of tomb and temple. The lion will have no chance in the tourist season, though the lizard may still hold his own, and as for 'Bahrám, that great Hunter', a new species of

> Wild Ass
> Stamps o'er his Head, but cannot
> break his sleep.

And I shall be something responsible for this, as, in casting around for a sufficiently alluring description of Petra, the authorities of the Hijaz Railway have sought my permission to reprint and circulate in pamphlet form that flowery little article from 'Wonders of the Past' which, in their considered opinion, is 'the best description of the place that has been written'! Not to the expert go they, but to the mere journalist. It flatters the vanity of one to think they may be right, and perhaps a day may come when I, too, shall join a touring party and go thither to see how Sir Alexander Kennedy's rusty-brown facts may tally with my rose-red fancies!

Eastbourne.

VIII

ON THE SCOTSMAN'S LOVE OF BURNS

To Sir Arthur Quiller-Couch

HERE in Biskra, on a sun-drenched verandah looking toward the pleasant greenness of the so-called Garden of Allah, with the sound of tom-toms from the street of the Ouled Naïls punctuating monotonously the still air, I am fingering a volume of Robert Burns: a last moment addition to my load of 'books to be read when away', because of a promise to give 'the immortal memory' to a certain Burns Club a few days after my return from Sahara sunshine to London fogs.

An odd place—this centre of the sordid-shoddy 'romantic'—to be re-reading the honest poetry of Burns, and yet I have found myself, in the detach-ment of distance, visualising the man and his work more vividly than I remember in any of my visits to his homes and haunts of Ayr and Dumfries.

These jottings, in which I shall seek to express some of the thoughts that have been stirring in my mind while contemplating the outline of my dis-course, I inscribe to 'Q', that liveliest of profes-sorial critics, as a question which he asks in his

'Adventures in Criticism' set me searching for an answer, which—with that confidence born of idleness and serene skies—I think I have found. But of this later.

Let me say at once, however, that I am no sort of Burns specialist. There are certain writers in whose works and lives I consider myself informed beyond the ordinary reader; but Burns is not one of these, and yet Scotland has produced a wilderness of 'Burns experts'. The fact that I was born by the banks of Loch Lomond might give me some title to discourse on Burns to an English audience, but before a Scottish audience that would be no manner of qualification. In some sort a Scotsman, however, I claim Burns as a birthright. Scotsmen do not need to be told anything about Burns. They absorb Burns with mother's milk in babyhood, with porridge in their youth, and with elements of greater strength in later years. But if there is no need to tell Scotsmen anything about Robert Burns, Scotsmen have certainly been telling all the world about him for a century and a quarter. Burns has become an integral part of Scottish pride and patriotism. It would seem that Burns was the veritable incarnation of the Scottish temper. It is no exaggeration to say that if ever a nation was made vocal in one man, that nation was Scotland in Robert Burns.

I believe that Burns celebrations, such as I have to face when I return to England, date back to the year 1802, and have been increasing continuously ever since. To contemplate the floods of oratory

that have flowed around the world on account of
Robert Burns would certainly suggest that there can
be nothing new to say of him or his poetry.   If that
is so, what chance will the Burns orators of the year
2002 have?   Yet I am reminded of Macready, the
great Shakespearean actor, who said, when he was
playing the part of Hamlet for the last time, that
even on that occasion he had detected new beauties
and subtleties in the character which in all the years
he had been presenting it had not appealed to him
before.   So if I were to revisit the glimpses of the
moon one or two hundred years hence, I should
not be surprised to hear the Burns orators of those
coming days expressing new thoughts concerning
his life and his work.   Every generation brings a
new point of view.   If Burns does not change, the
generations do.   Even the post-war view of Burns
must differ from the pre-war view unless we are to
suppose that the events of 1914–18 have done no
more than 'overcome us like a summer cloud'.

It is a solemn and a disturbing thought that in
every corner of the globe on the 25th of January
people are gathered together to celebrate the birthday
of a man who was unable to make a success of life,
and seldom had at his command the wherewithal to
clear his very humble household of debt.   In these
latter days, when money seems so easily made and
one has seen so many beggars take to horseback, it
is a sorry reflection that the mere matter of a cheque
which Mr. Kipling once received for a single column
of ephemeral parodies in the *Daily Mail* would have

put Burns on his feet for four or five years, and
might well have saved his life in those critical last
months.   Kipling 'fan' though I may be, I greatly
doubt if 130 years after he has passed away there
will be groups of admirers anywhere keeping his
memory green.   Hence arises the question: had
prosperity smiled on Burns as surely as the muses;
had his life been prolonged into the sixties, let us
say; would Scotsmen have assembled annually in
every corner of the world to toast his immortal
memory?   I think not, for reasons which will presently appear.

There is a phrase of some German philosopher
that I picked up in my youth and have on many
occasions successfully tested.   'Things produce
their opposites.'   Tyranny and oppression produce
fear and liberty, as the history of our own and
many another country will illustrate.   The morals
of Puritanism produced those of the Restoration.
Piety produces impiety.   Spengler's theory of historical cycles is merely the old idea freshly exploited.
Calvinism and John Knox were largely responsible
for Robert Burns; not for his poetry, Lord knows,
for there was little in Calvinism that gave birth to
poetry, but the whole temper of Burns is a revolt
from religious gloom and its attendant hypocrisy.
Burns, who was to know in his life so little of worldly
comfort, breathed a new spirit of joyousness into
Scottish life.   One might quote 'Man was made
to mourn' to the contrary, and indeed, I have at
times considered Burns as something of a pessimist,

but he is really the best sort of optimist who sees
things at their worst, and out of a great heart, brimming with sympathy for his fellow men, sees also
that life might be made worth living. 'Werna
my heart licht, I wad dee', sang Lady Nairne, and
all his life Burns was singing the same refrain in
different words.

On one of my visits to the British Front during
the War I found myself in a room with two officers,
one of whom was known to me. His name was
Luce, and when he left the room the other made a
pleasant observation on the oddness of the name
as derived from a fish, to which I responded
by quoting the 'luces' in Mr. Justice Shallow's
coat of arms, and remarking that in Scotland the
word might be confused with another of the same
sound denoting a very different member of animated
nature. Whereupon my interlocutor, an eminent
Scottish peer, recited the whole of Burns's address
'To a Louse'. So recently as the middle of last
century those well-known lines were actually printed
in more than one edition of the poems as 'To
a ————'. The vulgarity of one generation is
the good manners of another: a thought to recall
when we occasionally hear Burns accused of vulgarity. And I am old enough to remember a famous
Scottish divine delivering himself of this sort of
thing in the pulpit: 'Dancing! Music!—ay, ye
can dance and play, and sing and dance, but *there'll
be no waltz music in hell!*' That joyless cult of
gloom and intolerance darkened Scotland for many

a year, and soured the whole life of the country. That it did some good I am not prepared to deny. It produced its opposite eventually. Men are living in Glasgow to-day, and riding in the tramcars of that city every Sunday, who fought for years to prevent so dreadful a desecration of the Lord's day. I was in at the beginning of that fight, and remember the extremes of bigotry which were reached by those who thought they had a direct call from God to oppose Sunday trams in Glasgow as an institution that would upset the whole plan of salvation and greatly decrease the prospective population of Heaven.

Another thing those dark days of Calvinism did: they gave to Scotsmen many a touch of character that has served in anecdote and story to lighten the gloom, and to produce a certain rude philosophy of life in the unlettered folk, well expressed in the story of a Carluke worthy. He was fond of expatiating on life in these terms: ' It's just a case o' sinnin' and repentin'. Ye sin and repent. Sin and repent. Just sin and repent. Aye, an' if ye sin last, ye're gruppit! '

In our day there has been a great widening of the mind and incalculable increase in the spirit of tolerance, and Burns was one of the greatest forces, if not *the* greatest to bring this about. He was born in a century when artificiality both of thought and expression was rampant, and you will find many traces of its influence in his letters, but in his natural singing voice he speaks direct from nature's heart.

Anyone who has lived to see half-a-century can remember only the dying days, the last kick of that era of gloom. And if we can feel indignation rise in our hearts at the loveless powers that so shadowed the lives of our forefathers, what did not Burns feel who lived in the very heart of it all and was twice or thrice made to suffer the rebuke of an intolerant and inquisitorial kirk session? One is tired of hearing of Burns's weakness for fellowship. I love him for that above all things. That is where his real humanity shows. ' Good company ' was probably born out of the very gloom of ' auld licht ' Scotland. It certainly reached extreme lengths if we are to believe Dean Ramsay. You will recall a story of a drinking party at which one of the members remarked suddenly to the chairman: ' Garscaden's looking unco' gash ':

' Garscaden,' said the chairman, ' slippit awa' to his Maker an hour sin', but I did na want to disturb guid company by mentioning it.'

Pity, surely the supremest quality of any good religion, was the least noticeable of the virtues in Calvinistic Scotland. It is the most eminent quality in Robert Burns. No lines better convey it than these, ' To a Mouse ':

> Wee, sleeket, cowran, tim'rous beastie,
> O, what a panic's in thy breastie!
> Thou need na start awa sae hasty,
>   Wi' bickering brattle!
> I wad be laith to rin an' chase thee
>   Wi' murd'ring pattle!

> I'm truly sorry Man's dominion
> Has broken Nature's social union,
> An' justifies that ill opinion
>   Which makes thee startle
> At me, thy poor earth-born companion,
>   An' fellow-mortal!

I had begun to transcribe some lines from the two poems on Poor Mailie, ' the author's only pet yowe ', but refrain, for there would be no end to quotation if once I got fairly started. The pity of Burns is the only sort that is worthy of the name in being boundless. The very ' Deil ' (a conception which he inherited with his stock brand of religion according to Calvin handed on by his father, worthy man), yes, even the very Devil is an object of his pity, for he hopes he may ' tak' a thocht an' mend '.

Another quality of Burns in my estimation is largely responsible for the favour with which all classes of the community, indeed, all mankind, regard him and his work to-day. And this is the quality of wistfulness. That is the only name I can give it. It is that undertone of sadness which is present even in our happiest moments. The thought that time is passing, that ' pleasures are like poppies spread ', that ' had we never lo'ed sae kindly ', that this might have been and that could never be—that yearning and longing for a state of earthly bliss which, in our inmost hearts, we know to be illusory, unattainable—this quality of wistfulness is notably present in most of Burns's poems, and it is one of his many endearing qualities. It

is probably the real secret of the magic which all
critics from the earliest days of last century have
agreed in ascribing to his poetry.

So far I have been noticing qualities of the man
rather than the poet. I have no intention of attempting any ordered estimate of his poetry, and I am not
quite done with the man yet, but I may set down
a thought or two on one aspect of his poetry, and
especially would I like to touch on certain mis-
conceptions concerning it. Even Wordsworth, who
had a whole-hearted admiration for him, entertained
a suspicion that some of the Scottish words he could
not understand which he found as rhymes in Burns's
poems were inventions of the poet. Such words,
let us say, as ramfeezled, agley, blelum, and the
lave. While Cowper lamented that

> Poor Burns loses much of his deserved praise in this country
> through our ignorance of his language. I despair of meeting
> any Englishman who will take the pains that I have taken
> to understand him. His candle is bright, but shut up in a
> dark lantern. I lent him to a very sensible neighbour of
> mine, but the uncouth dialect spoiled all; and before he had
> read him through he was quite ramfeezled.

While one is glad to find so religious a poet as
Cowper admiring so outspoken a contemporary as
Burns, one must conclude either that Englishmen
have advanced since then in the knowledge of the
Scottish tongue, or that Cowper was singularly
unhappy in his notion of his brother poet's appeal.
Burns is not half so Scottish as Sir Walter in

hundreds of his pages, or R. L. S. in his Scottish romances, and not twenty-five per cent. so Scottish as S. R. Crockett or the author of 'Wee Macgreegor', which last mentioned character study was read and understood, if we are to believe them, by many thousands of English people. As a matter of fact Burns is a writer of the purest and most smooth-flowing English, and had nothing to learn in that respect from the author of ' The Task '.

> Thou ling'ring star, with less'ning ray,
> That lov'st to greet the early morn,
> Again thou usherest in the day
> My Mary from my soul was torn.
> O Mary! dear departed shade!
> Where is thy place of blissful rest?
> See'st thou thy lover lowly laid?
> Hear'st thou the groans that rend his breast?
>
> Flow gently, sweet Afton, among thy green braes,
> Flow gently, I'll sing thee a song in thy praise;
> My Mary's asleep by thy murmuring stream,
> Flow gently, sweet Afton, disturb not her dream.

' A dark lantern ', forsooth!   Why, in all the serious poetry of Burns there is hardly one Scottish word. He reserves the Scottish tongue for his lighter moods, his satirical vein, and it will be noticed in such a poem as ' The Cotter's Saturday Night ' that, as the thought changes in character or deepens in seriousness, the language changes also.   Thus, in one stanza where the poet depicts a humble Ayrshire interior, the intimate dialect is used:

With kindly welcome, Jenny brings him ben;
    A strappon youth, he takes the mother's eye;
Blythe Jenny sees the visit's no ill taen;
    The father cracks of horses, pleughs and kye.
The youngster's artless heart o'erflows wi' joy,
    But blate and laithfu', scarce can weel behave;
The mother, wi' a woman's wiles, can spy
    What makes the youth sae bashfu' and sae grave;
Weel-pleas'd to think her bairn's respected like the lave.

But in the succeeding stanza where the narrative
pauses and the poet reflects on human life, observe
the change of word medium:

O happy love! where love like this is found!
    O heart-felt raptures! bliss beyond compare!
I've paced much this weary, mortal round,
    And sage experience bids me this declare
If Heaven a draught of heavenly pleasure spare,
    One cordial in this melancholy vale,
'Tis when a youthful, loving, modest pair,
    In other's arms, breathe out the tender tale,
Beneath the milk-white thorn that scents the ev'ning
    gale.

Surely no despicable flicker from a dark lantern!
But I must not be tempted too far into the consideration of the technique of his poetry, since a
bulky volume rather than a brief note would be
involved; yet there is another point, touching the
artistry of Burns, on which I may permit myself
a sentence or two.   He tells us, in that famous
dedication to the noblemen and gentlemen of the
Caledonian Hunt, that the poetic genius of his

country bade him sing the loves, the joys, the rural scenes and rural pleasures of his natal soil in his native tongue, and he tuned his wild, *artless* notes as she inspired.

There has been a tendency to accept him a little too readily at his own valuation in the matter of art, and artlessness. Personally, he appeals to me as one of the most finished of English poets, and his prose is obviously—I might say, too obviously—that of one who is an artist in words. I maintain that he is a conscious artist and not an untutored genius of the plough. Remember, he was no infant phenomenon of the muse. The bulk of the poetry on which his fame is based was written round about the age of twenty-five—by no means an early age for a poet of genius—when his inspiration was at its freshest and his education had been carried far beyond the average of his class, both in reading and in writing. He was already an artist when he made his bid for fame. That is an aspect of the poet which I commend to students. Burns was a ploughman, but in the Scotland of his day, and perhaps in the Scotland of our day, the ploughman may be a man of culture as well as agriculture. Burns was no Scottish counterpart of the English Hodge, plus inspiration. He was a well-educated, bookish young Scotsman of poor but decent parentage.

And now I address myself to the matter of ' Q's ' inquiry as to the curiously different places occupied by Burns and Scott in the hearts of their countrymen.

We shall agree, I think, that no person, Scottish or English, will dispute that, of the two, Sir Walter is the worthier man.   In all the gallery of literary heroes, I know no more beautiful or more manly figure than that of Sir Walter Scott.   I take but little account of his poetry, which has long since fallen into comparative neglect, except for certain historical passages that still have a vogue in school reading-books.   But his novels are a treasury of imaginative grandeur which every Scotsman must thrill to think were written in his native land.   ' Q ' wonders why Scotsmen celebrate Burns with all his faults, in preference to Scott.   He thinks it is the sureness with which Burns touches the tenderest chords of pathos in such verses as ' Thou'lt break my heart, thou bonnie bird ', or in ' Highland Mary ':

> O pale, pale now, those rosy lips
>   I aft hae kissed sae fondly!
> And closed for aye the sparkling glance
>   That dwelt on me sae kindly:
> And mouldering now in silent dust
>   The heart that lo'ed me dearly!
> But still within my bosom's core
>   Shall live my Highland Mary.

Sir Arthur thinks such pathos Sir Walter could not touch.   It is more than thirty years since he wrote the study I am citing, and as soon as it was published a Scot came along to tell him where he was wrong.   The Scotsman told the English critic that the pathos was all very well, but the stuff that

made Burns superior to Scott in human appeal and
accounted for the world-wide Burns gatherings was
' Scots Wha Hae ', ' Auld Lang Syne ' and ' A Man's
a Man for a' that '.   He was a real, wild, untamed,
perfervid Burnsite.   ' I would rather be the author
of these three lyrics,' he declared, ' than I would be
the author of all Scott's novels.'   No wonder ' Q '
was constrained to give up inquiring why Burns
was the more favoured of Scotsmen!   It is folly
to suppose that if these were the only three things
Burns had written his name would be more evocative to-day of thrilling admiration than that of
Allan Ramsay, of Fergusson, aye or Tannahill.   I
incline to agree with ' Q ' that there is a good deal
of excellent rant in ' Scots Wha Hae ', and I am
not mightily impressed with the verse beginning
' Ye see yon birky ca'd a lord ', when I read else-
where in Burns :

> This wot ye all whom it concerns,
> I, Rhymer Robin, alias Burns,
> October twenty-third—
> A ne'er to be forgotten day—
> Sae far I sprackled up the brae,
> I dinner'd wi' a Lord.

When I reflect that Burns says ' Man was made
to mourn ', I am glad to have been alive to experience the imaginative delights of ' Ivanhoe ', of ' Guy
Mannering ', of ' Redgauntlet ', of ' Waverley ', yes,
even of the least of them, such as ' Count Robert
of Paris '.   There is no good purpose in searching

for points of contact between the Sahara and Switzer-
land. And Burns and Scott are well-nigh as
different. Scott would have been one of the grandest
characters that ever lived, even if he had written
nothing better than his not very great poetry, but
he was born to distinction, his young years were
not years of bitter struggle for bread, he earned
immense sums of money by his writings; he lived
in lordly state, and he was a good man. To his
son-in-law as he lay on his death-bed, he said ' be
a good man; nothing else will give you any comfort
when you come to lie here.' There is no Lockhart's
' Scott' among my books at Biskra, so the words may
be wrong, but the meaning is there.

Scott was remote from the average man in his
very goodness, as well as in his greatness. Burns
was a fellow sinner, a man of like passions, with a
quenchless love of mankind. We love him for his
companionable character, for his faults, for the
frankness with which he reveals himself to us in
his writings, for his humaneness. He comes nearer
to us than Scott even when we feel he is least worthy,
as in some of his gibes at those who were better
circumstanced than he, which was ever a sore point
with him, as it is with so many poor bodies this
very day. I would say also that I can imagine myself
meeting Burns in the Elysian fields and giving him
a slap on the shoulder, but imagine slapping Sir
Walter on the shoulder!

Sir Walter was a social success and Burns was
a social failure. That is one of his strongest pulls

on our affection: the beloved vagabond. He described himself as ' a man who had little art in making money and still less in keeping it. He was, however, a man of some sense, a great deal of honesty, and unbounded good will to every creature, rational or irrational '. I simply refuse to believe that if Burns had made ' pots of money ' and lent it out at interest, as Mr. Wm. Shakespeare did, had worn fine clothes, sported a heavy gold watch and chain, and ridden to kirk in a braw carriage, there would be a single gathering anywhere on the 25th January toasting his memory. It is because he was one of the most remarkable geniuses that have appeared in these islands, and because he was a poor, unfortunate, kind-hearted, honest, sinful man, that he dwells in the hearts of his countrymen.

While the author of ' Waverley ' with all his advantages of birth and estate and his divine genius for romance may and does compel our admiration, Robert Burns, penniless, but conscious of his poetic power, battling against hypocrisy and shame in the life around him, against his worse self at times, offending by his implacable honesty the very folk who could have made his life more pleasant, compelled, as he felt, to voice the cause of the poor and downtrodden, content to stand for the class into which he had been born, enriching all our lives with sweetest song and making rather a hash of his own, demands and receives the fullest measure of our sympathy. We should have liked him to have lived a very different life, to have had all the

comfort, happiness, admiration, which his unrivalled
lyric gift so well deserved; yet we know, in our own
hearts, that there was nothing else for him but that
which happened, and what happened made him
what we know. The poets learn in sorrow what
they teach in song, and those who have sorrowed
most can teach us best.

There is an anecdote of Burns, told by John Brown
in ' Horæ Subsecivæ ', which I copied out and
placed in the old Scott–Douglas edition of his poetry
that is lying on my table here. As it is an unfamiliar
story I shall tag it on to this closing page:

The father of the Rev. Mr. Steven of Largs was the son
of a farmer, who lived next farm to Mossgiel. When a boy
of eight, he found ' Robbie ', who was a great friend of his,
and of all the children, engaged in digging a large trench in
a field, Gilbert, his brother, with him. The boy pausing
on the edge of the trench, and looking down upon Burns,
said ' Robbie, what's that ye're doin'? ' ' Howkin' a muckle
hole, Tammie.' ' What for? ' ' To bury the Deil in,
Tammie! ' (one can fancy how those eyes would glow).
' Ah ' but, Robbie,' said the logical Tammie, ' Hoo're ye to
get him in? ' ' Ay,' said Burns, ' that's it, hoo are we to get
him in? ' and went off into shouts of laughter; and every
now and then during that summer day shouts would come
from that hole, as the idea came over him.

That is a charming story, in harmony with the
lovableness which the poet, by the direct and personal appeal of his lyric medium, makes to each one
of us, and young Robbie spoke truer than he fancied,
for Robert Burns the poet, more than any of Scotland's

L

men of genius, howked a muckle great hole for the Deil and eventually, by the force of his poetic indictments, got the Deil into it: for I think sufficiently well of the progress we have made towards a more charitable view of life since Burns's day to suggest that we of this later generation have been in some sort assisting at the burial of the devil of hypocrisy and religious intolerance.

Biskra,
  Algeria.

IX

OF BARRIE'S FIRST BOOK

To Coulson Kernahan

MORE than a quarter of a century has passed since the days when I used to visit Jean and you at that cheery Westcliff home which, in your admiration for J. M. Barrie, you had christened 'Thrums'. And it strikes me as an odd thing that your picturesque retreat at Fairlight— that 'Christmas card cottage' where Jean and you, my dear Coulson, are meeting the advance of years serenely, amid so many memoried treasures of a full and eager life—should have been named 'Frognal' by others long before your coming there. For I never think of Frognal without thought of Robertson Nicoll, who at Frognal, Hampstead, was a literary figure I still like to picture as a reality that endures. And no other name is so closely related with Barrie's rise to fame, excepting only that of Greenwood. Yes, there is another, F. W. Robinson, the editor of *Home Chimes*, to which, like Barrie in those distant days, you also were a contributor, but if Robinson and Greenwood were

the counsellors and encouragers of his beginning
time, Nicoll, with his unerring judgement and
infectious enthusiasm, was the strongest individual
force in helping the young exponent of Scottish
character and sentiment to establish his wide and
enduring literary reputation.

It was at your Frognal retreat, I think, in one
of our literary colloquies, that we were speaking of
those ' glad, confident mornings ' when Jerome and
Barr were providing new ideas for English editors
in *The Idler* and *To-day*, and they had no happier
thought than that which inspired *The Idler's* fascinating series of autobiographic papers, entitled
' My First Book '. The shyness of Barrie kept
him out of a distinguished company that included
R. L. S., Kipling, Conan Doyle, Hall Caine,
Zangwill, and seventeen other famous writers—
twenty-two in all, of whom, alas, fifteen are now
no more. If Barrie could have been induced to
join in that symposium I think we might have had
a quaintly amusing chapter in which he would
probably have made self-deprecatory fun of his
own initial effort, and encountered some pretended
difficulty in deciding whether ' An Edinburgh
Eleven ' by one Gavin Ogilvy or ' Better Dead '
by J. M. Barrie was to be the subject of his
contribution.

In the same year (1896) that Jerome and
Barr were organising the famous *Idler* series,
Barrie had already attained to the dignity of a
' collected edition ' in America, and in his intro-

ductory notes thereto he writes thus of 'Better Dead':

> This juvenile effort is a field of prickles, into which none
> may be advised to penetrate.   I made the attempt lately in
> cold blood, and came back shuddering. . . . And yet I have
> a sentimental interest in 'Better Dead', for it was my first,
> published when I had small hope of getting anyone to accept
> the Scotch; and there was a week when I loved to carry it
> in my pocket, and did not think it a dead weight.   Once I
> almost saw it find a purchaser.   She was a pretty girl, and
> it lay on a bookstall, and she read some pages and smiled, and
> then retired, and came back and began another chapter.
> Several times she did this, and I stood in the background
> trembling with hope and fear.   At last she went away without
> the book, but I am still of opinion that, had it been just a
> little bit better, she would have bought it.

He had earlier said that 'weighted with "An
Edinburgh Eleven" it would rest very comfortably
in the mill-dam', but you will perceive a strain of
affection for it in the passage I have given above,
and the tender paternal avowal of it as 'my first'.
As such it should hold peculiar interest for students
of contemporary letters, and for those who have
not made acquaintance with the little book itself
this slight sketch of it may prove an appetiser.

Barrie is a writer who is both humorous and witty.
There is a very subtle distinction between the two
qualities.   Sydney Smith we may esteem as witty,
so too Sheridan; but Dickens was a humorist; Carlyle
was a humorist; Hood, like Barrie, was both wit
and humorist.   Wit, as it seems to me, concerns

the outwardness of things, humour lies deeper. Thus the dictionary: ' wit is the association of ideas in a manner natural but unusual and striking, so as to produce surprise joined with pleasure; humour is a deep, kindly, playful sympathy of feeling and fancy, with all kinds of, especially lowly, and even outcast, things.' I think we shall agree on these definitions and on the strength of them it may be said that humour is the Scottish attribute, wit the English, speaking in very general terms, of course. There is more ' heart ' in humour, more ' head ' in wit. While you may admire the wit you do not so readily grow to love him as you do the humorist. Who that has read ' A Window in Thrums ' or ' Auld Licht Idylls ' can fail of affection for their writer? But Barrie has written books that are only witty. He might have produced a dozen ' Better Deads ' and ' My Lady Nicotines ' without winning his way to the hearts of his readers.

' Better Dead ' we must regard as his first book; for although ' An Edinburgh Eleven ' was written about the same time, and parts of ' My Lady Nicotine ' even earlier, the former was merely reprinted journalism, a collection of character studies; and the latter he published in order to assert his right to a series of newspaper articles, the credit of which had been claimed by more than one unprincipled scribbler. It was so long ago as the winter of 1887 that ' Better Dead ' went trembling into the critics' dens in the guise of a little shilling book with a coloured cover very suggestive of a ' shilling shocker '

of that time, the device containing a sanguinary
sword, a revolver, and a nihilist figure with a
dagger in his hand, comic silhouettes of Sir William
Harcourt and Lord Randolph Churchill giving
the clue to the diverting nature of the pages within.
It was the first book that carried on its cover
the words, ' by J. M. Barrie', which in 1887
meant so little and a few years later signified so
much.

Its author was no infant prodigy when it appeared.
He was then twenty-seven years old, and in these
days when precocious girl-authors become ' best
sellers ' in their 'teens, twenty-seven seems quite a
venerable age to venture upon authorship.

There were probably many and good reasons why
the book did not make any particular hit and has
remained one of the least read of his writings. The
average reader is not partial to ' having his leg
pulled ': he doesn't feel quite easy with an author
whose fooling is cast in the form of solemn narrative, and it would be difficult to name a finer piece
of sustained fooling than ' Better Dead '. True, it
is but a tiny book, containing no more than twenty-
four thousand words; but the subject is so delicate,
the root idea so difficult of treatment, that few writers
could have expended so many words on it without
unpleasantness. To make assassination the subject
of a *jeu d'esprit*, and to write about it to the extent
of ten chapters with no suspicion of offence, is to
carry through triumphantly a risky task. And that
is what the author of ' Better Dead ' has done. The

germ of the story may be found, more than two years before the book appeared, in a sketch which Barrie published in the *St. James's Gazette* for 21st April, 1885, wherein is suggested the formation of a society for getting rid of people who would be better out of the way, Mr. Mallock being proposed as a good beginning, though in the book his name is only mentioned casually, and he receives no place of prominence.

The story introduces us without parley to Andrew Riach (a name probably suggested by that of the then editor of the *Edinburgh Dispatch*, who was one of Barrie's early friends in the world of journalism), a young Scotsman just 'come to town' intending to become private secretary to a member of the Cabinet, and 'if time permitted, he proposed writing for the Press'. Then forthwith we are whisked away to 'Thrums', but here we find the famous little town endowed with the less happy name of 'Wheens'. Andrew is at the manse with the Rev. Mr. Eassie and his daughter Clarrie, who is in love with Andrew, though he, since his return from Aberdeen University with M.A. at the end of his name, has become a slave to logic, and makes a strange wooer. Andrew possesses in fullest measure that dominant characteristic of the Scots people, the bump of argument, abnormally developed by his study of logic. Fortified perhaps by a reading of Plato's 'Symposium' he is arguing on love with Mr. Eassie, cleaning his pipe the while with a hair-pin 'that his quick eye had detected on the carpet'

—a favourite fancy of the author. Andrew main-
tains that love is folly, and for the moment seems
to have routed Mr. Eassie, as the author turns again
to describe his hero.

Andrew had a very long neck, a fact which is
of importance in the story. His face was 'as
inexpressive as book-covers'—this was long before
the days of these multicoloured 'jackets' for current
fiction. 'A native of Wheens and an orphan, he
had been brought up by his uncle, who was a weaver,
and read Herodotus in the original. The uncle
starved himself to buy books and talk about them,
until one day he got a good meal, and died of it.
Then Andrew apprenticed himself to a tailor.' When
his time was out he walked to Aberdeen and got a
bursary. He was nearly rusticated for praying at
a debating society for a divinity professor who was
in the chair. ' " O Lord! " he fervently cried, " open
his eyes, guide his tottering footsteps, and lead him
from the paths of folly into those that are lovely
and of good report, for lo! his days are numbered,
and the sickle has been sharpened, and the corn
is not yet ripe for the cutting." ' All gross exaggeration, of course, but the germ of truth to be found
in it suggests a characteristic Scot of the 'dour',
argumentative kind.

Mr. Eassie had at Andrew again in a different
way, hinting that if he didn't become engaged to
Clarrie before leaving for London he might find
her the banker's wife when he came back. 'The
banker was unmarried, and had once in February

and again in June seen Clarrie home from the Dorcas
Society. The town talked about it.' So Andrew
lingered with Clarrie at the gate that night. 'The
only objectionable thing about Clarrie was her long
hair. She wore a black frock, and looked very
breakable. Nothing irritates a man so much.
Andrew gathered her passionately in his arms, while
a pained, puzzled expression struggled to reach his
face. Then he replaced her roughly on the ground
and left her. It was impossible to say whether
they were engaged.'

Arrived in London, Andrew took lodgings at the
top of a house in Bernard Street, Bloomsbury, and
immediately set about finding a Cabinet Minister
in need of a secretary. He met disappointment
everywhere, although he latterly 'offered to take a
pound a week less than any other secretary in London '.
He had fifty-eight testimonials with him, but couldn't
get anybody to read them; so he spent a great part
of his time reading them over to himself. ' He
had a yearning to stop strangers in the streets and
try a testimonial's effect on them.' With the Press,
it was no better. ' One of the finest things that
was ever written on the " Ontology of Being " '
he could induce no editor to publish. Eventually
he supplied the dailies with mendacious anecdotes
of great people who were dying, but 'as often as
not the invalid got better, and then Andrew went
without a dinner '.

But Andrew's ingenuity found other ways of
raising the wind:

Once he offered his services to a Conservative statesman; at another time he shot himself in the coat in Northumberland Street, Strand, to oblige an evening paper (five shillings).

He fainted in the pit of a theatre to the bribe of an emotional tragedian (a guinea).

He assaulted a young lady and her aunt with a view to robbery, in a quiet thoroughfare, by arrangement with a young gentleman, who rescued them and made him run (ten shillings).

It got into the papers that he had fled from a wax policeman at Tussaud's (half-a-crown).

Riach was now sunk in the blues, and failure had embittered him against everybody, but Queen Logic still reigned at the back of his brain. ' Even in his worst days his reasoning powers never left him. Once a mother let her child slip from her arms to the pavement. She gave a shriek. " My good woman," said Andrew testily, " what difference can one infant in the world more or less make? " '

While prowling about the streets in this despair there was a man whom he encountered frequently, and who began to exercise a nameless fascination on him. Rounding the upper end of Chancery Lane one evening he ran into him. ' Andrew had been dreaming, and the jerk woke him to the roar of London. It was as if he had taken his fingers from his ears.' The stranger was evidently hurrying somewhere, and Andrew involuntarily hurried after him. In Arundel Street he discovered that the stranger in turn was also shadowing someone. Along the deserted Embankment went the trio, each at some distance from the other. The first leant over the Embankment and gazed on the flood beneath, ' the next moment the stranger had darted forward, slipped his arms round the little man's legs, and toppled him into the river '. Andrew bounded forward, but the stranger exercised a mesmeric spell over him. ' " He was a good man," he said, more to himself than to Andrew, " and the world has lost a great philanthropist; but he is better as he is." ' It was in this fashion that Andrew became acquainted with the President of the Society for Doing Without Some People.

Andrew told him his story; they had many ideas in common; the president was most considerate; ' only once an ugly look came into his eyes. That was when Andrew had reached the middle of his second testimonial.' He was willing to assist Andrew to become a probationer of the society, whose noble aim was to punctuate with a full stop the lives of famous people who had reached the goal of their legitimate ambitions, lest they might live to recede from their greatness. Some of the most distinguished men of the time were associated with the organisation, and the far-seeing ones got themselves elected honorary members, as these were free from the attentions of the society, only ordinary members being eligible for ' removal '. Gladstone, in ' a very kind letter ' to the president, hoped that Salisbury would not be admitted an honorary member. It was a dangerous thing to admit one so young as Andrew to the society even as a probationer. The president mentioned the case of an excellent young man, ' discreet

beyond his years', who came to them for a time.
'It went to his head. He took a bedroom in
Pall Mall, and sat at the window with an electric
rifle picking them off on the doorsteps of the clubs.
It was a noble idea, but of course it imperilled the
very existence of the society. He was a curate.'

But Andrew is duly admitted a probationer,
thanks to the good offices of the president. He
attends a meeting of the committee at its house
in Bloomsbury. The description of the locality is
in Barrie's most characteristic vein. 'The London
cabman's occupation consists in dodging thoroughfares under repair. Numbers of dingy streets have
been flung about to help him. There is one of
these in Bloomsbury, which was originally discovered by a student while looking for the British
Museum. It runs a hundred yards in a straight
line, then stops, like a stranger who has lost his
way, and hurries by another route out of the neighbourhood.'

That long-neck of Andrew's is now a trial to
him, as the members of the committee can't keep
their eyes off it, and even the president insists on
his muffling it up. Mrs. Fawcett came and lectured
to the society, and protested against their debarring
women from its benefits. 'You call yourselves a
society for suppressing excrescences. Your president tells me,' she said, 'you are at present inquiring for the address of the man who signs himself
"Paterfamilias" in the *Times*; but the letters from
"A British Matron" are of no account.' She

also reminded them of a recent paper by Mrs. Kendal on the moral aspect of the drama in the country —written forty years agone and these famous ladies happily still with us!—and went on: 'I do not know how the paper affected you. But since reading it I have askéd, in despair, how can this gifted lady continue to pick her way between the snares with which the stage is beset?' Mrs. Lynn Linton she likewise commended to the attention of the S.D.W.S.P.

Andrew's first subject was Labouchère, and the chapter in which his first interview with the founder of *Truth* is recorded is one of the most amusing in the book. Andrew 'argued' with him one Sunday, but used in vain the logic he had acquired at Aberdeen. He pointed out that Labby was at the pinnacle of his fame, and now was the time to avail himself of the good offices of the society. 'Think of the newspaper placards next morning!' he urged, 'some of them perhaps edged with black; the leaders in every London paper and in all the prominent provincial ones; the six columns obituary in the *Times*; the paragraphs in the *World*; the motion by Mr. Gladstone or Mr. Healy for the adjournment of the House; the magazine articles; the promised memoirs; the publication of posthumous papers; the resolution in the Northampton Town Council; the statue in Hyde Park. With such a recompense where would be the sacrifice?' But Labouchère refused; he ordered Andrew to leave his house. 'Think of the public funeral!' cried

Andrew in despair. Andrew was shown to the door by the footman, but as he was leaving he put his head in at the doorway again: 'Would you mind telling me,' he said, 'whether you see anything peculiar about my neck?' 'It seems a good neck to twist,' Labby answered a little savagely.

His attempt to assassinate Lord Randolph Churchill was no more successful. It was to be his great effort, as he had failed with Sir George Otto Trevelyan and several other celebrities. He shadowed the statesman for days, and finally decided to do the deed between the Grand Hotel and the House. Lord Randolph left the hotel and wandered through the small thoroughfares lying between Upper Regent Street and Tottenham Court Road, stopping curiously to make notes at every tobacconist's window. After an hour of this he hailed a cab, and as he stepped into it Andrew rushed forward and snatched the notepaper from his hand. He wanted to read it before he slaughtered his victim. This is what he read when he found himself safe from pursuit up a back alley:

'Great Titchfield Street—Branscombe, 15; Churchill, 11; Langtry, 8; Gladstone, 4.

'Mortimer Street—Langtry, 11; Branscombe, 9; Gladstone, 6; Mary Anderson, 6; Churchill, 3.

'Margaret Street—Churchill, 7; Anderson, 6; Branscombe, 5; Gladstone, 4; Chamberlain, 4.

'Smaller streets—Churchill, 14; Branscombe, 13; Gladstone, 9; Langtry, 9. Totals for to-day: Churchill, 35; Langtry, 28; Gladstone, 23; Branscombe, 42; Anderson, 12; Chamberlain, nowhere.' Then followed, as if in a burst of passion, 'Branscombe still leading—confound her.'

Andrew saw that Lord Randolph had been cal-
culating fame from 'vesta' boxes: those vestas that
are now as antiquated as the flint and tinder, and
whose highly decorated boxes were a sort of popular portrait gallery, fore-runners of the modern
cigarette cards.   In the end he only managed to
get a cut at his lordship's heels as he entered his
hotel after the adjournment of the House.

At the next meeting of the S.D.W.S.P., Riach
was a candidate for admission to full membership,
and read his thesis, in the course of which he said,
' What shall we do, Society asks, with our boys?   I
reply, Kill off the parents.   There can be little
doubt that forty-five years is long enough for a man
to live.   Parents must see that.   Youth is the time
to have your fling.'   But Andrew had to flee from
the committee; in the end his neck had told against
him, and while he was waiting election in the side-
room they were drawing lots for him.   The president came to his aid, hustled him away in a cab
to King's Cross; and took a ticket for him to Glasgow.   It was Andrew's only chance, the president
assured him, his own fingers itching.   The committee were only human, he exclaimed.   ' Your
neck,' he cried, ' cover it up!'   And Andrew
only understood when the president's fingers met
round his throat, and ' he murmured in a delirious
ecstasy, " what a neck, what a neck!"   Just then
his foot slipped.   He fell.   Andrew jumped up
and kicked him as hard as he could three times.
. . . Andrew never thought so much of the presi-

dent again. You cannot respect a man and kick him '.

In the end, of course, Andrew Riach went back to Wheens, where, the master of the Grammar School having conveniently died, he got the post and married Clarrie: ' He was humbler now than he had been, and in our disappointments we turn to women for solace.' ' Domesticated and repentant he has renounced the devil and all her works. . . . For Andrew has told Clarrie all the indiscretions of his life in London, and she has forgiven everything. Ah, what will not a wife forgive! '

Such, then, is a brief outline of this most diverting trifle; from which it will be seen that the root idea is as whimsical as any ever conceived by W. S. Gilbert, while the manner of its working out is characteristic of none but Barrie himself, the fun being sustained without effort from first to last, and every page with its sparkle of wit.

The Thatched House,
  St. James's, S.W.

M

X

THE NAUGHTINESS OF 'WALKER, LONDON'

To W. Francis Aitken

MOST vigilant of book-worms, to your incurable habit of burrowing in catalogues of old books I am indebted, my dear Aitken, for many an item of Barriana which has gone to the enrichment of my library and has contributed to the completeness of a long-planned critical biography that may some day, attain to the dignity of an entry in one of these catalogues which so much delight your bookman's heart: '. . . 530 pp. octavo, full cloth, gilt title, fine copy, *uncut*, SCARCE, 15s.' To you, it may be, I owe the possession of an acting edition of Barrie's delightful comedy 'Walker, London', which I came upon in looking through my shelves the other day, and dipping into the green wrappered booklet found myself back in the days of my youth as magically as any wizard's wand could have transported me. For an hour or so of the pleasantest reverie I let wait the urgent matters of my desk and had a moon-glimpse of those far Victorian days.

We must admit, I think, that the Victorian was a mealy-mouthed age. A mincing insincerity characterised its speech. It used 'unmentionables' for trousers, it 'hanged' and 'dashed' when it really meant to damn, and it perverted physiology by substituting 'stomach' for belly. In a late Victorian book of essays which I looked into an hour ago I came across the old familiar interchange of brevities between Quin, the actor, and Rich, from whose management at Covent Garden he had withdrawn in pique, recorded thus:

> Quin to Rich—' I am at Bath.'
> Rich to Quin—' Stay there and be hanged.'

The idea of softening the authentic 'damned' with this foolish evasion is peculiarly Victorian. We know how Miss Ailie made Sentimental Tommy, when reading aloud to her, use 'stroke' for 'damn' and replace 'darling' and such like language of passion with 'words we have no concern with': a proper proceeding for that lavender lady. Indeed an instructive study in changing manners need not range beyond the works of J. M. Barrie, for I know not where the ebbing tide of Victorianism can be better observed than in his books and plays.

'Walker, London' is a sad time-marker for us who were young in the naughty 'nineties and can recall J. L. Toole's 'Oh, it's nothing' and the antics of that very young actor Seymour Hicks when, as Andrew McPhail, he had news that he had not failed. I remember also the ill-fated Laurence Irving, Hicks' friend and admirer, in the same part, and a mere mention of the other names in the cast at Toole's Theatre on February 25th, 1892, evokes a cloud of wistful memory: Mary Brough, Eliza Johnstone, Irene Vanbrugh, Mary Ansell and the rest!

But I propose to concern myself here with one feature only of ' Walker, London '—its notion of naughtiness. Early in the first act we are met with this quaint bit of dialogue, in the writing of which Barrie was already a master, as we perceive by its unforced naturalness:

ANDREW: ' Take a stomach; remove the——'
NANNY [putting fingers to her ears]:   Disgusting!
ANDREW [coming to]:   We all have them, Miss O'Brien.
NANNY: I suppose we have, but, sure, we needn't let on! That's the worst of being a doctor.
ANDREW: I'm not a doctor yet.   Oh, to be one, to prescribe, to operate.   To cut off legs!

That snatch of talk is perfectly in tune with the temper of the time in which the play was set, and Bell Golightly, B.A., was perhaps the first, as she certainly was the most engaging, stage presentation of the ' brainy ' young women who were the pioneers of the great movement that attained, through broken windows and hunger strikes, to triumph in the political equality of the sexes some three decades later.   Listen to her when Kit Upjohn and she are in the thick of their courtship:

BELL   [stamping her foot]: No!   Promise, Kit, that you will never again call me such names.
KIT: But——

BELL: They are degrading!

KIT: Nonsense, child!

BELL: Child! Do you not see that you are insulting me?

KIT   [kissing her]: My beautiful!

BELL: You must never pay those infantile compliments to my personal appearance. If you love me, let it be for my mind alone, for all other love is founded on an entological misconception.

KIT: We can settle all these little matters when you are my wife, Bell.

BELL: No, let us understand each other now. I must be your helpmate in all things. Should I seem unreasonable you must never humour me. No laughing me out of *my* arguments, nor kissing away *my* judgement. You will never yield to me for that most despicable of all reasons, because you think me pretty.

KIT: I will do my best to make you happy.

BELL: You will give up smoking?

One would like to read aloud that love scene to a young lady of to-day as she sat sipping her crème de menthe, while she flicked the ash from her cigarette and displayed her ' nude '-silked shapeliness to an indeterminate line above her knees. ' Give up smoking? What priceless rot! ' Can't you hear her? Manners have changed noticeably since the young wizard of Thrums made the first of his many stage successes some five and thirty years ago.

There is further play with the naughtiness of smoking, and a faint forecast of a still distant day when the charming Nanny O'Brien encounters Jasper Phipps, the barber masquerading as an African explorer, smoking his pipe on the deck of the house-boat. Toole's embarrassed look as he made to put his pipe in his pocket on Nanny exclaiming 'Smoking again, Colonel,' still lingers in one's memory and also his unctuous slyness, as she added 'Don't! I like it!' whereupon he whips out a cigarette-case and holding it to her says: 'Then perhaps——'

Here observe stage directions and ensuing dialogue:

> [She signs caution, goes on tip-toe to saloon door, looks at Mrs. Golightly, shuts door, comes back and takes cigarette which he lights for her, sitting on bank C.]

NANNY: I am sure I look horrid!

JASPER: Beautiful!

NANNY: Is this the right way?

JASPER: So exactly right that if I did not know better, I should think you had tried it before.

NANNY: Never! [looks suspiciously at him.]

Sad is the thought that such delicious naughti-ness as this may not happen again. And picture if you can such a soliloquy as Kit's when he comes back in the third act to push his wooing of Bell to its final stage:

KIT: Hallo! I am smoking and Bell dislikes it! Never again! [Flings cigar into water and sighs.] After all, it is an objectionable habit! [Produces cigar case, and flings away another cigar—sighs.] Making a chimney of one's nose! [Lights a cigar.] It will be no deprivation to me—none at all. [Takes cigar out of his mouth and looks at it.] How did this come about? [Flings it

away and sighs.] Bell will be pleased. [Takes
another cigar from case.] This is the last. [Makes
as if to fling it away.] It—it seems to stick to
my fingers! [Sound of singing in distance—rises
and goes to bow.] I hear their voices! They
are coming back! Bell is coming. [Looks from
cigar to place whence singing comes.] Bell—
cigar—cigar—Bell. [Falters, then flings cigar
into river, tries to catch it, misses, groans.] It is
nothing to give up smoking for the girl one loves!

All this was delightfully amusing when the farce
was first staged, and though the fun of it has not
yet evaporated, the laughter it would awaken in action
to-day would be mingled with a strain of amused
contempt for a compunction that cannot be trans-
planted into the manners of a more sophisticated age.

There are other instances of Victorian naughtiness in this delightful play which is so truthful a
mirror of its time, and these may profitably engage
us further. The timorous touch upon the once
barred topic of nudity will here be noted:

NANNY: And is it true that the ladies dress—ah—lightly?
JASPER: Mostly in telegraph wires——
NANNY: What is the costume?
JASPER: Oh, it's nothing.
W. G. [Bell's young brother]:   Fancy!
MRS. GOLIGHTLY: No, you mustn't.

Entirely proper to the time and the play is Nanny's
confession to W.G., in begging him to pull her
waistband tighter, that it is 'in honour of Mr.
McPhail's success I have decided to make my waist

smaller'. Yet the girl of to-day would read it with wonderment.

As indicating how the costume of the play has acquired with age a dramatic value, we find Nanny's stage direction when Jasper gallantly admires her little feet reads: ' *She pulls them beneath her dress !* '

But the last act ' cows a',' as they say in Thrums, for boldness. I had forgotten that the author did grit his teeth and in a daring moment let fly a word we had no concern with; nor can I now recall the effect of it—it must have been devastating—though later we were to hear it without wincing in ' What Every Woman Knows ', thus blazing the trail for a still naughtier bit of naughtiness which an even bolder dramatist introduced just twenty years on in his ' Pygmalion '. The course of true love is smoothing for Kit, who speaks to Bell as she is about to step into the punt alongside the house-boat:

KIT: And Bell, prove that your mind is made up at last by repeating the words I used.

BELL: What words?

KIT: Damn Logic!

BELL: Oh!

KIT: Logic has been the curse of our love. Bell, say it and be free.

BELL: I can't *say* it!

KIT: Yes, say it! [She hesitates then whispers in his ear.] Good!

Worst of all is the sentence given to that *enfant terrible* ' W. G.' to speak in the closing scene when the engagements of Bell and Kit, Nanny and Andrew are announced, and the engaged couples are looking out of the saloon windows. ' Look here all of you, I had better tell you this at once, if you should have any babies—(*They pull down their blinds*) or—or that sort of thing, you needn't expect me to hold the little beggars.'

A few minutes before they had been seen within the saloon of the house-boat dancing a minuet! Did we really dance minuets in the early 'nineties? Surely not. The very thought of it makes me feel like a survival from a lavendered past. The pulling down of the blinds was entirely harmonious then, but it would be a gesture of pure hypocrisy in an age when the Charleston has ousted both minuet and polka.

Perhaps, after all, these dear shades and phantoms of a late Victorian day were not less sophisticated than their daughters who are now kicking up their heels so brazenly, and they were surely their equals in charm. If ' Walker, London ' can be re-staged to-day only as a ' costume play ', and if it reflects a social life and a set of ideas that are as dead, and seem almost as remote, as the days of Nell Gwyn, the book of this farcical comedy, which is truly an abstract and brief chronicle of its time, is still evocative of pleasure and of beauty to us of the older generation, who, with our knowledge of the generation now shaping, may smile at those quaint contrasts I have pointed out, but with a smile in which a tear will glisten.

Savage Club,
 Adelphi.

XI

A MEMORY OF NEWSTEAD ABBEY

To John Drinkwater

KNOWING you as a skilled student of Byron
and one who has added, even after a crowded
century of other writers, to our knowledge of both
the poet and his poetry, I feel, dear Mr. Drinkwater,
that if you have happened in your newspaper reading
upon a certain brief but sinister paragraph that
caught my eye the other day, you must have suffered
some pangs of sorrow at the thought of time's muta-
tions. More than any item of news since the Great
War, this paragraph seems to me to advertise the
strangeness of our times. ' Newstead Abbey, once
the home of Lord Byron, is to be turned into flats.'
With true economy of words the laconic paragraphist
dealt his blow and passed to his next ' newsy ' trifle.
I have seen no other reference to the matter anywhere and there are times when I find myself doubting
whether I did read these direful words; and half-
hoping that they might be a wisp of memory left floating in my mind from some phantasm of the night.
Thirty years have passed like a film upon my
screen of life since I made a pilgrimage to Newstead:

just six years less than the total span allotted by a niggard fate to that most alluring of our great poets; and some notes made so long ago (when, like yourself some three years later, I resided in the old-fashioned town of Nottingham) may serve me to-day to recall my impression of a mansion which, in any land that had proper pride in its men of genius, would surely have been preserved as a ' national monument '.

Nature, art, and the aura of genius had all combined to make of Newstead Abbey a sacred place. By reason of its fine situation, and the memories that clustered round it as thick as the ivy upon its walls, it was a lovely bit of historic England; but as the scene of years of an immortal poet's pilgrimage, celebrated in one of his finest works, and enriched with the glamour of his fame, how many of our ' stately homes of England ' could compare with it?

A word or two of its history. It was in 1170 that Henry II granted a charter for the foundation of a priory at Newstead, in the very heart of that romantic woodland, the Forest of Sherwood, and no doubt its monkish inhabitants a few years later had occasional visits from Robin Hood and his merry men, so often the uninvited guests at abbey or mansion in this green land of adventure. But, thanks to husbandman and forester, and many another contributor, Newstead stands no longer in Sherwood Forest, and what remains of that great woodland has now retreated some miles to the northeast. The monks who won the favour of the second Henry were canons regular of the Order of St. Augustine, and doubtless enjoyed many privileges, as Henry was a frequent visitor to the neighbourhood —perhaps with a jealous eye upon his deer—and he was seldom there without being prevailed upon to extend the possessions of the monks of Newstead, so that in time these good men were able from their fat revenues to erect a church and monastery, which, in their flourishing days, must have been among the finest in the land.

One Henry gave and another took away, the Eighth of them writing a hasty finis to the long tale of monastic devotion, and in 1540 Newstead Abbey was added to the possessions of the Byron family, who had held lands in the county since they came to England with William the Conqueror. Sir John Byron, of Colwick, Steward of Manchester and Rochdale, and Lieutenant of Sherwood Forest, who then became owner of the Abbey, and set about transforming it into a mansion, was known as ' Sir John Byron the Little with the great beard ', although his portrait, I recall, shows him without beard of any kind.   Lord Byron wrote better lines than those in which he records this event:

> One holy Henry reared the Gothic walls,
>   And bade the pious inmates rest in peace;
> Another Henry the kind gift recalls,
>   And bids devotion's hallowed echoes cease.

Centuries were to pass before ' devotion's hallowed echoes ' woke again in Newstead and the last of

the Byrons lay in his grave, having builded something that will outlive all stone and mortar.

The history of Newstead Abbey from its coming
into the hands of the Byrons and the poet's succes-
sion to the title need not engage us; enough that
during these years the prosperity of the Byrons had
its ebb and flow, and at the death of the 'wicked
Lord', the poet's grand-uncle, it was at its lowest.
This nobleman's clouded career furnishes one of
the many tragic chapters in the annals of the Byrons.
His foolish quarrel at the Star and Garter, a Pall
Mall tavern, in January, 1765, with his neighbour,
Mr. Chaworth, of Annesley—a name fated to be
closely knit in romance with that of Byron—is familiar
to all readers of biography. Chaworth had ventured the opinion that Sir Charles Sedley had more
game on five acres than Lord Byron had on all his
manors, an insulting statement of truth which the
wicked lord could consider only on the duelling
ground. Chaworth died from wounds received in
the encounter, and before expiring he gave an account
of the affair that was most discreditable to the conduct
of his challenger. Byron was tried by his Peers
and dismissed on paying his fees; but his remaining
years were spent as a recluse at Newstead, where
he pleasured himself by doing a maximum of damage
to his estate, already much reduced by his gambling.
Abbey and grounds fell into decay. While his
passion for destroying trees was boundless, the
famous Pilgrims' Oak, which stood—and I hope
still stands—at what is now the eastern entrance

to the estate, was saved from destruction only by the public spirit of some local gentlemen.

So deplorable was the state of Newstead when the fifth Lord Byron died that he was occupying the one room that was not open to the rain, the old Xenodochium and the Great Refectory being at that time stocked with forage, while in the entrance hall and the Monks' Parlour cattle were stabled. Such was its state when the poet became sixth Lord Byron. His lines barely conjure up an adequate picture of the ruin that was his heritage:

> Through thy battlements, Newstead, the hollow winds whistle,
> Thou, the hall of my fathers, art gone to decay:
> In thy once smiling garden the hemlock and thistle
> Have choked up the rose which late bloom'd in the way.

He was a lad of ten when, in 1798, he came with his foolish mother to Newstead as owner of the old Abbey and its still extensive domain. A brief portion only of his youth was spent in the halls of his fathers; for after a year at the Abbey his mother packed him off to the boarding-school at Dulwich, and thence, in two years to Harrow, where he remained till 1805, when he entered Trinity, Cambridge. But the long vacations were often spent at Newstead, whose surroundings exercised so strong a spell on the young poet. His mother finding the expense of maintaining the place more than her narrow means allowed, little was done during those years to reduce its dilapidation, but

when the poet came of age he wrought many improve-
ments, though no Byrons were to be thanked for
the splendid condition in which the Abbey stood
at the time of my visit. That was the work of
strangers; and the poet asked ' Who could suppose
that a stranger would feel? '

Newstead estate is about nine miles north of
Nottingham. The village I recall as a dirty little
place on the west of it and a walk of a mile and a
half through the private grounds brought one to
the Abbey. The surrounding scenery is essentially
' English ', pleasingly diversified, green, tree-fringed
hills sweeping gently to little vales; the streak of
road, now losing itself in a patch of forest, and again
twisting through open meadow lands, with cattle
at pasture. We went along a grove of magnificent
beeches, with a prattling stream tumbling over a
rocky ledge to a pool beneath, and thence to the
little lake that shimmered—it was a sunny day of
June—in front of the Abbey. A scene of tender
beauty. Ah, how will it figure in the House Agent's
advertisements of ' Flats to Let '!

The west front is the more imposing, notwith-
standing its mixture of architecture. Standing east
and west, the old church formed the north end of
the Abbey; but its western gable, a bit of fine English
Gothic, was all that remained, and the stone-tracery
of its great window was softly mantled in ivy, while
in a niche above it the Madonna and Child, to
whom the antique sanctuary was dedicated, remained
intact; the lower niches tenantless.

I wonder if the vendor of the adjoining flats-to-be will quote the poet:

A glorious remnant of the Gothic pile
    (While yet the Church was Rome's) stood half apart
In a grand arch, which once screen'd many an aisle:
    These last had disappear'd, a loss to art:
The first yet frown'd superbly o'er the soil,
    And kindled feelings in the roughest heart,
Which mourn'd the power of time's or tempest's march,
In gazing on that venerable arch.

Within a niche, nigh to its pinnacle,
    Twelve saints had once stood sanctified in stone;
But these had fallen, not when the friars fell,
    But in the war that struck Charles from his throne,
When each house was a fortalice—as tell
    The annals of full many a line undone,—
The gallant cavaliers, who fought in vain
For those who knew not to resign or reign.

But in a higher niche, alone, but crown'd,
    The Virgin Mother of the God-born child,
With her son in her blessed arms, look'd around,
    Spared by some chance when all beside was spoil'd;
She made the earth below seem holy ground.
    This may be superstition, weak or wild,
But even the faintest relics of a shrine
Of any worship make some thoughts divine.

The old west front of the Abbey extends south from the gable of the old church, which it adjoins, the south end being entirely modern. The Norman tower was erected by Colonel Wildman, who bought the estate from Byron in 1813. But ancient and

NEWSTEAD ABBEY

modern are blended as effectively in the exterior
as they proved to be within. One entered a noble
hall through the Gothic porch, and it was difficult
to picture it as the shelter for cattle which it had
been a hundred years before. Mr. Webb, owner
of the estate, thirty years ago was a noted hunter
of big game and he had turned the hall into a veritable museum of his trophies.

After going up the grand staircase to the western
corridor, we had to climb the spiral stone stairway
that gave access to the poet's rooms. One of the
loveliest things in Newstead I noted here: a window
of stained glass, old as the Abbey, and aglow with
that lustrous light which the modern glass so seldom
admits.

Byron's dressing-room and bedrooms, and the
little ante-room known as the Haunted Chamber,
were all preserved in the same condition as he left
them. His bedroom was once the abbot's lodging.
It was simply furnished, the gilded Elizabethan
bedstead with its coronets being the one touch of
ostentation. In the oriel window stood the poet's
writing table, surely an emotional object to all who
have been touched however lightly by the finger
of romance. The view from this window was so
charming that it must have stayed rather than speeded
the pen.

> Before the mansion lay a lucid lake,
>   Broad as transparent, deep, and freshly fed
> By a river, which its soften'd way did take
>   In currents through the calmer water spread

N

> Around: the wild fowl nestled in the brake
>   And sedges, brooding in their liquid bed:
> The woods sloped downwards to its brink, and stood
> With their green faces fix'd upon the flood.

Although such was the scene that daily greeted the poet's eye on his late rising from his lordly bed, it will be noted that his muse something faltered in its description.

From the bedroom one passed into the gloomy little apartment long reputed to be haunted by the ghost of a black friar. (What will become of that poor ghost when all the flats are let?) This little chamber looks upon the site of the old sanctuary, and in monastic days served as an oratory, where the aged or infirm were able to perform their devotions and could even join in the services that took place in the church below, since the window opened into it. You will recall, perhaps, how Byron introduces the Newstead phantom in ' Don Juan ':

> As Juan mused on mutability,
>   Or on his mistress—terms synonymous—
> No sound except the echo of his sigh,
>   Or step, ran sadly through that antique house;
> When suddenly he heard, or thought so, nigh,
>   A supernatural agent—or a mouse,
> Whose little nibbling rustle will embarrass
> Most people, as it plays along the arras.
>
> .   .   .   .   .
>
> Once, twice, thrice, pass'd, repass'd, the thing of air
>   Or earth beneath, or heaven, or t'other place;
> And Juan gazed upon it with a stare,
>   Yet could not speak or move; but, on its base

As stands a statue, stood: he felt his hair
  Twine like a knot of snakes around his face:
He taxed his tongue for words, which were not granted
To ask the reverend person what he wanted.

Returning to the west corridor, we were admitted through a massive oaken door to the great dining hall, anciently the monks' refectory. In Webb's time this noble room had a fine baronial atmosphere, rich in armorial shields and suits of mail. When Byron fell heir to Newstead, it was in use as a forage loft.

But a smaller dining-room opening off the larger interested me more, as this was always used by Byron in his days at the Abbey. Originally the Lord Abbot's parlour, and still so-called, its ceiling was deeply panelled, and richly decorated in gold and azure, the walls oak panelled. The mantelpiece was, I remember, a fine piece of work, but its character escapes my memory. In the centre it had the armorial bearings of the Byrons, with the words 'Sir John Byron, MDLVI', and three pro-jecting heads, the central one representing a Saracen, and those on each side a female and a European soldier, commemorative, so the legend runs, of an episode in the crusades, when an ancestor of the Byrons rescued an Egyptian maiden from a Moor. These carvings figure in the poet's 'Lines on Leaving Newstead':

Of the mail-covered barons, who proudly to battle
  Led their vassals from Europe to Palestine's plain,
The escutcheon and shield, which with every blast rattle,
  Are the only sad vestiges now that remain.

But there is no warranty for the crusading Byrons, and doubtless the poet in his Greek adventure was more of a crusader than any of his ancestors. It was in this room, and around this oaken table, that Byron and his boon companions made merry and indulged in pranks, which, however picturesque when seen through the mist of years, were still unworthy in an age that paid even less regard to the proprieties than is paid to-day. A good notion of the hectic hours at Newstead may be gained from a letter written by Charles Skinner Matthews, a companion of Byron, to a friend, describing a visit to the Abbey:

If the place itself (he writes) appears strange to you, the ways of the inhabitants will not appear much less so. Ascend then with me the hall steps, that I may introduce you to my Lord and his visitants. But have a care how you proceed; be mindful to go there in broad daylight, and with your eyes about you; for, should you make any blunder—should you go to the right of the hall steps, you are laid hold of by a *bear;* and should you go to the left, your case is still worse, for you run full against a *wolf!* Nor, when you have attained the door, is your danger over; for the hall being decayed, and therefore standing in need of repair, a bevy of inmates are very probably banging at one end of it with their pistols! so that if you enter without giving loud notice of your approach, you have only escaped the wolf and the bear to expire by the pistol-shots of the merry monks of Newstead.

Our party consisted of Lord Byron and four others, and was now and then increased by the presence of a neighbouring parson. As for our way of living, the order of the day was generally this: for breakfast we had no set hour, but each suited his own convenience, everything remaining on the table till the whole party had done—though, had one wished to breakfast at the early hour of ten, one would have been rather lucky to have found any of the servants up. Our average hour of rising was one. I, who generally got up between eleven and twelve, was always, even when an invalid, the first of the party, and was esteemed a prodigy of early rising. It was frequently past two before the breakfast party broke up. Then, for the amusement of the morning, there was reading, fencing, single-stick, or shuttle-cock in the great room—practising with pistols in the hall—walking, riding, cricket—sailing on the lake—playing with the bear or teasing the wolf. Between seven and eight we dined, and our evening lasted from that time till one, two, or three in the morning. The evening diversions may be easily conceived.

I must not omit the custom of handing round after dinner, on the removal of the cloth, a human skull filled with Burgundy.

After revelling on choice viands, and the finest wines of France, we adjourn to tea, where we amused ourselves in reading or conversation, each according to his fancy; and, after sandwiches, &c., retired to rest. A set of monkish dresses, which had been provided with all the proper apparatus of crosses, beads, tonsures, &c., often gave a variety to our appearance and pursuits.

There's a pretty picture for the moralists: is it matter for marvel (they might ask) that the poetry born of such a life might bring the blush to the maiden's cheek and have pernicious reactions on the mind of youth? Perhaps it was over-squeamish of Mr. Webb to have the monkish skull, which had been put to such base uses, given decent interment; for the fevered hand of genius that once had touched it gave it a distinction its mouldered owner had failed to confer upon it. And yet we must concede that such goings-on as these are not likely to disgrace the Flats!

The library I remember as a long narrow room, panelled in light and dark oak, with some beautiful carving, and occupying nearly the whole of the north side of the Abbey. Then in the east corridor were the state bed chambers, a splendid suite of apartments, with eastward windows framing hill and copse enough to rejoice Old Crome. From the Abbey's earliest days these rooms had been reserved for the honoured guests who came to hunt in Sherwood Forest. There was Charles the Second's room; Edward the Third's room (more probably Edward the First's, the latter king having visited the Abbey in the eighth year of his reign), the Duke of Sussex's room and Henry the Seventh's lodgings, all, when I went through them, filled with historic pieces of furniture which in the present vogue for antiques would sell for more than the Abbey itself.

The saloon, or large drawing-room, was formerly the dormitory for the monks. Here, in due place of honour over the chimneypiece, hung the original of the familiar portrait of Lord Byron by Philips, while the poet himself has catalogued the other paintings in the room in this lively strain:

> Steel barons, molten the next generation
>   To silken rows of gay and garter'd earls,
> Glanced from the walls in goodly preservation;
>   And Lady Marys, blooming into girls,
> With fair long locks, had also kept their station;
>   And countesses mature, in robes and pearls:
> Also some beauties of Sir Peter Lely,
> Whose drapery hints we may admire them freely.

Generals, some all in armour, of the old
   And iron time, ere lead had ta'en the lead:
Others in wigs of Marlborough's martial fold,
   Huger than twelve of our degenerate breed:
Lordings, with staves of white or keys of gold:
   Nimrods, whose canvas scarce contained the steed;
And here and there some stern high patriot stood,
Who could not get the place for which he sued.

     .   .   .   .   .

Here sweetly spread a landscape of Lorraine;
   There Rembrandt made his darkness equal light,
Or gloomy Caravaggio's gloomier stain
   Bronzed o'er some lean and stoic anchorite:
But, lo! a Teniers woos, and not in vain,
   Your eyes to revel in a livelier sight:
His bell-mouth'd goblet makes me feel quite Danish,
Or Dutch, with thirst—What, ho! a flask of Rhenish.

In the south corridor the owner had set up a little
museum of Byron relics and also some of Dr.
Livingstone, for, strange as the collocation may
appear, that devoted missionary was also identified
with this resting place of the Pilgrim of Eternity.
There was the plain circular table whereon the poet
wrote part of ' Childe Harold ' and ' English Bards
and Scotch Reviewers ', the last cap he wore in
Greece, the brass helmet and sabretache used in his
fatal expedition there, the portion of the tree on
which he cut his own and his sister's names on his
last visit to Newstead, crockery ware, spill-cups,
candlesticks, inkstand, swords, single-sticks, boxing-
gloves, face-guards, his favourite dog's collar, the
rapier with which Mr. Chaworth was killed, carved

oak chairs, bearing the embroidery of Byron's sister, Augusta: all these and more were here displayed. Livingstone was the guest of Mr. Webb during his last stay in England, and here in a room in the Sussex tower he wrote 'The Zambesi and its Tributaries'. Stanley had also been a guest at the Abbey.

So much for the mansion, yet the description is far from complete, as much of it remaining unmentioned as might be cut up into numerous flats. The old chapter house, a dainty little Gothic building, had become the private chapel of the Newstead estate, and one wonders what use it will be put to for the new regiment of flat-dwellers. In the cloister court, on the east, a quaint old fountain stood, its waters splashing in the sunlight. Let the poet picture it:

> Amidst the Court a Gothic fountain play'd,
>   Symmetrical, but deck'd with carvings quaint—
> Strange faces, like to men in masquerade,
>   And here perhaps a monster, there a saint:
> The spring gush'd through grim mouths of granite made
>   And sparkled into basins, where it spent
> Its little torrent in a thousand bubbles,
> Like man's vain glory, and his vainer troubles.

But of all the many points at which the latter-day visitor to Newstead may feel 'in touch' with the romantic and pathetic personality that for so brief a space of time endured his destiny here and hallowed the place for ever, I think it is when we stand beside the memorial which Byron erected to his dog 'Boatswain'. This is placed amid the ruined walls

of the Abbey church where the high altar stood,
and in this choice of place there may be detected
a certain gesture of defiance.   In his restless craving
for love and friendship he encountered so much
that proved illusory, that we can forgive the extrava-
gance of this memorial in his genuine sympathy for
the lowly and the inarticulate, as marked in Byron
as his despisal of the canaille. The monument
is of marble, resembling a stunted obelisk set upon
a base of six broad steps, the slabs of which show
peculiar fissures said to have been the result of an
earthquake.   In the vault beneath Byron directed,
by a will executed in 1811, that his body should
be placed beside that of his faithful canine friend,
but it is doubtful if so extravagant a wish would
have been observed even though the sale of the
Abbey in 1813 had not put an end to the idea.   ' I
have built myself a bath and a *vault*,' Byron wrote
to a friend, 'and now I shan't be buried in it.   It
is odd that one can't be certain of a *grave*, at least
a particular one.'   The inscription sets forth Boatswain's many virtues in orthodox fashion, but
the ' Epitaph ' contains more than the ordinary
percentage of Byron's pessimism. Though it is
well-known, I shall give myself the pleasure of
transcribing it again; for it contains some memorable lines:

> When some proud son of man returns to earth,
> Unknown to glory, but upheld by birth,
> The sculptor's art exhausts the pomp of woe,
> And storied urns record who rests below;

When all is done, upon the tomb is seen,
Not what he was, but what he should have been:
But the poor dog, in life the firmest friend,
The first to welcome, the foremost to defend,
Whose honest heart is still his master's own,
Who labours, fights, lives, breathes for him alone,
Unhonour'd falls, unnoticed all his worth,
Denied in heaven the soul he held on earth:
While man, vain insect! hopes to be forgiven,
And claims himself a sole exclusive heaven.
Oh man! thou feeble tenant of an hour,
Debased by slavery, or corrupt by power,
Who knows thee well must quit thee with disgust,
Degraded mass of animated dust!
Thy love is lust, thy friendship all a cheat,
Thy smiles hypocrisy, thy words deceit!
By nature vile, ennobled but by name,
Each kindred brute might bid thee blush for shame.
Ye! who perchance behold this simple urn,
Pass on—it honours none you wish to mourn:
To mark a friend's remains these stones arise:
I never knew but one,—and here he lies.

In Byron's time there stood a grove of oak trees
some little way from the Abbey, a favourite haunt
of the poet as might be supposed, and in whose
gloomy nooks it pleased his fancy to set up leaden
satyrs and fawns, which was sufficient ground in
the local bucolic mind for its later title of ' the devil's
wood '. It still stood when Washington Irving
came to Newstead in the early 'thirties of last century,
but it was hewn away scores of years ago, when decay
had threatened its oaks, all save the stump of that
on which the poet had in sentimental mood carved

his own and his sister's name. Near by the site
of this vanished grove, and on the borders of the
lawn, there was another oak which had been planted
by the young master of Newstead when he arrived
at the Abbey in 1798. What 'more natural than
that sentiment should mark it for its own? In later
years the poet would link his own fate with that
of this oak tree. 'As it fares, so will fare my fortunes', and visiting the Abbey in 1807, when Lord
Grey de Ruthyn was the tenant, he was saddened
to find the oak choked up with weeds and almost
destroyed.

Young oak! when I planted thee deep in the ground,
  I hoped that thy days would be longer than mine:
That thy dark waving branches would flourish around,
  And ivy thy trunk with its mantle entwine.

Such, such was my hope, when, in infancy's years,
  On the land of my fathers I rear'd thee with pride:
They are past and I water thy stem with my tears,—
  Thy decay not the weeds that surround thee can hide

I left thee, my oak, and, since that fatal hour,
  A stranger has dwelt in the hall of my sire;
Till manhood shall crown me, not mine is the power,
  But his, whose neglect may have bade thee expire.

Oh! hardy thou wert—even now little care
  Might revive thy young head, and thy wounds gently heal:
But thou wert not fated affection to share—
  For who could suppose that a stranger would feel?

But a stranger did feel, for the little care was
shown by those who came to own his ancestral hall

in after years, and thirty years ago there was no more flourishing tree on the estate than Byron's oak. What may happen to it and to all these memory-haunted souvenirs if it is true that ' Newstead Abbey, once the home of Lord Byron, is to be turned into flats ' I dare not think.   It was the poet's hope that—

> Haply thy sun, emerging, yet may shine,
>   Thee to irradiate with meridian ray;
> Hours splendid as the past may still be thine,
>   And bless thy future as thy former day.

—a hope that was indeed fulfilled, for in the days when Mr. Webb was lord of the manor Newstead Abbey was better cared for than it could have been in Byron's own day and more worthy to have been the stately home of a prince of poets.

I am at least enough of a romanticist not to permit myself ever again to revisit the Abbey, preferring to remember it in all its opulence of beauty as I saw it thirty years ago, and to suppose that so it continues, for the true spirit of romance is to see all things just as one wishes to see them.

Meads,
 Eastbourne.

XII

OF AUCASSIN AND TARTARIN: ROMANCE AND THE COMIC SPIRIT

To St. John Adcock

WHEN we except such commanding writers of the past as Dumas and Hugo, and the occasional 'best seller' of to-day, as the author of 'Jew Süss', the English reading public spares but little of its time to continental writers, and that little is spent mainly with translated works. You, I am sure, will not be ready to suppose that I mention this by way of disparaging English taste, which is far from my intention; for if I wished to name a critic to whom his native literature had been all-sufficing, whose adventures in reading had not led him far beyond the rich fields of English, wherein he had great content, I should be inclined to mention you, my dear Adcock. And should I not be naming one who, in devotion to his native literature, was not without compensations which readers like myself, who have made many a haphazard excursion into half-a-dozen tongues, may have missed? One who knows English literature as you know it, whose acquaintance with every school and individual of the modern period especially is so intimate that surely you must read even in your sleep, such a one need not fear to be dubbed a literary stay-at-home.

Yet, why do I address a dear friend of old years and a critic so essentially English on a matter that concerns two writers of an alien tongue? It is because I am minded to-day to set down a word or two about a common friend of ours, first introduced to me by you a score of years ago, a man of genius whose mortal body we helped to lower ' into the breast that gives the rose ' one lovely Sussex morning a few springtides back.

Not many readers are familiar with the name of Edward Wright: he who wrote so much never wrote a book, so that at least he made no enemies. But relieved of the need to earn at the pen's point a livelihood ' for weans and wife ', he might well have added to the classics of criticism. There is no living critic in whom the qualities of perception and felicity of expression blend more harmoniously than they did in him. He had an uncanny gift of getting at the heart of a book while he seemed to be doing no more than cutting its leaves, and to read, as so often it was my business in the days of the War, the articles he had written after a few hours of fumbling among heaps of newspaper clippings was always to marvel at his power to give true literary shape to things amorphous. In all the years he was my colleague he seldom failed in the most forbidding

task. Hundreds of thousands of words he wrote
upon the progress of the war, displaying a knowledge
of military history that astounded all his associates,
and won the admiration of eminent experts. The
most abstruse scientific matters he could make clear;
there was no literary or historical subject he could
not touch with charm and persuasion; no foreign
tongue seemed to daunt him: he adapted many a
Scandinavian and Breton folk-tale, translations from
the French or German he could ' knock off ' with
astonishing ease, and indeed I often had the feeling
that he would have faced without a tremor a study
from Czechoslovakian or Hungarian had the need
been urgent, even if he had never seen either language
in print before! Yet, his efforts to speak French
were worthy of Stratford-atte-Bowe, as I remember
one day at Doullens just before the final German
' push ' began. A literary wonder was Edward
Wright, and some day I may be able to give evidence
for what at present, I am conscious, is mere assertion;
indeed I am now about to put in a minor ' document
in the case '. It relates Edward Wright with a
scene of my wanderings in what I hope may be
thought an interesting way.

One of the first things in French with which I
made casual acquaintance after the poetry of André
Chénier, for which my teacher infected me with his
wise enthusiasm, was Bida's rendering of ' Aucassin
and Nicolete ' into modern French. That little
jewel of the old romantic ages is worth a wagon-load
of modern sophisticated verse in the pleasure it has

spread throughout the world. When I see the
academy portraits, the newspaper photographs and
the 'Epilepstein' busts of latter-day 'piddling
poetasters' (the phrase is Henley's) not a line of
whose verse will survive a century hence, I feel how
rascally Fame can be that let the author of 'Aucassin
and Nicolete' pass nameless into limbo.   A wandering
minstrel of the late thirteenth century who sang
and recited in the halls of the great nobles of
northern France, this lovely product of his art is
preserved in a unique medieval manuscript in the
Bibliothèque Nationale of Paris.   There must have
been many copies in circulation, and perhaps we owe
to some untidy servant, who neglected to burn it
at a late medieval 'spring cleaning', its survival
into the age of mechanical reproduction, a sure
source of enchantment for all time to come.   In
such casual fashion has the modern world come
by most of its ancient treasures, from the Bible
onward.

Do not be alarmed if I seem heading for a biblio-
graphical study of 'Aucassin and Nicolete', although
I doubt if even I could make that unattractive.   It
is far too big a matter for a paragraph; Bourdillon
gives packed pages to it.   I must note, however, that Andrew Lang's English version, like
Bourdillon's, dates back to 1887, since when there
have been another eight or nine.   Of these the
most widely circulated is possibly the least known
to collectors, as it has not yet had separate existence.
Its author is Edward Wright.   My old enthusiasm

for the song-story of the two young lovers of Provence
bade me include a complete version of it in my
' Masterpiece Library of Short Stories,' and in making
that translation I think that Wright produced a
work of exceptional literary merit. He had written
earlier a condensed version for inclusion in ' The
World's Great Books ' and it is probable that more
readers throughout the English world owe their
knowledge of ' Aucassin and Nicolete ' to these two
sources than to all the others combined.

As it might be charged against me that, in a moment of editorial weakness, I allowed him in his
later version to give a reading of the Picard original
which offers a more fanciful description of its *jongleur*
author than scholarship will accept, I may permit
myself a word on this. In the original the song-story
begins:

> Qui vauroit bons versoir
> Del deport du viel antif,
> De deus biax enfans petis,
> Nicholete et Aucassins,
> Des grans paines qu'il soufri,
> Et des proueces qu'il fist
> Por s'amie o le cler vis?
> Dox est li cans, biax (est) li dis,
> Et cortois et bien asis.
> Nus hom n'est si esbahis,
> Tant dolans ni entrepris,
> De grant mal amaladis,
> Se il l'oit, ne soit garis,
> Et de joie resbaudis,
> Tant par est douce.

o

This, with close eye on the original and a deliberate effort to suggest an antique English, Andrew Lang thus renders:

> Who would list to the good lay
> Gladness of the captive grey?
> 'Tis how two young lovers met,
> Aucassin and Nicolete,
> Of the pains the lover bore
> And the sorrows he outwore,
> For the goodness and the grace
> Of his love, so fair of face.
>
> Sweet the song, the story sweet,
> There is no man hearkens it,
> No man living 'neath the sun,
> So outwearied, so foredone,
> Sick and woful, worn and sad,
> But is healed, but is glad
>   'Tis so sweet.

Here is Wright's rendering of the opening snatch of song:

> Hear a tale of joy and grief
> By the minstrel Old Antif,
> Telling how two lovers met,
> Aucassin and Nicolete,
> And the dolours undergone,
> And the deeds of prowess done
> By a lad of noble race
> For a lady fair of face!
>
> Sweet is the tale and finely told.
> Though a man be ill and old,

Sick of body, sad of mind,
And to moody thought inclined,
If he hear it, he shall be
Healed and filled with jollity.
It is so sweet!

It will be observed that he has boldly set capitals
to *viel antif* and made them stand for ' Old Antif ',
the name of the minstrel, while in Lang's version
they are freely rendered as the ' captive grey '.
A vast deal of scholarship has been expended upon
these two words, Lang having evidently preferred
a reading of the manuscript which gives *viel caitif*,
though the weight of opinion favours *viel antif*
(or ' ancient old man '), while the fanciful ' Old
Antif ' was first thought of by Hermann Suchier,
the German professor, who between 1878 and 1909
produced some seven editions of the original text
with many illuminating notes.   In any case it does
not carry us any nearer to the authorship of this
immortal tale, as nothing is known of a *jongleur*
named Antif, and we remain in this particular where
we were.

But this I do know: that Edward Wright's version
of the whole song-story which he rendered into
modern English with no attempt to create an antique
atmosphere by the use of old and archaic phrases,
stands not unworthily beside Andrew Lang's masterly
version.   And what an astonishing tale it is; so
packed with incident, so naïve in character and yet
so appealing to our sophisticated age! Aucassin is
the son of Garins, Count of Beaucaire, Nicolete the

daughter of the Moorish King of Carthagena,
bought by the captain of Garins' soldiers in some
expedition when he found her a captive, and reared
as his own daughter. She is—need it be said?—
most wondrous fair:

> Nicolete of the bright face,
> Lily of love and rose of grace!
> Sweeter than grapes my Sweetheart is,
> Or wine in carven chalices!

And in one of the prose passages—for the story
moves briskly forward in alternate passages of prose
and verse, the prose being recited, the verse sung
(to a somewhat monotonous tune I believe)—the
heroine is thus minutely pictured:

Her yellow hair fell in little curls; her eyes were blue and
laughing; and her face finely curved, with a proud, shapely
little nose; her little lips were more tenderly red than cherries
and roses are in summer-time; her teeth were white and
small; and her firm little breasts swelled beneath her mantle
like two nuts of a walnut-tree. So slim was her waist that
you could have clipped her in your two hands; and the daisies
that snapped beneath her toes as she passed, and fell on the
arch of her foot, looked quite black beside her feet and legs.
So very white the maiden was.

That Childe Aucassin, the Christian youth, should
love the Saracen maid was as inevitable as the count's
efforts to wed him to another. Nicolete is pent
up in her godfather's tower at Beaucaire:

> In the vault where Nicolete
> Prisoned is, may no one get.

Pleasant is the place to see,
Carved and painted wondrously;
But no pleasure can she find
In the room, for grief of mind.
Look! for she is leaning still
From the marble window-sill!
Delicate brows and yellow hair
She has, and delicately fair
Her face is, and no man can see
On earth a lovelier thing than she
In the woodland far below
She can see the roses blow,
And the pretty birds that sing,
While she is 'reft of everything.
' Ah me! Poor slave! ' she cries. ' Ah me!
Why should I a prisoner be?
Aucassin! My lord! My knight!
Heart's desire, and eyes' delight!
Because you do not hate me, I
In a prison cell must lie,
All with grief and pain fordone.
But, by God, sweet Mary's Son,
Here for long I will not stay:
          Love shall find a way!

While Wright makes too much of the last line of
the verse—*Se jel puis fare*—Lang makes not enough
—' If I may flee '—though following the metre
more faithfully. But, again, that matters little.

Nicolete does break prison in the good old way,
and Aucassin in turn is thrust into confinement for
persisting in his love. But it falls out happily that
he is able to go in pursuit of her into the dark forest
whither she has fled, and, finding her in the bower

which she has prepared in hope of his coming, he carries her with him on his horse into the distant land of Torelore, which is an interlude of unrestrained fantasy. The Saracens sack Torelore, and while Aucassin is thrown into a ship that is wrecked at sea and finally drifts to his own Beaucaire, Nicolete in turn is taken back to Carthagena and her father's court. All this is the very stuff of romance, and it is told with the prettiest detail of circumstance. Aucassin's parents are dead, and he is acclaimed by his people as the Count of Beaucaire, but he is sad without Nicolete who, to evade being married to a pagan king, takes to the road in minstrel guise, carrying her viol, her lily skin stained dark with juices, and so arrives at Beaucaire to sing to the love-lorn Aucassin:

> Under the tower of Beaucaire town,
> Aucassin in state sat down:
> And around him gathered then
> The great lords who were his men.
> Seeing all the flowers of spring,
> And hearing all the small birds sing,
> He called to mind the happy days,
> When he rode the woodland ways
> With his sweetheart, Nicolete,
> Till his eyes with tears were wet.
> And look you! Nicolete was there,
> Standing on the castle stair!
> She took her viol and her bow,
> And cried: ' Fair Barons, listen now!
> Yes, those beneath and those above,
> Please listen to a tale of love,

Of Aucassin, a gallant knight,
And Nicolete, a lady bright!
Long their love endured, and he
Sought her beneath the greenwood tree:
But from the tower of Torelore
The pagans the two lovers bore.
Of Aucassin is nothing known.
Nicolete is in Carthage town,
Where her father reigns as King,
And loves her more than anything.
Fain is he to marry her
To Caliph, Sultan, or Emir:
But she takes no thought of this.
All her love and all her bliss
Are set upon a Christian lad—
Aucassin was the name he had!
And in the Name of God she vows
Never a lord will she espouse,
Save one she now knows nothing of,—
            Her own true love!'

The end, as you will perceive, is now a few lines
off, and though capable of being foretold by the
densest, there would always be a long-drawn sigh
of satisfaction and surprise from the ladies and their
gallants that listened to the minstrel, as he brought
his charming story to so sweet a close:

Tender and long was his embrace:
He kissed her eyes and mouth and face:
So the night sped. Then Nicolete
And Aucassin at the altar met:
And she, the bride beyond compare,
Became the Lady of Beaucaire.

> Long was their wedded life and sweet,
> And great the joy they had in it.
> Thus has Nicolete her bliss
> And her Aucassin has his.
> Our song-story now o'er.
>   I know no more!

Believe me, that when I started my intention was to give but a paragraph to ' Aucassin and Nicolete,' and here I am pages on, with many a thing unsaid of it that I had a mind to mention. You will agree, I think, that whether it be read in the Picard French of the original, in the modern French of Bida, or in the English of Andrew Lang, of Laurence Housman or Edward Wright, it is a story that no reader of taste should fail to make better acquaintance with. And to the amateur of letters I can think of no better introduction to that alluring field of study: the *cante-fable* or song-story, which takes one as far afield as Arabia, by way of Saracenesque Spain and the Moorish lands of North Africa.

' I like your book: you " do go on so " ', an Australian lady wrote to me not long ago, and I took it as a compliment. To make a pigeon hole of your mind with all your accumulations of fact and fancy neatly docketed, and when a piece of writing is toward, to choose the nice number of those required, blow the dust off them, and give each its paragraph of relative length, is not my notion of how an interesting essay may be put together. I have compiled many an encyclopedia, as you know, and do not undervalue orderliness,

nay, I hold it in such regard that I believe it to be
of the very essence of literary style, and I think I
have Stevenson with me here; but just now I am
not seeking after the ideal of *la pièce bien faite* which
Sarcey so much admired in French drama.   Besides,
I am writing this in an armchair in my favourite
corner of a Southern ' Pullman ', from whose wide
windows I look upon the lovely green places of
Sussex so many mornings and evenings of the year:
those sunlit, kine-peopled fields with their ' gigantic
smile ', ' broad as ten thousand beeves at pasture '.
This does not conduce to composition that marches
with the mechanical progression of a train—its pace
was more leisurely if less smooth when Trollope
was composing his novels in his corner seat—but
it does enable one to ' go on so ', and there is a
certain merit in that.

Though my eye has just been resting on the bosky
slopes of the South Downs as the train is slowing
with the approach to Lewes, whose fine old castle
guards the gate to Downland, my mind's eye is
seeing a castle far-away, which has the virtue of
bringing me back to the subject of these pages—
Beaucaire!

The years are many since I first came upon
Beaucaire, after some dusty hours a-wheel through
olive groves and vineyards.   And as I looked upon its
jauntily upthrusting tower and not too closely pried
into the ruins of the ancient castle of Bellicardo,
which belonged to the Dukes of Toulouse, I was
little disturbed by the knowledge that ' Old Antif ', or

whoever the minstrel was, knew no more about
the site of Beaucaire than Shakespeare did about
the coast of Bohemia. It is thought that he may
have been a captive in Barbary, or in Spain, and
there have come by both the content and the form
of his immortal story, but the waves of the sea that
cast Aucassin's bark so fortunately beneath the
turrets of his own castle were more than thirty miles
away from Beaucaire, which stands that distance
up the Rhône. Still, the river which in places runs
wide and shallow bears craft to-day as large as any
that went down to the seas in the days of Torelore
and at Beaucaire, now a prosperous and well built
little town with spacious wharves for its trade in
wines and oils, it is wide enough and might well
have been rough enough to provide the setting for
a shipwreck.

We shall not inquire too closely into these details,
however, for across the bridge another castle stands,
and the home of another hero of romance is beckon-
ing. It may be a far cry from the pale loveliness
of ' Aucassin and Nicolete ' to the robustious humour
of ' Tartarin of Tarascon '—with only a suspension
bridge between!—and yet both are in essence of
the same eternal stuff of romance.

Now an English reader who may have enjoyed
to the full the famous trilogy of Tartarin books
might well suppose that the town of Tarascon is
largely a creation of Alphonse Daudet's imagination,
so little are we accustomed to our novelists naming
the actual scenes of their stories. But all who

have travelled from Paris to Marseilles by way of
Lyons and Avignon must have passed through
Tarascon, with its wide and open station perched
high on a viaduct, and the porter bawling in his
rich, southern tongue, ' Tarascon, stop five minutes.
Change for Nîmes, Montpellier, Cette.' And if
the traveller has—and how can he fail to have?—
happy memories of the incomparable Tartarin, his
feet will itch to be out and wander the dusty streets
in the hope of looking upon the scenes of that hero's
great days; to peep perchance at his tiny white-
washed villa on the Avignon Road with its green
Venetian shutters, where the little bootblacks used
to play about the door and hail the great man as his
portly figure stepped forth, bound for the Alpine
Club ' down town '. There would be small other
reason for tarry at this ancient town; such interest
as it possesses it owes to the genius of Daudet, whose
inimitable humour has vivified and touched it with
immortality.

It was only to be expected that when I had gone
to Nîmes to visit Daudet's birthplace there a gentleman from Tarascon whom I met at an hotel perspired
with indignation as he denounced ' that Daudet '
for libelling the good folk of Tarascon. ' Tartarin!
The whole thing's a farce. There never was such
a man! ' The town itself was well worth seeing,
he assured me, if I could but forget Daudet's ribald
nonsense.

You must know, of course, what a rare fellow
this Tartarin was—*coquin de bon sort!* I am not sure

that I should speak of him in the past tense; although his Creator eventually gathered him to his fathers, Tartarin was built for immortality, and at most his passing was a translation; he is for all time the archetype of southern character, and Tarascon is still alive with him. Of medium height, stout of body, scant of hair on the head, bushy-whiskered and jovial-faced, you may see his like any day sipping his *petit verre* at any café on the promenade of the sleepy old town, or playing a game of billiards with the grand manner of a Napoleon figuring out a campaign.

Blessed with all the imagination of the generous South, Tartarin was indeed an ineffectual Bonaparte in the body of a good-natured provincial. ' We are both of the South ', he observed to Pascalon, when that faithful henchman, at a crisis in his hero's career, pointed out the similarity between him of Corsica and him of Tarascon. Daudet makes him, in a bright flash of self-knowledge, describe himself as ' Don Quixote in the skin of Sancho Panza ', and Henry James has in this wise elaborated the point with his usual deftness:

There are two men in Tartarin, and there are two men in all of us; only, of course, to make a fine case, M. Daudet has zigzagged the line of their respective oddities. As he says so amusingly in ' Tartarin of Tarascon ', in his comparison of the very different promptings of these inner voices, when the Don Quixote sounds the appeal, ' Cover yourself with glory! ' the Sancho Panza murmurs the qualification, ' Cover yourself with flannel! ' The glory is everything the imagination regales itself with as a luxury of reputation—the *regardelle* so prettily described in the last pages of 'Port Tarascon', the flannel is everything that life demands as a tribute to reality—a gage of self-preservation. The glory reduced to a tangible texture too often turns out to be mere prudent under-clothing.

It is true that a good deal of the humour that attaches to Tartarin is of the unconscious sort. He and his brethren of Provence stand in relation to their fellow-countrymen much as the Irish to the English in the matter of humour, but in that only. They are often the butt of northern witticisms, and are said to be experts in drawing the long bow: Tarascon in this respect no more than many a score of little towns in the Midi; but it suited the author's purpose admirably to locate the home of his hero there, as the place possesses many quaint little peculiarities of its own which fitted in admirably with the scheme of Tartarin's remarkable career.

Since the days of my pilgrimage the Tarasconians have proved worthy of their reputation, as a picture postcard has been put in circulation bearing a photograph of 'La Maison de Tartarin'. It shows a square and comfortable white house, flat-roofed, with a series of loop-hole windows that give it a murderous look. In front is a large garden, where an old baobab stretches forth its branches and innumerable exotics mingle their strange leaves in the beautiful disorder of the primeval forest. So, at least, I gather from a French journal. Yet, while pointing out the mendacity of the picture postcard, the journal in question publishes, with every evidence of sincerity, an equally apocryphal account of the real Tartarin, who, we are told, was a person named originally Jean Pittalouga, a native of the south of Sardinia, not a Frenchman at all. He was bought out of slavery by the Brotherhood of the Trinity, and came to Tarascon to manage the property of the fraternity in that town. As Sidi-Mouley-Abdallah was the superior of Morocco and that country was part of Barbary, Pittalouga became known in Tarascon, because of his romantic experience among the Moors, first as *Sidi-Barbari*, and then as *Barbarin*. The time came when the Trinity fraternity had to clear out, and with them Barbarin, who now rented a neighbouring farm on the outskirts of the town— the veritable '*Maison de Tartarin*' of the postcard. But he did not die there. He went away with the Trinity fathers into Africa, and is believed to have been devoured entirely by some terrible wild beast, with whom he had disputed the sovereignty of the desert. To all which, as Daudet remarks of the member of the Jockey Club travelling *avec sa nièce*, 'Hum! hum!'

One may note here that the author did first write of his comic hero as Barbarin; but as the French law affords the fullest measure of protection to living people whose names may be introduced in works of fiction, and as there lived in Tarascon a certain M. Barbarin, who wrote to Daudet a letter worthy of his hero, wherein he threatened the utmost rigour of the law unless the novelist ceased to make sport of 'what was dearer to him than life itself, the unspotted name of his ancestors', Daudet altered the name to Tartarin, and was inclined to think in after years, when the fame of his creation had travelled around the globe, that his hero would never have been so popular under his original name. It may have been a case of apt alliteration's artful aid; but one may suppose that Tartarin would have been equally popular by any other name. He embodies the extravagant, and not the least lovable, side of French character, as truly as Uriah Heep and Mr. Pecksniff represent English humbug and hypocrisy; he has many points of similarity with Mr. Pickwick, who can hardly be compared with him as reality seen through the eye of kindly caricature.

Tartarin was, in a word, an epitome of innocent vanities; large-hearted, generous, he had the Cæsarian ambition to be the first man in his town; he was imbued with the national hunger for '*la Gloire*', and many were the amusing ways in which he sought to demonstrate his prowess. To impress his townsmen, the dear old humbug surrounded himself, as you will remember, with all sorts of foreign curiosities. His garden was stuffed with exotics from every clime, most notable of all the wonderful baobab which he grew in a flower-pot, although that is the unmatched giant of the tree kingdom. His study was decked with the weapons of many strange and savage peoples, and, like a miniature museum, his possessions were ticketed: 'Poisoned arrows! Do not touch!' 'Weapons loaded! Have a care!'

His earliest exploits were as chief of the ' cap-
hunters ', for, you see, in those days the good
folk of Tarascon were great sports, and the whole
countryside having been denuded of game, they
were reduced to the device of going forth in
hunting-parties, and after a jolly picnic they would
throw up their caps in the air and shoot at them
as they fell!

The man whose hat bears the greatest number of shot
marks is hailed as champion of the chase, and in the evening,
with his riddled cap stuck on the end of his rifle, he makes a
triumphal entry into Tarascon, 'midst the barking of dogs and
fanfares of trumpets.

Tartarin, however, determined to cover himself
with glory—as well as with flannel—by making an
expedition into Algeria and Morocco, there to try
his prowess on the lions of the Atlas. His ludicrous
adventures on this great enterprise—how he shot a
donkey and a blind lion, and returned to Tarascon
pursued by his devoted camel—form the theme of
the first of Daudet's three charming stories. And
when, a few years ago, I made my first acquaintance
with North African shores, I was reminded of
Tartarin's adventure with the donkey by finding that
the country on the outskirts of Algiers was vividly
familiar to me through Daudet's description. We
were more fortunate than Tartarin in encountering
a fine jackal, which, startled by our car, stood for a
moment or two in the middle of the road before
disappearing in a neighbouring plantation.

TARASCON: THE MARKET PLACE

The years pass with Tartarin lording it at Baobab
House, and at the club every evening spinning his
untruthful yarns, beginning: ' Picture to yourself a
certain evening in the open Sahara '. Then come
the further adventures of ' Tartarin in the Alps ',
and I confess that when, a good many years ago,
I first clambered up a portion of Mont Blanc it was
of Tartarin's famous ascent I thought rather than
of Jacques Balmat's; the fiction was more vivid in
my mind than the fact; and again at the Castle of
Chillon the comic figure of Tartarin imprisoned
there was no less intriguing to the imagination than
that of Bonnivard; and, by the by, in the famous
dungeon one can see scratched on the wall the signa-
tures of both Lord Byron and Alphonse Daudet.

The last, and in some respects the best, of all
the Tartarin books—like Mulvaney, his fame is
' dishpersed most notoriously in sev'ril volumes '—
is ' Port Tarascon ', wherein are detailed the mirthful
misadventures of the great man and many of his
townsmen who, under his direction, set sail to found
a colony in Polynesia, an undertaking that proved fatal
to his fame, and ended eventually in his self-exile
across the Rhône bridge to Beaucaire, where he died
soon after; of sheer melancholy we are to suppose.

The rivalry between the two towns of Beaucaire
and Tarascon, their long-sustained mutual jealousies,
furnished Daudet with many an opportunity to poke
fun at them. ' Separated by the whole breadth
of the Rhône, the two cities regard each other across
the river as irreconcilable enemies. The bridge

P

that has been thrown between them has not brought
them any nearer. This bridge is never crossed—
in the first place, because it's very dangerous. The
people of Beaucaire no more go to Tarascon than
those of Tarascon go to Beaucaire.' As the gentleman I met at Nîmes would have said, ' Zut! It is
not true.' But that is neither here nor there.

Up to his forty-ninth year, Tartarin had never
spent a night away from his own home. ' The
very limit of his travels was Beaucaire, and yet
Beaucaire is not far from Tarascon, as there is only
the bridge to cross. Unhappily that beastly bridge
had been so often swept away by the storms; it is
so long, so rickety, and the Rhône so broad there
that—zounds, you understand! . . . Tartarin preferred to have a firm grip of the ground.' But this
must have referred to the old bridge that made way
for the present magnificent structure, which crosses
the river in four spans and is 1,456 feet in length.
However, it was this suspension bridge, and no
other, across which the hero's crony Bompard came
with such bravery to witness for his friend, when
Tartarin, fallen from his high estate, was on trial
at the court of Tarascon for having been party to
a gigantic swindle in the great colonising fraud of
Port Tarascon, a charge of which, as we know,
he was rightly acquitted. Bompard, at the time of
the trial, was in hiding at Beaucaire, where he had
become conservator of the Castle and warden of the
Fair Grounds—Beaucaire's annual fair is famed all
over France—' but when I saw that Tartarin was

really dragged into the dock between the myrmidons of the law, then I could hold out no longer; I let myself go—I crossed the bridge! I crossed it this morning in a terrible tempest. I was obliged to go down on all fours the same way as when I went up Mont Blanc. . . . When I tell you that the bridge was swinging like a pendulum, you'll believe I had to be brave. I was, in fact, heroic.'

The view from the bridge as one crosses to Tarascon is as pleasant a picture as may be seen in any part of old France. The noble stream, broken by sedgy islands, sweeps on between its low banks, and rising sheer from the water's edge on a firm rock-base, almost opposite the picturesque mass of Bellicardo, are the massive walls of the ancient castle of Tarascon, founded by Count Louis II in the fourteenth century and finished by King Réné of Anjou in the fifteenth. Like many another palace of kings, it is now fallen to the condition of a common prison. Within these grim walls Tartarin passed some of his inglorious days, but days not lacking romance, for was not Bompard from the opposite height signalling o' nights to him by means of mysterious lights?

The scene along the Promenade, with its far-reaching rows of plane trees, is one of peaceful and happy life, and it is good to look upon people who are in no hurry to do business and seem to take things easily. Across the way, there, the chemist is standing at his door, with those great glass jars of coloured water, now long gone out of fashion in England, shining in his window, while he rolls a cigarette for the white-trousered postman who has stopped to give him a letter, and chats with him in the passing. He might be Bezuquet himself did we not know of the misfortune that befell the latter, when he was tattooed out of recognition by the South Sea Islanders, and had to wear a mask when he came home.

St. Martha and the Tarasque are the peculiar glories of the Tarasconians, and we cannot do better than go to Daudet for the legend of St. Martha and the beast:

This Tarasque, in very ancient days, was nothing less than a terrible monster, a most alarming dragon, which laid waste the country at the mouth of the Rhône. St. Martha, who had come into Provence after the death of our Lord, went forth and caught the beast in the deep marshes, and binding its neck with a sky-blue ribbon, brought it into the city captive, tamed by the innocence and piety of the saint. Ever since then, in remembrance of the service rendered by the holy Martha, the Tarasconians have kept a holiday, which they celebrate every ten years by a procession through the city. This procession forms the escort of a sort of ferocious, bloody monster, made of wood and painted pasteboard, who is a cross between the serpent and the crocodile, and represents, in gross and ridiculous effigy, the dragon of ancient days. The thing is not a mere masquerade, for the Tarasque is really held in veneration; she is a regular idol, inspiring a sort of superstitious affectionate fear. She is called in the country the Old Grannie. The creature has herself stalled in a shed especially hired for her by the town council.

Isn't all this perfectly in tone with Tartarin? And also with Aucassin; for, as I have said already, they are of the same essence. They are but two sides of the same coin, the comic and the serious and a toss-up is all that is needed to regulate our pleasure in either if we have the necessary modicum of romance in us. Myself, I find that I can enter as joyously into the adventures of Tartarin as I can surrender myself to the patterned medievalism of Aucassin and Nicolete, or St. Martha and the Tarasque. There is an unlaughed humour in these latter, the deeper soundings of the comic muse that are made with a fine show of seriousness; and of all the god-like things that man has evolved since he came down from the primeval tree and set himself upon his hind legs the power of happy laughter and the solemn enjoyment of the comic are immeasurably the most precious.

One of the oddities of Tarascon is its railway station on the outskirts of the town. It is situated some thirty feet above the level of the street, and you gain the platform by climbing several long flights of stairs. I have never since passed through the station on my way to Marseilles without recalling my climbing of these same stairs so many years ago carrying a heavily-burdened bicycle on a hot and dusty day of June. During most of the day, I fancy, there is but little life in or around the station, for a clerk would cheerfully devote a quarter of an hour to explain to you the absurdities of the railway time-table; but half-a-dozen times a day it wakes up with the arrival of a train from or to the capital, for all trains in France seem to have a connection, however remote and tardy, with the octopus of Paris Then there is much ringing of bells and blowing of trumpets, and you almost expect to see the quaint and portly form of Tartarin himself returning from his great adventure in the Sahara or from his ascent of Mont Blanc. But you reflect that these and many other of his doings were much too good to be true, and take your place in the corner of the carriage, making yourself comfortable for the long and dreary journey to Paris.

The last thing you see as the train steams out is the white stretch of the Avignon Road between the railway and the river, its little white houses and modern villas close-shuttered and growing indistinct in the soft southern twilight.

The Corner Seat,
  Victoria—Eastbourne.

XIII

THE STREET OF ADVENTURE

To Hamilton Fyfe

I AM sending back to you, my dear Fyfe, ' The Street of Adventure ' by Philip Gibbs, which you were good enough to lend to me a fortnight ago, on my admitting, to your surprise, that it was one of the many modern novels I had neither read nor felt any stirring desire to read. I am thus proving myself of that rare brotherhood—the honest borrowers. Most of the books that have been borrowed from my own library have resembled Noah's ultimate dove, in so far as they have not returned to their ark.

I must apologise, however, if perchance you set any store by this particular copy of ' The Street of Adventure ', for having annotated it somewhat freely, a habit I have, even in reading for recreation, as I cannot repress the critic in me. Perhaps, by the way, a good part of the enjoyment which we who have given our years to the making of books derive from any sort of reading, arises from the exercise of this critical faculty.

You warned me that I should find the earlier part of this particular book somewhat heavy going, as

the story *qua* story was no great affair, but that I
would be well repaid for my patience in the latter
half of it.   Frankly, I have to confess that although
I was not uninterested even from the first, and do
not grudge the time given to its reading, I cannot
discover wherein I have been enlightened or even
adequately rewarded.   As a story, I think you will
agree with me that it is flat, stale, and unprofitable;
as a picture of journalistic life it strikes me as a
piece of lurid and exaggerated painting, not much
closer to the realities than Cubism is to nature.

Those of us who have spent some thirty years
in the by-ways of Fleet Street are almost as familiar
with the facts which the author of ' The Street of
Adventure ' uses for his material as any of the actors
in the pitiful little drama of the death of *The Rag*
—if one may apply the word drama to anything
so formless and inconsequential as the shutting down
of a badly managed and badly edited daily newspaper.   Perhaps there are few journalists who could
have made better use of their own personal experience than Philip Gibbs does in these concluding
chapters, although they lose in vivid reality by having
to carry the fag end of a feeble plot, which at no
moment of its development can grip the discerning
reader.

But my chief criticism of this book is the entirely
objectionable attitude of its author to the profession
in which he has spent his life, and whence he has
derived his livelihood.   ' It's an ill bird that files its
ain nest.'   This note of querulous discontent with the

facing p. 216

FLEET STREET

vocation one has accepted, repeated in varying keys throughout the book, eventually 'gets my goat', as your admired friends the Yankees say:

I think few men were ever so quickly inoculated with the subtle poison of Fleet Street as young Frank Luttrell. His temperament could not withstand it, and I had the melancholy satisfaction of seeing that all my forebodings about him were realised. To those who have never lived in the Street of Adventure, having only passed down its highway to St. Paul's or Charing Cross, it is difficult to explain the effect which its atmosphere has upon educated men of highly-strung temperament. It produces something of the same symptoms as the drug habit. The victim loathes the poison, but craves for it. He knows that he is yielding to a habit of life which will inevitably drag him down, and he is filled with self-pity and remorse; but if the phial is withheld from him he becomes feverish, restless and miserable. As with the opium-smoker all his higher instincts tell him to avoid his evil haunts. He knows that the temporary thrill of excitement will be followed by deadly depression, and by the degradation of his intellect and imagination, and that his will-power will be inevitably weakened so that at last it will be impossible to break or attempt to break his habit of life. Such a simile would be laughed at by men who have breathed the atmosphere of Fleet Street all their working lives. They have never known the purer air. They have been so long fettered that at last like enslaved animals they lick their chains.

Between ourselves, this sort of stuff is merely a pose. Neither you nor I have any delusions as to the power of the press—that favourite topic of suburban debating societies—but surely we do know that the greatest civilising agency of all times has been the printed page used wisely by men who have had some true thing to say and have said it in good plain language.

There is no particular reason why every sub-editor and every reporter and every descriptive writer on the staff of a Conservative daily newspaper should not be an extreme Radical, or Communist for the matter of that, since his part in the production of the paper is in no wise concerned with the political views which its editorial writers express. In most cases those journalists whose business it is to give utterance to political views are men who have per-suaded themselves, wisely or otherwise, that the opinions they are expounding are sound. Because my milkman may be a sidesman in the Church of England, and I might be a Plymouth Brother, I cannot imagine that the lacteal fluid would undergo any unusual chemical change.

Then listen to this:

A man who has seen bright visions in enchanted woods does not go joyfully into mean streets, into the squalor and filth of human by-ways. Other men of education and ideals would not have suffered so acutely. With stronger fibre they would have resisted the influence of such a life more manfully, but Frank was so sensitive that every nerve in him quivered at the least touch. Every rebuff in a profession, where rebuffs are constant, hurt him frightfully. Every insult, in a life of ceaseless insults, left him with an open wound. To be born a gentleman, with instincts of pride and dignity and delicacy, is the greatest misfortune to those who write history day by day.

When I recall the brilliant work of Arthur Machen in the London *Evening News*, and your own fine descriptive writings in the *Daily Mail*, and remember that Rudyard Kipling was also ' born a gentleman ', but has never repented of his early decision to become a journalist, passages like this make me feel that Philip Gibbs, with his bilious view of the newspaper press, was not quite the man to tell the story of the street of adventure as it might have been told.

He has occasional glimpses of sound sense, and rightly enough one of these is revealed to us by ' Mother Hubbard '—an altogether charming, but highly improbable personage—when she is made to say one night to the shadowy hero of the story:

It is disgraceful. You young men have no self-respect. If you can't get on to another paper just yet, why don't you write novels, or plays, or stories for the *Family Herald Supplement*, or penny dreadfuls, or advertisements for Pink Pills? Something—anything rather than bemoaning your fate. Do you know what I am doing to keep my end up?

Mother Hubbard was doing some typing, and thereby proving herself a much better type of humanity than Codrington, the gossip-monger, or Frank Luttrell, the feeble journalist. The author, by the way, in rather bad taste, as I think, introduces his own name several times into the story, as in some sort the procurer of Frank Luttrell for that life of literary prostitution which he would have the layman believe to be synonymous with journalism. And here we have the kernel of the whole thing; of life itself, in every walk of it—character! There is nothing wrong with journalism, and there is nothing wrong with engineering or coal-mining, if the journalist or the engineer or the miner is a person of some virility. Anyone with red blood in his veins must despise your so-called dreamers and flabby senti-mentalists, without whom nine-tenths of the modern novelists would have nothing to write about.

Little though I feel I have profited by the reading of ' The Street of Adventure ', there is much that I could find to say about it, and of course, the work is far from lacking in merit, though its humour is a bit exaggerated at times and tends to cheap effect. A book that irritates one as this has irritated me is probably not unprofitable reading. To have one's antipathies roused is even more salutary than to be appealed to entirely on the sympathetic side. But this letter has run sufficiently long to be in danger of boring you, and I shall make an end by noting two curious slips of the author, which I cannot set down to his credit as an acute observer.

' He was smoking a cigarette, and the third finger of his left hand was deeply stained with nicotine.' I may be wrong, but have you ever noticed that the third finger is the one that receives the stain? I should say it was the second, unless, indeed, we must here consider the thumb a finger.

Then perhaps you will remember that Luttrell is sent by the editor of *The Rag* to ' write up ' an omnibus accident in Hornsey. ' He had not an exact idea where Hornsey was. He guessed vaguely that it was somewhere in the East.' This was good enough for an uninformed and dreamy youth from the country, but the author, who had himself been through the mill of London journalism for many years, proceeds to tell us that 'he turned his face eastward', and again, 'he had gone down to Hornsey'. I am writing this in the parish of Hornsey, and as every junior reporter on any London 'Rag' ought to know that Hornsey lies along the 'northern heights', I begin to wonder if the author of 'The Street of Adventure' was the most reliable member of his staff on the topography of the great city in which the Street of Adventure occupies so tiny a space.

It is many years since I read Merriman's 'Slave of the Lamp', and much of it has faded from my memory, but it was a story, and as a novel of the journalistic life I am backing it at 20 to 1 against 'The Street of Adventure'. Do not you think that in growing lachrymose and pathetic about the death of *The Rag* Philip Gibbs gives away his case? All his admirable description of the last days of that ill-fated journal gives the lie to his preceding attack on journalism as a profession. If journalism is the low and contemptible thing he would have us believe, why all this pother about a shop shutting up? It is because journalism is *not* all a mean and dirty business that the death of a daily newspaper, employing a large staff of workers and many men of more than ordinary intellectual gifts, is worthy of more consideration than the closing of a draper's store.

Kenmore,
    Highgate.

XIV

'AN INLAND VOYAGE': A NEW NOTE AND AN OLD MEMORY

To C. E. Lawrence

IN addressing the ensuing pages to you, my dear Lawrence, the intention is certainly not to offer you any reflections upon the vagaries of literary taste and criticism, since few can rival your own experience as a literary 'taster'. Your long association with one of our most distinguished publishers has made you so familiar with the uncertainties of critical judgement that I can have nothing new to submit to you there anent. If, then, my immediate remarks would seem to be a carrying of coals to Newcastle, you will know that they are not exclusively for your eye, and that your name stands above for quite another reason, which will presently appear.

I have been spending an hour or two with 'An Inland Voyage' to-night because I had read yesterday some disparaging criticism of that work, which is properly Stevenson's first book. Stevenson himself, when joining in *The Idler's* famous symposium, chose to assume that he was expected to write about 'Treasure Island '—' My paymaster, the Great

Public, regards what else I have written with indifference, if not aversion . . . and when I am asked
to talk of my first book, no question in the world
but what is meant is my first novel.' Now first
books, as you know, are always suspect of immaturity. Sometimes the discerning critic delights to
tell you how an author has fallen short of his ' splendid
promise ' or the achievement of his first book, or
he may choose to show you (as the mood serves)
how an author has advanced immeasurably since
his initial attempt to make the world give ear. It
is all so easy. Well, the dispraise of ' An Inland
Voyage '—which I am assured is not only below
the literary mark of ' Travels with a Donkey ' (as
I am ready to admit), but that ' The Silverado
Squatters ' is astonishingly ahead of both—has sent
me to the book again to find those crudities of
reflection, those affectations of style, that stiffness
of the descriptive passages, and that forced gaiety
which I had failed to detect in many an earlier
reading.

I was willing to believe that I might have been
so caught by the charm of the writer's personality
that I had been blind to the noticeable faults of an
artist in his experimental stage. Henley's unfavour-
able opinion was thrown in my face, and I began
to wonder what there could be in the book which
so pleased me more than twenty years ago that, with
a copy of it in my knapsack, I set out alone to follow
the course of the voyage, along the banks of the
canals and rivers where ' Arethusa ' and ' Cigarette '

had each paddled his own canoe some twenty-five years before.

Whether to say that I am disappointed or reassured by this latest reading is a delicate matter. If a hunt for weeds has left me almost empty-handed, and I have merely had further harvest of pleasure from a source that has already yielded me so much, what shall the stern critic say of me? Under his penetrating eye I proceed with trepidation; little cold shivers flickering along the spine of my literary consciousness.

' An Inland Voyage ' contains prose as good and reflections upon life as wise as any that Stevenson ever put upon paper in his seventeen after years of life. I find very little that is immature, but an astonishing deal that could come only from the seeing eye and the understanding heart. Nor do I find the quality of its humour strained. ' It is not badly written, thin, mildly cheery and strained ', says R. L. S. in a passage of self-depreciation, and certain critics have been quick to take the book at its author's valuation. Assuredly it is ' not badly written ': it is essentially characteristic of one who, in his tireless effort to select the right word, was apt to the end of his days to give an impression of virtuosity to those who have a less regard for qualities of style.

I remember Sir Arthur Conan Doyle warmly protesting against a phrase of Stevenson's which described a clock as being stopped by ' an interjected finger '. Conan Doyle seemed to find the adjective

ON THE SAMBRE AT QUARTES

facing p. 225

unnatural and affected. His own vigorous, forthright prose reveals no 'literary' quality, no delicate
choice of words, and, like many another, he would
seem to argue that to be 'natural' you must keep
close to the ordinary commerce of speech. There
is no greater misconception of literary style. Writing
is not talking. The finest writers invigorate their
prose with nicely chosen words that are meaningful
and sonorous, that give a lively pattern to what else
were a colourless mass; in short, they deliberately
avoid the 'naturalness' of every-day talk. No
parrot-cry of 'affectation' ever made Stevenson
falter in his choice of words, and for the life of me
I cannot see that he went wrong when he used 'interjected'. There are various ways in which you
could stop a clock with your finger without inter-
jecting it. He conveyed a distinct idea in a definite
way. He also knew the right moment to bring
in a longish word to relieve and articulate a sentence
which words of one or two syllables were tending
to make too slack.

As the canoeists paddled along the Scheldt 'cattle
and grey venerable horses came and hung their
mild heads over the embankment'. Is 'mild' an
affectation? Is it not here a lovely word, worth a
whole essay on kindness to animals?

Of the life of the canal folk:

There is not enough exercise in such a life for any high
measure of health; but a high measure of health is only
necessary for unhealthy people. The slug of a fellow, who

Q

is never ill nor well, has a quiet time of it in life, and dies all the easier.

Do you find that ' affected ', or this?—

How little we pay our way in life! Although we have our purses continually in our hand, the better part of service goes still unrewarded. But I like to fancy that a grateful spirit gives as good as it gets. Perhaps the Bazins knew how much I liked them? perhaps they also were healed of some slights by the thanks that I gave them in my manner?

And, tell me, is this sort of stuff foppish and immature?—

Bazin was a tall man, running to fat: soft-spoken, with a delicate, gentle face. We asked him to share our wine; but he excused himself, having pledged reservists all day long. This was a very different type of the workman-innkeeper from the bawling disputatious fellow at Origny. He also loved Paris, where he had worked as a decorative painter in his youth. . . . He had delighted in the museums in his youth. ' One sees there little miracles of work,' he said; ' that is what makes a good workman; it kindles a spark.' We asked him how he managed in La Fère. ' I am married,' he said, ' and I have my pretty children. But frankly, it is no life at all. From morning to night I pledge a pack of good enough fellows who know nothing.'

It faired as the night went on, and the moon came out of the clouds. We sat in front of the door, talking softly with Bazin. . . . Madame Bazin came out after a while; she was tired with her day's work, I suppose; and she nestled up to her husband and laid her head upon his breast. He had his arm about her, and kept gently patting her on the shoulder. I think Bazin was right, and he was really married. Of how few people can the same be said!

That there is a certain artificiality in the author's method, I will grant the critic, his little reflective passages following, perhaps, too regularly upon the descriptions of the incidents which suggest them to exclude the suspicion (though I feel it to be unworthy) that the one may have been invented for the sake of the other. But the work as a whole is full of enduring charm, a shy and gentle humour enlivens every page, and its descriptions are as pleasing to the mind as those old vignettes of the master-engravers used to be grateful to the eye. Such inequalities as it may possess serve rather to endear it to me. Is it not true that the irregular features of a loved one may have a beauty for the lover that is not apparent to others? And as for immaturity, it is worth remembering that in 1877 Stevenson was a man of twenty-seven—long past the age of the literary prodigy—already a practised writer, who had produced in ' A Lodging for the Night ', ' Will o' the Mill ' and ' The Sire de Malétroit's Door ', three of the finest short stories he ever wrote, to say nothing of many other essays and studies afterwards gathered into ' Virginibus Puerisque ' and ' Familiar Studies '.

All this, my dear Lawrence, has arisen from my desire to say a word or two in inscribing to you the following revision of a paper which I wrote in the late summer of 1918, and which, with a group of other little sketches of mine, found favour in your eyes that led to their publication in book form by the historic house of John Murray. In the welter of war books, I fear my 'Wrack of War' had little notice, though its contents had been already widely circulated in serial form, and in reprinting 'With R. L. S. in the Land of War' in the present collection, to which it properly belongs, I have ventured to associate your name with it.

.   .   .   .   .   .

Was there ever a book so informed with the delicate fragrance of peace as 'An Inland Voyage'? In remembering the quiet joy with which one first read that enchanting story of a canoe journey by sluggish waterways through the pastoral lands of Northern France, the heart is touched with a great longing for an end to these harassing days of war and a return to that care-free life when one might go a-gipsying for the pure delight of tranquil travel. If it be that such days may come no more for many of us, we can do no better than take this companionable book from the shelf and, yielding ourselves to its charm, live over again in imagination those glorious days by the Sambre and the Oise. There is no anodyne more potent than may be found in these pages of R.L.S. when the heart is seared with the 'latest official communiqué' from the blood-sodden fields of war.

Yet it is of war that I am about to write—of war and of long-lost days of peacefulness. Often since the German swept into Belgium and poured over the French frontier have my thoughts gone back to a pilgrimage that I made a dozen years ago along

the route of 'An Inland Voyage'. For it was
through 'this very smiling tract of country' which
R. L. S. pioneered so peacefully in the late August
of 1876 that the Teutonic hosts were to pass with
fire and frightfulness at the same season thirty-eight
years later. If he were alive to-day, to what great
issues would not the pen of Tusitala have been
engaged? His blood would have boiled at the foul-
ness which the German had spread over all that
smiling land—the enemy of whom he warned us
in 'A Footnote to History' and from whose clutches
the Great War was to save the mortal remains of
him who sleeps in far Samoa, where the Union Jack
soon supplanted the flag of Germany.

Well can I imagine what has happened along the
route of 'An Inland Voyage' since August 1914,
when I have seen the havoc which the war has wrought
in many another once 'very smiling tract' of France
and Flanders, but I purpose no imaginary voyage
by little rivers which so recently ran blood. My
aim is merely to recall the associations of R. L. S.
with places which were scenes set for his dainty
comedy of vagabondage, and which War was later
to use for the staging of the World's Tragedy.

The Inland Voyage began at Antwerp. Stevenson
had a companion, the late Sir Walter Simpson, and
each voyager paddled his own canoe. That of
R. L. S. was named 'Arethusa'—a name of old and
new honour in our sea story—Sir Walter's, 'Cigarette'.

'We made a great stir in Antwerp docks,' he
says, as they launched their canoes, when a squally

wind was blowing. He tied the sail despite the
obvious danger, though 'not without some trepidation ', and makes an excellent start in his philosophising
journey with the reflection :

It is certainly easier to smoke with the sheet fastened; but
I had never before weighed a comfortable pipe of tobacco
against an obvious risk, and gravely elected for the comfortable
pipe.   It is a commonplace, that we cannot answer for ourselves before we have been tried.   But it is not so common
a reflection, and surely more consoling, that we usually find
ourselves a great deal braver and better than we thought.

How many a time has this same thought come
to our gallant young lieutenants at their first going
' over the top '?   It has been the theme of countless
stories of ' trial under fire ' since the war began.

The wind served the canoeists well up the Scheldt,
he tells us, and thereafter up the Rupel as far as
Boom, where next morning they took to the still
waters of the Willebrock Canal.   Brussels was reached
by dint of much paddling in drizzling rain, which
did not damp his enthusiasm for the life of the canal
folk.   ' Of all the creatures of commercial enterprise, a canal barge is by far the most delightful to
consider,' he writes.   Alas, even these delightful
creatures have long been caught in the toils of war,
and many have I seen in inland waterways of the
war zone with great red crosses on their hulls, carrying such cargoes as R. L. S. had never imagined.
Others there are now on these same canals that
mount big guns or creak clumsily through the locks

laden with the baneful materials of destruction instead
of the fruitful things of ' commercial enterprise '.

From Brussels the canoeists took train to Maubeuge, their frail crafts being carried thither by rail.
Few names are more fraught with meaning for us
to-day than that of Maubeuge, the town of ' might-
have—beens '. If the French had been able to hold
it—as they might, had they put their faith more
in trenches and field fortifications than in stone walls
—how different the whole course of the war! But,
on the other hand, had the Germans been able to
crush Sir John French's little army of heroes against
it in the retreat from Mons, the story of the war
would have been as strangely different.

' There was nothing to do, nothing to see. We
had good meals, which was a great matter, but that
was all.' But what was there not to do and to see
there in the last days of August and during the first
week of September 1914, when the garrison of over
30,000 French troops sought in vain to hold the
place against the invaders! To-day also, there would
be much to do and to see; but the good meals
would be more difficult to come by—and that also is a
great matter. The driver of the hotel omnibus belong-
ing to the Grand Cerf, where the voyagers put up and
where Prussian officers have now swaggered for
four years, was the one person in Maubeuge who
interested R. L. S.

' Here I am,' said he. ' I drive to the station. Well.
And then I drive back again to the hotel. And so on every

day and all the week round.   My God, is that life?'   I could
not say I thought it was—for him.   Might not this have been
a brave African traveller, or gone to the Indies after Drake?

Whoever was driving the Grand Cerf 'bus when
the Great War began would have no need to com-
plain of the dullness of Maubeuge and the lack of
excitement.   Myself, I found Maubeuge none so
dismal as it is made to appear in Stevenson's pages,
where the only adventure that befell was Sir Walter
Simpson's narrow escape from arrest for drawing the
fortifications—those fortifications that were to give
so poor a return for the money spent upon them.
In the pleasant little square of the town I recall a
spirited monument to the sons of the countryside
who died for France in the last war.   It will be a
great day for France when Maubeuge can set up
another memorial to those who have laid down their
lives since the August of 1914.

The region of Maubeuge reminded me not a little
of some parts of England's Black Country.   'Look
you,' said a stout gentleman to whom I spoke by
the wayside, when, with my bicycle, I was setting
out along the canal bank in the track of the inland
voyagers, 'we have glass works, potteries, iron
foundries, engine works, copper and many other
industries here.'   Only too well the Germans knew
this, and the many industrial places that cluster
around the ineffectual forts of Maubeuge have now
long been used to help on the war against the country
of their hapless owners.   Indeed, the bitterest thing

THE 'GAUNT TOWER' AT
PONT-SUR-SAMBRE

about the war has been the way in which the enemy has turned France's resources against herself.

The first stage of their paddling along the canalised Sambre brought the voyagers at nightfall to the little hamlet of Quartes, whence they had to walk another mile to the village of Pont-sur-Sambre to find a lodging for the night. This Pont will always be associated in my mind with an odd incident of the war.

Late in 1914 a photograph came to me as editor of *The War Illustrated* from a correspondent in France. It represented a scene of military activity, and was vaguely described as ' British divisional headquarters, with dispatch riders setting out for the front '. A true enough description, no doubt, but a curious tower was shown in the background, and I knew that tower well, as R. L. S. had written of it and I had snapped a camera at it. ' Away on the left, a gaunt tower stood in the middle of the street,' he writes. ' What it had been in past years, I know not: probably a hold in time of war.' This gaunt tower identified the place in the war photograph as Pont-sur-Sambre, which had long ceased to be the headquarters of any British division, as Haig's Corps was retreating past it on the east and Smith-Dorrien's to the west on the 24th of August.

Perhaps the most interesting stage of the canoe voyage, reviewed in the light of later happenings, was that lying between Pont and Landrecies. When ' Arethusa ' and ' Cigarette ' paddled up the Sambre to this storied town, and nearly thirty years later when I went awheel through the same countryside,

it presented many signs of pastoral prosperity.   The
river at a point about six miles north-east of Landrecies skirts the forest of Mormal, which, as R. L. S.
observes, is 'a sinister name to the ear'.   How
sinister he little guessed when he wrote the word.
' The breath of the forest of Mormal,' he goes on,
' as it came aboard upon us that showery afternoon,
was perfumed with nothing less delicate than sweet-
briar '; its breath in the closing days of August 1914
would be acrid with the fumes of war.

Stevenson saw only the south-eastern fringe of
this great forest as he paddled along on his way to
Landrecies.   I had to traverse it awheel in the
gathering dusk and contrived to lose my way among
its maze of lonesome glades.   I can distinctly remember chanting in time to my pedalling as the shadows
deepened, and perhaps in an effort to intensify the
eeriness of the place and the hour :

> Enter these enchanted woods,
>   You who dare. . . .
> Thousand eyeballs under hoods
>   Have you by the hair.

When I recall to-day the little flutterings of concern
which then beset me at the thought of so slight an
adventure as being overtaken by the night in these
uncharted woodland paths, a vivid sense of dread
grips my imagination as I try to picture the immense
columns of the Second Corps stringing out in retreat
along the western confines of the forest to take up
position at Le Cateau for one of the greatest battles

in history, while the First Corps lumbered by the
eastern roads, through the valley of the Sambre to
Landrecies, Allenby's cavalry covering the retreat
and engaging in many skirmishes with the pursuing
Uhlans amid the sylvan ways of this forest of the
sinister name.

It had been a day of ' intense and glaring heat ',
as one historian records, when the British, weary
and battered, got past Mormal and reached the line
Le Cateau—Landrecies—Maroilles, with a dangerous
gap between the first two points.   Meanwhile the Germans had been marching steadily after them, behind
their cavalry screen, through the forests, thus avoiding
aerial observation, and there was to be no rest that
night for the tired Fourth Brigade, holding Landrecies,
when a steady drizzle of rain followed the sinking
of the sun.   What happened there on the night of
August 25th is admirably recorded by Mr. John
Buchan in his ' History of the War ':

The outpost line on the northern edge of the town had
just taken up position, but no patrols had yet gone to the
front.   Suddenly out of the shadows of the forest, veiled by
the rain and darkness, the German columns advanced with
a rush.   A spatter of rifle-fire from the pickets gave the
alarm, but the thin line was swept away, and while our
Guardsmen in the town were rushing to arms, a dense mass
of the enemy was pouring into the main streets.   It was one
of the most critical moments of the campaign, but the
splendid discipline of our men saved the situation.   In the
main street the German column found its advance checked
by fire from the front and from the houses.   They tried
to push on, and then a section of Maxim guns opened on

them, and tore a line of dead and wounded through their
ranks.

They fell back, rallied, and came on again, while other
columns tried to work through the side streets and round the
town. Everywhere they found their way disputed. Officers
and men, each group acting on its own initiative, improvised
a defence at all points, and in many places the British Guards
and the Germans crossed bayonets in hand-to-hand fight.
German batteries pushed close up to the town, and threw
shells into it, and soon burning houses gave light to the
combatants, who till now had been fighting in bewildering
darkness. The enemy's guns were so near that at one point
a party of our men, driving the Germans before them, came
under the fire of six guns at a range of less than two hundred
yards. . . .

The Guards held their own among bursting shells and
burning houses, and gradually beat off the German assault,
while Haig successfully held the long line towards Maroilles.
It was after midnight when the Germans at last realised that
their surprise attack had failed, and the firing gradually died
away along the front. They had paid dearly for their enterprise. In the main street of Landrecies alone there were
nearly a thousand of their dead and wounded, and one Jaeger
battalion had almost ceased to be.

Such was the dread business that stirred in the
sleepy old streets of Landrecies during the Retreat
from Mons—those streets that were so much livelier
when R. L. S. sojourned here at the old Hôtel de la
Tête d'Or, than when I came to the town many years
after its fortifications had been dismantled and its
garrison removed, to find it as dull a place as any in
all Picardy. Less than five years having elapsed
since the Franco-German War, when Stevenson

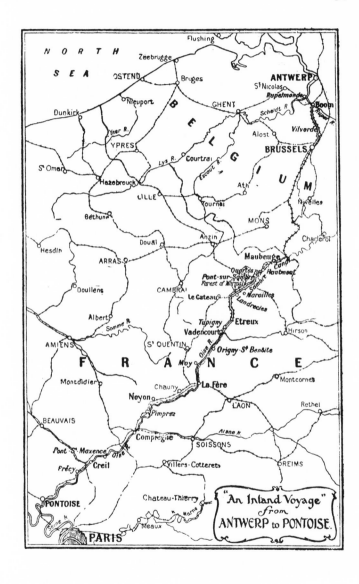

"An Inland Voyage"
from
ANTWERP to PONTOISE

steered his canoe into Landrecies, and the town
having been the scene of many a siege in old wars,
it still retained some military importance, which
prompted him to certain reflections that may be read
to-day as singularly apposite:

In all garrison towns, guard-calls, and *reveilles*, and such-
like make a fine romantic interlude in civic business. Bugles,
and drums, and fifes are of themselves most excellent things in
nature; and when they carry the mind to marching armies,
and the picturesque vicissitudes of war, they stir up something proud in the heart. But in a shadow of a town like
Landrecies, with little else moving, these points of war made
a proportionate commotion. Indeed, they were the only
things to remember. It was just the place to hear the round
going by at night in the darkness, with the solid tramp of
men marching, and the startling reverberations of the drum.
It reminded you, that even this place was a point in the
great warfaring system of Europe, and might on some future
day be ringed about with cannon smoke and thunder, and
make itself a name among strong towns.

Unhappily, Landrecies could not make itself a
name among strong towns, in a time when no town
remained 'strong' against the fire of modern artillery;
but the heroic story of the stand of the British Guards
there on the night of August 25th has given to it
a new and deathless glory.

The rattle of the drums which sounded so frequently during the two days R. L. S. tarried at
Landrecies, and the 'picturesque irony' that drums
are covered with asses' skin, led our sentimental
voyager to the writing of a memorable page which

we read again to-day with a keener sense of the truth
it carries under its veil of light philosophy:

> . . . Wherever death has his red flag a-flying, and
> sounds his own potent tuck upon the cannons, there also must
> the drummer-boy, hurrying with white face over fallen
> comrades, batter and bemaul this slip of skin from the loins
> of peaceable donkeys.
>
> Generally a man is never more uselessly employed than
> when he is at this trick of bastinadoing asses' hide. We
> know what effect it has in life, and how your dull ass will not
> mend his pace with beating. But in this state of mummy
> and melancholy survival of itself, when the hollow skin
> reverberates to the drummer's wrist, and each dub-a-dub goes
> direct to a man's heart, and puts madness there, and that
> disposition of the pulses which we, in our big way of talking,
> nickname Heroism—is there not something in the nature of
> a revenge upon the donkey's persecutors? Of old, he might
> say, you drubbed me up hill and down dale, and I must
> endure; but now that I am dead, those dull thwacks that
> were scarcely audible in country lanes have become stirring
> music in front of the brigade; and for every blow that you lay
> on my old greatcoat, you will see a comrade stumble and fall.

If the mere beating of drums in old Landrecies
led R. L. S. to such profitable reflection, to what epic
utterance may not some future genius of our race be
moved when he visits this little town where the
Guards Brigade performed those deeds of new renown
of which we have read above!

From Landrecies to Etreux the canoeists pursued
their voyage on the still waters of the Sambre-Oise
canal, and thence their canoes were carted by way
of Tupigny to Vadencourt, where they were launched
in the swift current of the upper Oise.

In my lonely pilgrimage I went awheel as far as Etreux, through a gently undulating country, rich in hop vines, with far views of thickly wooded fields and little hills, on the main road to Guise, along which Haig's Corps continued their retreat after the heroic night at Landrecies, while Smith-Dorrien was staying the German avalanche, half a dozen miles to the west, in that marvellous battle of desperation at Le Cateau. I do not recall a pleasanter picture of rural content than Etreux presented that day, with the clatter of the weavers' shuttles coming through the open doors of little cottages and the thuds of the threshers' flails sounding in farm steadings on the sunny outskirts of the town.

The road through Tupigny and Vadencourt kept me close by the Oise of my hero's adventures, and it was here, he assures us, on this sedgy stream, wriggling its devious ways by field and woodland, he had some of the happiest moments of his life—where so many of his countrymen were to find the veritable Valley of the Shadow. He could have shouted aloud for pure joy of living, as he felt himself ' scoring points ' against ' the old ashen rogue ' death, with every stroke of his paddle. The insistent humanity of the man is seen in this passage which conveys the spirit of our life in these days of the Great War better than any contemporary comment I can call to mind:

I think we may look upon our little private war with death somewhat in this light. If a man knows he will sooner or later be robbed upon a journey, he will have a bottle of the best in every inn, and look upon all his extravagances as so

much gained upon the thieves. And above all, where instead
of simply spending he makes a profitable investment for some
of his money, when it will be out of risk of loss. So every
bit of brisk living, and above all when it is healthful, is just
so much gained upon the wholesale filcher, death. We shall
have the less in our pockets, the more in our stomach, when
he cries stand and deliver. A swift stream is a favourite
artifice of his, and one that brings him in a comfortable
thing per annum; but when he and I come to settle our
accounts, I shall whistle in his face for these hours upon the
upper Oise.

Stevenson came near enough to settling accounts
with the old ashen rogue on that reach of the Oise,
for he narrowly escaped a watery grave by tumbling
out of his canoe. But he scrambled to safety still
clutching his paddle. ' On my tomb, if ever I have
one, I mean to get these words inscribed : " He clung
to his paddle." '

By Origny Sainte-Benoite, some eight miles east of
St. Quentin, through which the broken but unbowed
remnant of Smith-Dorrien's Corps retreated on Noyon
from the shambles of Le Cateau, the paddlers were
borne on the swelling flood of the Oise to Moy, a
little village dear to my memory, as there I was most
hospitably received at the Golden Sheep, though the
landlord, knowing nothing of its fame in ' An Inland
Voyage ', had changed its name to the uninspiring
' Hôtel de la Poste '. ' Sweet was our rest in the
Golden Sheep at Moy,' says R. L. S., and I could
echo this at that later day; but there has been no
sweet rest at Moy since the fateful autumn of 1914,
and as the Allies' trenches cut athwart the village

R

before the Germans swept westward again in the spring of 1918, I fear that the Golden Sheep, the quiet old château, and all the cottage homes of that pleasant little village now make a rubbish heap beside the Oise.

Even by the winding river to La Fère the journey is only a matter of nine or ten miles, and here R. L. S. had one of his happiest adventures. Turned away from a busy inn as ' pedlars '—which I am sure they looked—the canoeists were warmly welcomed at the little auberge kept by Monsieur Bazin. ' We were charged for candles,' he says, ' for food and drink and for the beds we slept in. But there was nothing in the bill for the husband's pleasant talk, nor for the pretty spectacle of their married life '.

When I went there, M. Bazin had long since passed away, his ' pretty children ' were now fathers and mothers themselves, but Madame Bazin was still active and calmly contented with her lot, like those splendid provincial women of France who have shown a heroism in this time of war as sterling as the heroism of their valorous husbands and sons. Here another Stevenson shrine may have vanished, for La Fère lay right in the foremost lines of the trench warfare. As Mme. Bazin explained to me, the town existed ' solely for the military '. I wonder how those children of hers, who won the heart of R. L. S. in 1876, have fared in the terror that has come upon their countryside. They have acquitted themselves well, I feel sure, and proved themselves worthy of the lovely pages Stevenson dedicates to the Bazins.

We next follow ' Arethusa ' and ' Cigarette ' by the winding river to ancient Noyon, one of the most picturesque towns of Picardy, whose austere and hoar cathedral has ever a foremost place in my affections.

It was on the evening of the sixth day (18th August) of the Retreat from Mons that the whole of the British Expeditionary Force came together along this river Oise between La Fère and Noyon, a battered but unbeaten army of heroes, who had foiled the most frantic efforts of a vastly superior foe to destroy them. In this ' Golden Valley ', as it is locally known, though it is a strath rather than a valley, they could snatch a little rest, and for one day it looked as though the retreat was at an end; but on Sunday morning, the 30th, the retreat had to begin again towards Compiègne and finally to the Marne (3rd September), where the tide turned at last and all the sacrifice of our glorious countrymen 'twixt Mons and Marne was splendidly redeemed.

The grand old cathedral and the beautiful town hall, which carried us back in its architecture to mediæval twilight and renaissance dawn, were the peculiar glories of this grey old city of Picardy, where, nearly twelve centuries ago, the great Charlemagne was crowned. Among all the dainty cameos of Stevenson's descriptive art, I know none more instinct with charm and the spirit of place than that of Noyon Cathedral:

I have seldom looked on the east-end of a church with more complete sympathy. As it flanges out in three wide terraces and settles down broadly on the earth, it looks like the poop of some great old battleship.   Hollow-backed buttresses carry vases, which figure for the stern lanterns.   There is a roll in the ground, and the towers just appear above the pitch of the roof, as though the good ship were bowing lazily over an Atlantic swell.   At any moment it might be a hundred feet away from you, climbing the next billow.   At any moment a window might open, and some old admiral thrust forth a cocked hat, and proceed to take an observation.   The old admirals sail the sea no longer; the old ships of battle are all broken up, and live only in pictures; but this, that was a church before ever they were thought upon, is still a church, and makes as brave an appearance by the Oise.

He confesses that he is never weary of great churches. ' It is my favourite kind of mountain scenery.'   And again: ' Mankind was never so happily inspired as when it made a cathedral.'

I could never fathom how a man dares to lift up his voice to preach in a cathedral.   What is he to say that will not be an anti-climax?   For though I have heard a considerable variety of sermons, I never yet heard one that was so expressive as a cathedral.   'Tis the best preacher itself, and preaches day and night; not only telling you of man's art and aspirations in the past, but convicting your own soul of ardent sympathies; or rather, like all good preachers, it sets you preaching to yourself;—and every man is his own doctor of divinity in the last resort.

Truly, to-day ' the dead have all the glory of the world ', for it was good to die in the belief that the Gothic glories of Rheims and Ypres, and of Noyon, were imperishable.   What would Stevenson's pen have written had he lived to suffer the knowledge that the Teutonic tribes that swept westward in a

facing p. 244

NOYON CATHEDRAL:
WEST FRONT

mad orgy of destruction heralding the Great War,
made the loveliest cathedrals of Flanders and Northern
France the chief targets of their artillery? One of
the few happy moments that I experienced in the
third year of the war was the news that Noyon, which
in the triumphant recoil from the Marne the Allies
had failed to retake, was rescued safely on March 18th,
1917; and one of the saddest came just one year
later, when I read that the gallant French had to
withdraw, that the enemy was enclosing Noyon once
again, and the old grey cathedral was burning. ' In
the little pictorial map of our whole inland voyage,'
says R. L. S., ' which my fancy still preserves, and
sometimes unrolls for the amusement of odd moments,
Noyon Cathedral figures on a most preposterous scale,
and must be nearly as large as a department. . . . If
ever I join the Church of Rome, I shall stipulate to
be Bishop of Noyon on the Oise.' I am glad to
think that the gentle writer was long removed from
the strange world of new horrors and sleeping securely
far away on Veae Top when Noyon Cathedral was
given to the flames by the vandal invaders.

At Compiègne, that charming, historic town which
has lain in the war zone from the beginning of
September, 1914, when there was hard fighting in
the woods near by, and where civilian life so long
endured amidst endless alarms, the ceaseless thunder
of guns and the stir of military movement, Stevenson
set down some observations on the military prepara-
tions of his time, which one reads again with quickened
interest to-day:

Reservery and general *militarismus* (as the Germans call it) were rampant. A camp of conical white tents without the town looked like a leaf out of a picture Bible; sword-belts decorated the walls of the *cafés*; and the streets kept sounding all day long with military music. It was not possible to be an Englishman and avoid a feeling of elation; for the men who followed the drums were small, and walked shabbily. Each man inclined at his own angle, and jolted to his own convenience, as he went. There was nothing of the superb gait with which a regiment of tall Highlanders moves behind its music, solemn and inevitable, like a natural phenomenon. Who that has seen it can forget the drum-major pacing in front, the drummers' tiger-skins, the pipers' swinging plaids, the strange elastic rhythm of the whole regiment footing it in time—and the bang of the drum, when the brasses cease, and the shrill pipes take up the martial story in their place? . . .

But though French soldiers show to ill-advantage on parade, on the march they are gay, alert, and willing like a troop of fox-hunters. I remember once seeing a company pass through the forest of Fontainebleau, on the Chailly road, between the Bas Breau and the Reine Blanche. One fellow walked a little before the rest, and sang a loud, audacious marching song. The rest bestirred their feet, and even swung their muskets in time. A young officer on horseback had hard ado to keep his countenance at the words. You never saw anything so cheerful and spontaneous as their gait; school-boys do not look more eagerly at hare and hounds; and you would have thought it impossible to tire such willing marchers.

There was much else that occupied his roving thoughts and ever-beguiling pen at Compiègne, but to-day the passages above chosen have a more imme-diate appeal than his whimsical reflections on the

Gothic quaintnesses of the old town hall. 'I doted
upon the town hall,' he confesses. Though Compiègne may escape the utter ruin that has overwhelmed so many other places of beauty and ancient
story in this land of War, it will not emerge scathless
as Stevenson beheld it, for German heavy batteries
were not trained upon it without achieving some
destructive result. But it is an arresting thought
that the rampant 'reservery and general militarismus'
which he witnessed so long ago as 1876 were prepara-
tory for the Great War that took nearly forty years
more to burst into a world conflagration, lighted by
the blood-thirsty leaders of a predatory nation.

The inland voyagers found a packet of letters from
home awaiting them at Compiègne, and these broke
the spell of vagabondage. The later stages of the
journey seem suddenly to lessen in interest. Their
canoes were bearing them along the widening waters
of the Oise not to unknown, adventurous things,
but homeward to old familiar ones.

You may paddle all day long; but it is when you come
back at nightfall, and look in at the familiar room, that
you find Love or Death awaiting you beside the stove; and
the most beautiful adventures are not those we go to seek.

At Pont Sainte-Maxence and at Creil they lingered
amid scenes where the now familiar horrors of this
war were to be enacted. From Précy to Pontoise,
where they 'drew up their keels for the last time
out of that river of Oise that had faithfully piloted
them through rain and sunshine so long', they were

leaving behind them that land of old romance which in these later years was to be known by a name of manifold terrors—'the war zone'.

The spirit of the fruitful peace that breathed throughout all that 'very smiling tract of country' in the years before the war is preserved for us with rare literary art in the pages of 'An Inland Voyage', though we of this generation may never know it again as R. L. S. revealed it to us. Literature offers no service more precious to the mind that is seared with the dread realities of these times. Stevenson's ancestors built certain of our great coastwise lights that guide the adventurous mariner home, and he himself in such pages as we have been re-reading has lighted many a beacon to cheer and hearten when the shadows fall.

Savage Club,
  Adelphi.

XV

ROLLING DOWN TO RIO—AND THEREAWAY

To J. Kennedy Maclean

YOU will remember my South American adventure, my going and returning, and the lapse of well nigh two years between. I gratefully recall that you were of those whose 'letters from home' served to cheer my days of exile. Never for a day, nor for an hour of that time, did I suffer a lowered interest in the unfolding of the panorama of life in those distant lands where I abode or wandered, yet I was never without the wistful feeling of the exile. 'The hills of home' are terribly remote when you sit alone on the historic Cerro de Santa Lucia at Santiago de Chile and contemplate the wonder of a Pacific sunset upon the mystic masses of the Andes, as so often I did in those days that now seem not less remote in time than I was then in place. So that the letters from you and other friends had a value which you could hardly have guessed.

One of you enclosed a newspaper cutting the lines of which remain etched in my memory, so sensitive was I to their mood at the time. They were written

by a poet-painter whose book ' Through India with
Pen and Brush ' had attracted favourable notice not
long before I went ' rolling down to Rio '—Mr.
A. Hugh Fisher, who will not be hard on me, I
trust, if I venture to enrich this chapter with them.
I can remember now the thrill of comradeship with
which I read them first in Santiago:

> Time tames the beast and ripens
>   The fruit upon the bough,
> Time wears the flint and lessens
>   The sharpness of the plough.
>
> Time mitigates men's anger,
>   They say, and conquers woe,
> But I two years am exiled
>   And still my torments grow.
>
> Bulls bow their necks to labour,
>   And lions lose their ire;
> And Indian monsters bend the knee,
>   And coursers ply for hire.
>
> Big grapes break from their bunches,
>   Juice runs to purple waste;
> And ears of corn grow ruddy
>   And apples sweet to taste.
>
> Far distant is the city,
>   Home, wife and friends are far.
> I hear the Scythian rabble
>   And watch an unknown star.

Well, here I am talking about the end ere I have
begun. The unknown stars that I watched most

eagerly—at first—were they that stood over the
South American continent.   I was not more anxious
to return than I had been to go!   But it is only of the
going that I wish to tell at present.

When I was a boy in that old Glasgow where your
early years in journalism and mine also were passed,
many a time did I roam among the docks, inspecting
with the eager eyes of youth the great ships assembled
there from the far reaches of the seven seas.   There
were always to be seen some big East Indiamen,
with their coolie crews, picturesque 'windjammers'
that had roughed it round the Horn, and all sorts
of odd craft that traded as far away as Australia and
South America.   For me those last had a peculiar
attraction.

Often have I watched them loading up with mighty
crates of sugar-crushers for Tucumán, or agricultural
machinery for the vast *estancias* that lie beyond the
River Plate.   I fancy it must have been an early
delight in the tales of the buccaneers and 'the
Spanish Main' that awakened in me this interest
in all things South American, for the mind of youth
makes as little concern of the thousands of weary
leagues that stretch between the Argentine and the
Spanish Main as does that of the average ill-informed
person of mature years who might be sorely pressed
to distinguish between Rio de Janeiro as the capital
of the Argentine and Montevideo as the capital of
Brazil. (You will observe that I here use 'the
Spanish Main' in its proper sense as applied to the
islands of the Antilles which frame in the Caribbean

Sea north and east, and not to the vast, vague ocean of the boys' story-writers.)

Naturally, I had my dreams of visiting that enchanting land which lay so far across the seas and held such possibilities of romance. In maturer years, when I thought I knew it better in the stories and sketches of Cunninghame Graham, and when I had read much of its sanguinary history, I still cherished some remnants of these boyish buccaneering fancies, and somehow the river down which Candide reached his Eldorado seemed in my mind to issue far off in Argentina. The very name of the River Plate was potent to stir one's imagination. Thus, when in time I became the counsellor of youth, I was much given to recommending young men to learn Spanish so that, buccaneering being no longer popular and 'pieces of eight' out of currency, they could still 'go west, young man' and make fabulous fortunes in *pesos !*

It is many years since I proffered these counsels, and I trust I may have misled none, though now that I have myself adventured in that land of fortune, I shall in future qualify my advice. Yet, it may be, that in this I builded better than I knew.

Having persistently disregarded a gipsy's warning given to me in my youth that I should have to seek my fortune abroad because my teeth were somewhat widely set, I had long settled into the way of London life—surely as interesting and satisfying as any!—with no least little notion that the gipsy was right and that I should myself set out in quest of

Spanish gold. How or why the occasion arose is neither here nor there in the present narrative, but it sent me back to school, to pick up as quickly as I could the very language whose usefulness I had so often impressed upon ambitious youth. Endowed with a certain faculty for acquiring languages, this proved a simple and delightful occupation, and in the end it was the only Spanish gold that I did pick up.

But I was to be no 'emigrant'. I had always entertained a lurking, and, perhaps, unreasonable, contempt for the man who cannot fight his battle in his own country and is driven abroad to find an opening he is unable to make for himself in the fierce competition at home, and I have often declared that I should prefer to be a moderately successful citizen of London than a wealthy rancher of Texas, a millionaire of the Pampa, or a sheep-farming magnate of Australia, if any of these involved my having to live far away from London. And this I reiterate to-day, when I have made my home upon the Sussex downs after having refused in cold blood several offers which would have led to very considerable fortune had I cared to reside in either of the Americas for a period of years.

Thus, in that month of March when my wife and I set out for Buenos Ayres, via Paris, and thence to Lisbon for the ocean liner, we left our home as though we might be returning in a week or a month; our address remained, during our year on the River Plate, 'Highgate, London', and so continued while I went farther afield alone through Chile and the

west coast republics before returning to London,
after the lapse of nearly another year, by way of
Panamá and North America.

I wish to lay some emphasis on this, although it
may seem a trivial and purely private matter. In
reality it makes all the difference in one's point of
view. Sell or let your house, part with your furniture, store it even, before leaving for the other side
of the world, and you have taken a fatal step towards
cutting adrift from the old life. Your thoughts will
no longer orient from your home, but from the new
environment in which you find yourself. Given
two men of very similar temperament who had both
come to the Argentine on the same boat: the one
under contract to carry through a certain undertaking
in a given time and return home, the other to manage
a great Argentine enterprise for a period of years,
tailing into an indefinite future; the one having his
home in London still bright and waiting for the
happy day of his return, the other having left an
empty and desolate house, sold or stored his household gods, and looking forward to making himself
as comfortable as possible in the new land which
might yet claim him for its own; is it reasonable to
suppose that the outlook of these two men would
be the same? I believe the impressions of the former
will be the more unbiased, because he looks at everything dispassionately, knowing that in a few months,
a year or so, nothing that is happening in this foreign
country will greatly concern him, and he will be
snug again within the four walls of his own established

home. The other will excuse this and that to himself, knowing that the sooner he gets used to this
and that, however he may hate them, the better for
his ultimate comfort. He will become a biased
witness, struggle he never so bravely to convey a
truthful impression.

But with what a load of preconceived opinions
one steps aboard the ship that is to carry him into
a far land, where he will have to get rid of these
impedimenta as quickly as he is able. In my case
the accumulations of years of reading had to be
jettisoned at a much more rapid rate than I took in
my new load of Spanish lore. Somehow, when we
were aboard the ship that was to carry us across the
seas of my old desires, it did not look so fine and
nowise so romantic as the vessels I used to watch
sailing away to ' South Ameriky ' from the sullen
river Clyde, in the days when I dreamt dreams by
that ' long black river of the night '.

Lisbon looked a veritable city of dream as we
steamed out of the beautiful estuary into the Atlantic.
Seen from the water, there are few finer prospects
than the long and diversified coast-line of Lisbon,
culminating in the castled height of Cintra. A
soft haze of heat blurred the outlines of the hills
and touched them much in the manner of those
hazy landscape engravings that used to adorn the
albums and ' Keepsakes ' of early Victorian days.

The dinner-bell rang soon after we had settled
in our new quarters, and for two weeks or so our
days now slipped away, punctuated by the ship's

bells. This 'orderly division of time' speedily produces a mental condition that makes for calm and good health. With nothing to do but engage in an occasional game of deck golf, or lounge in your canvas chair reading a novel, and be prompt to answer the summons of the bells that ring you to your meals, the days fade into each other, like the old-fashioned dissolving views.

I smile when I think of the plans I made for reading and writing on that voyage! Robert Barr —does his name mean anything to this generation, to whom I am sure his pseudonym 'Luke Sharpe' means nothing?—had some years before produced a book of stories which he was supposed to have written or told 'In a Steamer Chair'. I liked the title and had a vision of myself a-stretch in one of these chairs writing, writing, writing as the steamer went upon its way and, if not writing, then reading, reading, reading! I took with me a bundle of elaborately prepared notes for a book I had contracted with a London publisher to furnish, hoping so to advance the work in these idle days at sea that I should have no more than a little 'polishing' to do when I came to my journey's end. That packet travelled with me some twenty thousand miles and lies to this day unopened in a study drawer among other might-have-beens. Not a line did I write, nor can I now recall any book that I read on that long and pleasant voyage. It was with a great content that I found it impossible to fix my mind on any thought of work in those serene days of sailing over sunny seas. Nothing seemed to matter; even the frequent ticking of the wireless was somewhat of an intrusion on our ocean peace.

There are those, I believe, who can and do contrive to write in a steamer chair. I remember asking your friend Dr. F. B. Meyer, whose gracious character I esteem almost as much as I now differ from his religious opinions, to write me an article for a magazine I was editing twenty-five years ago, and his replying that he was about to start for America, but would try to write it on the voyage. He was as good as his word and I had the manuscript 'on time'. It was in type and ready for press when another manuscript came from him, now lecturing in Chicago, together with a letter saying that he had just come across my original request, which he thought had escaped his notice, so he had sat down at once and made amends by writing the article desired. He had quite forgotten that he had handsomely fulfilled his promise *en voyage*! The two articles, I remember, had points of resemblance, but except in their common theme —which I have now forgotten—they might have had different authors; and both were in his own handwriting.

We know that R. L. S., Jack London, Lady Brassey, and many another who went a-sailing in yachts upon sunlit waters, wrote whole books on board their craft. But that is a different matter: they were in a measure withdrawn from contact with strangers, and had merely transferred their

s

dwelling-places from substantial homes of brick
and mortar to floating homes of wood or steel.
They had, moreover, no objective other than to
voyage; each day's log did not bring them nearer
a journey's end. So that we must rule out such
cases in considering this strange matter of the
paralysing effect of an ocean voyage on the activities
of the writing man. I am offering no explanations
and content myself with the statement of personal
experience.

And what of ' romance ' in this rolling down to
Rio? Alas, not a gleam! There is more that is
romantic in a bus-ride from Hornsey Rise to Chelsea
than in the long voyage to the River Plate, and if
you like to look into ' the bright eyes of danger ',
you will find more stimulus in steering your motor-
car from Hampstead Heath to Brighton. A more
hum-drum, a safer, or less exciting voyage could
not be imagined. You could put a child of seven
aboard at Liverpool or London with as much sense
of security as you could see him on the tram to be
met by his mother at the terminus a mile away.
The seeker after adventure is hard put to it in these
steamship days to get a taste of the old spirit he
imbibed from Marryat, Clark Russell, and Kingston.

We seemed to be lying off Las Palmas before
the beautiful picture of Lisbon in sunshine had
quite faded from our vision, and at this distance
of time I would not undertake to say whether it
was two or three days that had passed between the
two ports, so dreamy was our progress. The sight

of Las Palmas, with its grateful greenness of hill and valley, and far southward, cloud-high in a gorgeous flood of sunshine, the mighty mass of Teneriffe, thrusting itself boldly into the sky from the heaving wilderness of water, gave to the beholder one of those rare moments of spiritual exaltation which a first sight of such natural grandeur must always awaken in the sensitive mind.

St. Vincent was a different story. Fully two days more steaming brought us thither to that vile haunt of malaria and all things unlovely. The Cape Verde Islands, of which St. Vincent is the principal, dishonour the name they bear, as there is scarce a speck of verdure to be seen upon them. Presumably there must be some natural reason for the naming of the Cape itself, on the African coast, off which, nearly five hundred miles north-westward, these scabby isles show their horrid heads above the blue Atlantic. They are of a dirty red colour, and at a distance resemble some humpy monsters of the deep wallowing in the sunshine. The port is useful as a coaling and cable station. A town of shanties, it swarms with negroes and ships' pedlars. Here a small colony of young Britons is marooned in the cable service, and a less attractive destiny could not be imagined for a bright young Englishman. At first the young cable operator is no doubt delighted to find how much more picturesque he has become than he was at home. To have to wear white duck suits and a pith helmet, and look like Stanley on his way to discover Livingstone, is extremely attractive

to the mind of youth! Even the gentleman who
sells coals to the liners comes on board looking for
all the world like a colonial governor or the leader
of a mission to Timbuctoo. But when the debilita-
ting effects of the climate make themselves felt,
when the novelty of the life has gone, what remains?

St. Vincent gave us our last glimpse of the Old
World. Its very ugliness sent our thoughts zest-
fully forward to the undiscovered beauties of the
New, then so full of promise, now so—but that's
a later story. It was pleasant to hear again the
long soft swish of the water running past the vessel's
sides as it resumed its tranquil voyage into the
sunset. Now succeeded many days of idle lolling
in the deck-chair, watching through the binoculars
the swarms of flying fish skimming over the surface
of the ocean like tiny aeroplanes. It was my first
sight of these little marvels of the story-books, and
I recalled the anecdote of a sailor friend of my
youth who, telling his grandmother of the wonders
he had seen in his travels, was pointedly informed
by her that she was listening to no ' sic nonsense as
fishes that could flee.'

' Will you believe, then, that when we were going
through the Red Sea the water was so clear that we
could make out many of the chariots lost there when
the hosts of Pharoah were overwhelmed by the Lord?'

' Oh, I'll believe that ready enough, for it's in
the Bible.'

Bird life in these ocean solitudes is rare, yet we
not only saw several birds flying on confident wing

some hundreds of miles from land, but for two or three days we were forcibly reminded of ' nature red in tooth and claw ', by witnessing a little drama in feathers. One day out from St. Vincent a bird, about the size of a pigeon, gorgeously coloured and sporting a plume of orange-red, alighted on the rigging of the ship, pursued by a larger hawk-like creature. Evidently the pursuit had lasted for a long time, as both were land birds and seemed very exhausted, for we were now several hundreds of miles from the African coast, whence hunter and hunted had no doubt flown. For two or three days an exciting game of hide and seek ensued, the hunted, with the skill of desperation, cleverly selecting different positions in the rigging or on the smoke-stacks, which offered no opportunity to the hunter to swoop down on him from above. There were violent chasings at times around the ship, when the essential cruelty of the Spanish emigrants was displayed in their efforts to strike the pursued bird with all sorts of objects hurled at it as it swept past the bows. Eventually the hawk gave up and disappeared, and soon afterward the bird of brilliant plumage took wing away.

Early on the sixth day out from St. Vincent, on going on deck before breakfast, we were not a little surprised to find that we were steaming close to a long and narrow green island on which many signs of careful cultivation were evident. In a cove the white houses of a township showed clear and inviting in the morning air, the blue smoke curling from

some of the chimneys giving one an intense pang
of home hunger. With the binoculars it was easy
to make out people going about their tasks in the
fields, others walking towards what seemed to be a
signalling station. The surprise at this sudden
coming upon a bit of the habited globe in what, for
all we had supposed the night before, was still mid-
ocean, sent us questioning to the officers of the ship.
The island turned out to be Fernando de Noroña,
notable chiefly as a Brazilian penal settlement. A
Brazilian—the only one among our company—told
me a story about Fernando de Noroña which, speaking
in Spanish, he considered *muy graciosa*. An Englishman in Pernambuco killed a native in a quarrel and
was sent to the penal isle, but, in the course of a year
or less, he was granted his liberty, that being a matter
of simple negotiation; a little influence and a modicum of money can always save a criminal in that
happy clime. But the Englishman, having long
suffered a shrewish wife, found so much peace in
prison that he refused to quit the island! Fernando
de Noroña lies some two hundred miles off the
north-eastern shoulder of Brazil, so we were soon
to be touching at Pernambuco and hugging the
Brazilian coast for the rest of our voyage.

The first sensation of crossing a great sea and
making land on its farther shore once experienced—
and it is a ' thrill ' that never comes again—we sank
back into the half-indifferent contemplation of the
long, indented coastline of this prodigious land of
Brazil. For hundreds of miles it is unchanging in

its character of palm-fringed shores, with great dim mountain masses inland, a soft blur of heat over-hanging all. There is plenty to suggest mystery and romance, and yet, somehow, beauty is lacking: I mean the wild beauty of peak and crag which we find along the coasts of Scotland, where the con-formation is continually changing. These mountains of Brazil have that volcanic sameness which only becomes magnificent when you can ascend to some commanding pinnacle and look down upon a veritable wilderness of mighty earth mounds, as it was my good fortune once to do from the tower of the ancient castle of Polignac in the volcanic heart of France.

The sight of Bahia, about one day's steam from Pernambuco, was peculiarly pleasing. It might have been a bit of the French or Italian Riviera, with its rich verdure and bosky hills, while the residential suburbs looked quite European as seen from the ship. Two more days brought us to Rio de Janeiro, full of expectation and curiosity for the pearl of South America. For once we were not disappointed. The bay of Rio has been so often photographed, so frequently described, that every reader must have a good mental picture of the place, and that picture will resemble very closely the actuality.

Here, indeed, is something entirely unlike any bay we have in the Old World. The fantastic islands of volcanic origin that peep up through the broad waters of the bay, or impudently flaunt their grassy cones high above sea-level, in the most unexpected

places, give to Rio, as seen from the bay, an aspect
that is unique. The town spreads itself out with
picturesque irregularity among the gentle valleys
lying between the many hills that rise swiftly
upward some little way inland from the shore, the
noble height of Corcovado crowning the whole
lively and diversified scene. These hills being mostly
tropical in the richness and character of their vege-
tation, the art of man had no great task to transform
the situation into one of the world's most beautiful
cities.

About noon of the day after leaving Rio, we were
steaming up the picturesque estuary of Santos. A
Frenchman on board had promised me that here I
should see something *tout à fait originale*, and much
though I had been charmed with the actual sight of
Rio, so long familiar to me in picture, the approach
to Santos proved even more interesting, due perhaps
in some degree to the lure of the unknown and
unexpected. There is also a touch of romance in
slowly approaching a town that lies up a river, instead
of coming upon it suddenly from the sea.

The country through which the river runs (it is
more an arm of the sea than a river) is undoubtedly
' original ', abounding in low volcanic hills, with
prodigality of verdure, broken now by palm groves
and swampy flats. Here one is conscious of being
in a strange land, and it is easy to imagine with what
tense interest and straining eyes the first bold adventurers sailed up this narrow and beautiful waterway
to found the city that has become the second port

of Brazil. The city itself stretches by the riverside
around the foot of a great green hill, disfigured by a
monstrous advertisement announcing to adventurers
of a different kind and a later day that somebody's
biscuits are the best. A considerable part of the
town lies on land that still looks suspiciously swampy
and used to be a haunt of yellow jack, though I
was told that to-day it would be difficult to find
a healthier spot. That may be so, but I think I
could succeed if I tried hard enough.

Two days more and we found ourselves at anchor
in the roads outside Montevideo, which presents
a most engaging picture from the sea, the town
covering a lumpy tongue of land that juts seaward,
with a rocky shore rambling inland in many
directions and along the bay, which culminates in
the conical mass known as the Cerro, crowned by
an antique fortress and a modern lighthouse. At
night, when the myriad electric lamps are lighted,
the Cerro lighthouse throwing its broad and regular
beams athwart the bay, innumerable red and green
lights blinking on the buoys in the harbour, much
flitting of motor launches, and brightly illuminated
liners lying at anchor, there is no scene I know that
better suggests one's juvenile fancies of fairyland.

Here we bade good-bye to the ship that had been
our most pleasant abode for so many days, and made
our first acquaintance with things Argentine by
transferring ourselves to a musty river-steamer. It
was small comfort to discover that your bug-haunted
cabin, like the rest of the vessel, had been fashioned

on your native Clyde. The passage up the river—which, seaward of Montevideo, is some 150 miles in width, narrowing suddenly to 60 opposite the city, and to the eye has no farther shore, so that only the discoloration of the water distinguishes river from sea—was made in the roughest weather we had experienced, the steamer tossing like a cork and its paddle-wheels beating the waves with feeble irregularity.

Highgate,
    London.

XVI

OF BUENOS AYRES AND THE LITERARY SLIPSHOD

To J. K. M.

IT was an early autumn morning when we walked off the gangway at the Dársena Sud to suffer the passing of our impedimenta through the customs. The wind bit as shrewdly as on a midwinter's day in London, and, believing in this land of sunshine with a simple faith that had yet to suffer rudest shocks, we had to remain there, an hour or more, clothed for summer, chattering with cold. But we were actually in Buenos Ayres, and soon all the marvels of the 'Paris of South America' were to reveal themselves to us starveling Britishers who knew nothing better than our own London and the Paris of France.

So much had been written about this ever-changing city, and usually in terms of the grossest flattery to its citizens, that I sought in my 'Argentine Through English Eyes' (from which this chapter is in part derived) to present a truthful picture of the life of Buenos Ayres and found myself, as I had expected, denounced by the native press in characteristic fashion; nor were my efforts at honest description

received at home with any marked degree of sympathy.   There has long existed a sort of unwritten
rule that English writers must ' puff ' all things
Argentine, and the Argentine authorities have been
alive to the uses of advertisement. ' They speak
very highly of it in the advertisements,' as the old
lady in *Punch* naïvely observed.   I did not write
my Argentine book to please the Argentines, who
are indefatigable in listening to the praise of their
country, but make a metaphorical move for their
puñalejos if a word of frank criticism be spoken.
So ' The Argentine Through English Eyes ' was not
a popular book in Buenos Ayres, and having the bad
fortune to appear while the Great War was still
dragging its sanguinary course it had no noteworthy
success in England, but it has sold well and still
sells in America under the title of ' The Real
Argentine ', so that I may claim to have poured at
least a cupful of diluent into the buckets of praise
of the Argentine with which we have been swilled.
What I wrote, I wrote, and I have no regrets; though
it is probable that at this later date I might find
Buenos Ayres so vastly changed that my impressions
now would be entirely different.   I gather from my
Argentine friends on their frequent visits to London
that the ' Paris of South America ' is certainly a
less flattering label for Buenos Ayres than it was
during the year I spent there.

   But the chief thing that interested me then, and
the only thing I wish to dwell upon here, was the
palacio of *La Prensa* ; for I were no true journalist

if my first concern in any modern city was not related to its press.   The journalism of Buenos Ayres is more remarkable than that of London, Paris or New York, and as I came to have a peculiar knowledge of it I could write much thereon that might occupy you as a journalist, but would be less likely to engage the bookman.   Journalists are inclined to imagine that their 'shop' is of common interest and that they 'talk' it with general acceptance.   This is a matter in which we scribes can easily deceive ourselves.

Yes, I confess that, as a journalist, I had more desire to inspect the famous building of the great Buenos Ayres daily than any other sight in the city. During my stay I was in frequent touch with the management of *La Prensa*, and was privileged to examine every corner of its wonderful home, on one occasion spending some hours there after midnight, when the sight of Buenos Ayres from the globe on which stands the *Prensa's* goddess of Light, who holds aloft her flaring torch over the restless city, is surely one that can rarely be equalled in the world.   No doubt if one were to look at Paris by night from the top of the dome over Sacré Cœur, or London, say, from the Clock Tower at Westminster, the sight might be more beautiful, but it could scarcely be more impressive, as the extraordinary flatness of Buenos Ayres permits the observer on the *Prensa* tower to survey the whole vast city to its utmost limits and even to distinguish the twinkling lights of La Plata, the provincial capital twenty-four miles away.   I shall not readily forget that starry night when, at two o'clock, I stood up there in the look-out beneath the goddess of Light and saw the great, noisy, cruel city as a prodigious map of stars. The prodigality of Buenos Ayres in electric light was evident even at that hour, for mile upon mile the eye could follow the main streets with their double lines of radiant dots, thinning gradually as they flickered into the boundless plain beyond, while on the fringes of the mighty metropolis appeared numerous constellations betokening the distant suburbs which the Federal Capital threatened to engulf.

The interior of the *Prensa* building is almost everything that our English ideas would expect a newspaper office not to be. If you enter from the front, there is nothing in the business department to strike your attention. We have newspaper offices in England by the score quite as imposing. Nor is there anything particularly worthy of note in the reportorial rooms, the library, or any of the worka-day departments, though the note of luxury is probably more pronounced in the apartments of the editor and the editorial writers than in most English offices. The machine-room is splendidly equipped, and I was pleased to notice that the assis-tant overseer was a fellow-countryman. The over-seer, I was told, was an Argentine, but I suspect he was of British or German parentage, for the native has little aptitude for mechanics.

There is a series of ' show ' rooms which makes it hard for one, like myself, whose life has been spent in newspaper offices at home amid the odour of printer's ink, to imagine himself within a building devoted to the production of a daily newspaper. At two o'clock in the morning what a scene of hustle is a daily newspaper office in Fleet Street! Here everything was as quiet and orderly as a museum when the visitors have gone. And in truth it reminded me not a little of a museum. There was a magnificent concert-hall superbly decorated with painted panels, for the doing of which artists had come especially from France. Here many of the most famous operatic stars who have visited Buenos Ayres have appeared before select audiences invited by the *Prensa* ; celebrated actors have tried new plays, and illustrious visitors from foreign lands have addressed privileged audiences in many different tongues. The value of such a hall to a newspaper is so obvious that it is surprising none of our London journals has yet attempted anything of the kind. I think the *Prensa* salon accommodates an audience of some five hundred, and it is smaller than the very charming little theatre of *Femina*, the Paris ladies' journal, in the Champs Elysées.

Then there is a suite of living-rooms, fronting to the Avenida, worthy of a prince. These used to be placed at the disposition of distinguished visitors to the Argentine with a liberality that was not always appreciated, for I was told that this very pleasant custom of honouring the country's guests had more than once been abused by a visitor staying so long that he threatened to become a permanent boarder of the *Prensa*. A sports-room for the staff includes appliances for every variety of indoor sport and exercise, from billiards to fencing; nor need one ever be at a loss for a cooling bath in the hot summer days, as the bathrooms and lavatories are worthy of a first-class London club. But, most curious of all, perhaps, are the medical and dental departments. The rooms for the physicians and surgeons on the staff of the *Prensa* are supplied with all the latest medical and surgical appliances, and readers of the paper can come here free of charge for advice and treatment. There is also a legal department, where skilled lawyers look into the troubles of the newspaper's subscribers.

In short, the *Prensa* building is one of the few really interesting and distinctive sights of Buenos Ayres, and a notable ornament of the Avenida. It is an epitome of Argentine progress. A matter of sixty-five years ago the journal was a badly printed four-page sheet, issued from some scrubby little shanty, while to-day it is one of the wealthiest, as it is one of the largest, newspapers in the world, housed in a palace that cost some £300,000 to build. Its enterprising founder, the late Dr. José Paz, died at Nice a week or two before I left England, and I was, later, present at the ceremony of receiving his remains in Buenos Ayres for interment at Recoleta, the last resting-place of the Argentine's aristocrats. He had built another palace for the whole Paz family in the Plaza San Martin, one of the most princely private residences I have seen in any land, but he was not spared to occupy it.

The whole atmosphere of the *Prensa* building and
of the great journal itself is very un-Spanish: there·
are no loose ends, no unfinished corners. The
Spanish have inherited from the Moors—their
superiors in so many ways—the oriental indifference
to the jarring note. There is no country in the
world that produces its books and periodicals in so
slip-shod a fashion as Spain. With Spanish editors
proof-reading counts for nothing. Their best books
and their most important journals are nightmares of
printers' devilries. The name of some eminent person
will be spelt in two or three different ways in the same
column and different kinds of type will be mixed together in the composition of one word in a way that
would justify the immediate shooting of the slovenly
compositor. The South American press, with some·
noteworthy exceptions—as *La Prensa*, *La Nacion* and
Caras y Caretas—is lacking in taste to a degree that
no English or German printer could conceive. There
is little evidence of the capacity for taking pains.

An Argentine gentleman will build himself a
fine house, which, thanks to the concrete universally
used, he can make extremely attractive, copying the
elaborate details of the most plastic modelling. He
will be apt to muddle together half a dozen styles of
architecture, thinking nothing of joining bits of
Italian and French Renaissance to Gothic and
Moorish, and spending a large sum of money on a
monstrous massive door, with florid carvings, without
which no Buenos Ayres mansion is complete. But
even when his house is a perfect copy (originality

T

of course is out of the question) of some European style, there will be some detail that will offend a proper taste; the door will be stained a wrong colour, the window-frames will be painted out of harmony. More likely still, the windows will be splashed with paint, an old gas-pipe will be left sticking out of the wall somewhere. Depend upon it something will remain ' to give the show away '. These paint spots will never be removed from the window; that old gas-pipe will endure as long as the noble mansion of cement.

Or go out on a Sunday afternoon to Palermo, the much-vaunted resort of the Buenos Ayres *mundo elegante*, and note how seldom one sees a really faultless ' turn-out '. It will be a gorgeous motor, as big and imposing as money can buy, but the chauffeur will be dirty and unshaved, or some notice-able detail will be awry to strike the jarring note. Look at the young dudes, those *jovenes distinguidos*, seated to scrutinise and ogle the passing *señoritas :* they will be over-dressed in the most flashy manner, and their boots will be highly polished, the top parts of them being filled in with loud-coloured cloth. Every detail of their clothes will speak of expense and swagger, but notice those that have crossed their legs and you will see that each is displaying an offensive knot of white tape wherewith he has tied his cotton drawers over his socks.

I had been thinking of this lack of finish when I read and made some notes about Flora Annie Steel's ' The Hosts of the Lord '. It was one of the bundle of latter-day novels I stuffed into my boxes

on leaving home, and although I read it merely to
pass an idle hour in my rooms at the Phœnix (that
hotel which is familiar to every British visitor in
Buenos Ayres), I remember that I was agreeably
entertained.   But a slip-shod and peculiarly feminine
style marred in some measure my enjoyment of the
story.   I hope I am right in saying 'peculiarly
feminine'.   The slip-shod in life and literature may
not be an exclusively feminine characteristic, but
there is no doubt that the capacity for taking pains
to finish the ship down to the last bolt and the last
ha'pennyworth of tar is not common in womankind.

Before reading 'The Hosts of the Lord' I had
formed no very clear opinion of Mrs. Steel as a writer,
save that I recalled a certain graphic power to realise
large events and dramatic atmosphere in 'On the Face
of the Waters'.   And now when I was reading her
purely as a distraction in the dozy hours I found myself
critical of her manner.   Her use of italics becomes most
irritating after a few chapters.   No really competent
male writer offends in this respect.   No masculine
novelist with even half of Mrs. Steel's power would
strew his pages with such needless italics as one finds
in the following sentences, taken quite at random:

And if he was the '*god of her idolatry*,' she was to him the
'*dearest morsel of earth.*'

This was Erda Shepherd herself, the woman who was the
'*dearest atom of God's earth*' to him.

For after all that idyll in the garden had been, bar its
environments, commonplace enough—which had landed him
—*in an Adelphi drama!*

Must I marry you to—to *him ?*
He had learnt *thus* much in these latter days of grace.
He was equally at the man's mercy if he *chose to brave results.*
There was nothing to be gained by doing so *as a rule!*

The pages of the book literally pullulate with italics, and out of all the hundreds of instances in which Mrs. Steel underscores her words, like some lady of scant vocabulary writing to a friend, there is scarcely one in which there is justification for the emphasis. As a rule the English language is of sufficient strength to express the strongest emotions without necessitating the disfigurement of the printed page with such artificial emphasis. Note also in the above quotations how the novelist in one page makes her hero dub the heroine his 'dearest morsel of earth', and a few sentences later changes morsel to atom. Atom is repeated again a little farther on.

But the quaintest bit of slip-shod runs through chapters XVIII, XIX and XX. In the first of these Erda is described walking back to the house from the river-side.

As she did so an *orange* caught her eye under a tree, whence it had fallen from sheer gold-ripeness, and, knowing how Mrs. Campbell mourned a single loss, she gathered it up and took it with her.

I have put a word in italics in this sentence for a reason that will appear when, in the following quotation from the next page of the story, I put two other words in italics, which somehow Mrs. Steel prints in ordinary type. Erda stands before the mirror in her room, with the orange still in her hand—

It was a woman, tall, slender, robed in white; a woman with red-gold hair, edged by the light behind her; a woman with a red-gold *apple* in her hand.

She stood arrested before herself; helpless before the memory of a voice—

' All straight folds—the sunshine on your hair, and a red-gold *apple* in your hand—the World's Desire! '

For twenty-two pages more that orange masquerades as an apple, until at the end of the scene ' she still held in her hand the useless, foolish, unnecessary *orange* ! '

This ' red-gold ' business is overdone, you will agree, and Mrs. Steel, with all her cleverness, cannot gull me into mistaking a red-gold orange for a red-gold apple. I don't even believe Erda had red-gold hair! Nor do I believe for one moment that her hero, Lance, was such a don at quotations that he could cite Shakespeare, Milton and Tennyson as glibly as the editor of ' Familiar Quotations '. And I am sure she did not believe so herself when she wrote:

He pointed to a *gosain* who was forming the centre of a group of gossipers round a syrup-seller's shop, and added— for he knew his Milton as well as his Shakespeare—' The superior Fiend who gives not Heav'n for lost! '

Mrs. Steel's italics for the Anglo-Indian word are here quite justifiable; but I was tempted to put the parenthetical sentence in italics, because I am sure it was thrown in merely as an excuse for putting most improbable poetry into the mouth of one who could not have remembered two lines of Milton to save his neck. This is not playing the game with one's readers; it destroys the illusion of reality. But it is Mrs. Steel's method and it brings her work down into the category of the slip-shod and the unenduring. She has great gifts of imagination, but they are not so great that they lift her among the giants who can afford to be slip-shod. Such a sentence as this, for instance, is conclusive evidence of a complete lack of instinctive style:

But ere the second foil matched its fellow on the armoury wall, he would have seen as pretty a bit of sword play as could well be seen.

And it is only one of many that strew the pages of ' The Hosts of the Lord '.

As touching Buenos Ayres and fiction, I have one more note to add. Since I rolled home again from that far land I have often derived amusement from the efforts of novelists to give ' local colour ' to their tales of South American scenes which were unfamiliar to themselves. This passage, which I copied from ' The Crescent Moon ', a novel by F. Brett Young, that I read eight or nine years ago on one of my many visits to Ayrshire, but of which I retain no vestige of memory, is perhaps the most hilarious of these ' bloomers ':

. . . Over there, in the heart of that wild darkness, Arran lay. The shoulders of Goat Fell stood up against the storm;

Kilmory Water should be in a brown spate; there, in the Clachan they would all be sound asleep, all but the two sheep-dogs lying with their noses to the hearth, where fiery patterns were stealing through white ashes of peat. M'Crae stood waiting in the cold for the expected thrill. It didn't come . . . He could only think in that perverse moment of sun-shine and light; of the green mountain slopes above Buenos Ayres and blue, intense shadows on the pavement of the Plaza where dark-skinned ranchers from inland *estancias* lounged at the scattered tables of the cafés. His utmost will was powerless to enslave his imagination. He shivered, and turned gratefully to the oily heat of the engine-room.

Now I happen to know both scenes well; indeed I could see Goat Fell and all the lovely island as I read that page and I will pass the Goat Fell allusion; but when I remind you that so far as the eye can see from the tallest building in Buenos Ayres the land is as flat as a table top, that no least little hill breaks the horizon; and that a *ranchero* should never be confused with an *estanciero*, you will see how bad a break even a masculine novelist may make. Mr. Brett Young might have taken the pains to look up some guide book to South America, or even to spend ten minutes with an encyclopedia before inventing these ' green mountain slopes above Buenos Ayres '. How the Buenos Ayrians would welcome them if, by some magic like that which produced Mr. Lob's wood in ' Dear Brutus ', they were to awake one morning and have their eyes refreshed with a sight so pleasing and so unexpected!

Highgate,
London.

XVII

ON AND IN 'THE PURPLE LAND'

To Richard Curle

IN greater measure than it has been meted out to me, you have had the fortune to wander the world and to look upon strange scenes in far lands. I fancy that the bond between you and Joseph Conrad may have derived much of its strength from your common *wanderlust*, the love of roving which both of you had been able to indulge so thoroughly: Conrad as his accepted vocation, you as the most agreeable of avocations. You must have noticed—since indeed it is your inquisitive business to notice everything as a daily writer in one of our most famous newspapers—that despite most systems of mnemonics being based upon 'association of ideas', or the relating of similar things, we are more often inclined to associate dissimilar things. Example: I find that when I am thinking of W. H. Hudson my thoughts will wander to Conrad, or that when Hudson has come into my mind Conrad has been first in my thoughts.

I should be hard put to it to give a reason for this. They have nothing in common either in their

lives or their art: Richard Jeffries and Hudson, yes.
I am merely stating an experience, not offering an
explanation. But it explains in a way why I am
inscribing these pages to you, my dear Curle, although
I do not know if you are greatly interested in Hudson.
In our too-rare confidences I doubt if his name
has ever been mentioned. I know, however, from
your preferences, and without your telling me in
set terms, that Hudson must be among your favourite authors. Not your beloved Conrad, nor any of
his generation will outlive him in the affections
of reading folk. Nay, just as his progress to fame
was slower and his arrival there delayed beyond
that of most of his great contemporaries, so do I
believe will his reputation continue to grow and,
in the end, outshine and outlast that of others
who have in their own day enjoyed wider renown
and incomparably greater worldly reward.

It has often been a matter of regret to me that
my own enthusiasm for Hudson had not taken hold
of me before I went venturing to the River Plate.
It would certainly have given a different turn to
my Argentine days, and with 'The Naturalist in La
Plata' as my guide I should have been tempted
more afield during my sojourn in Buenos Ayres.
I should probably have come away with memories
more agreeable than those I have of the life of its
larger towns, to the study of which most of my
leisure was devoted. It is since my return to England
that my Hudsonian enthusiasm has awakened, and
although there is a keener edge to my enjoyment

of that lovable autobiography of his boyhood, ' Far Away and Long Ago ', in the fact that much of the ground over which he moves in his matchless narrative of young life is familiar to me, I should have looked upon it with a better understanding, or at least a more friendly feeling, had I seen it first through that magic haze which his rare descriptive art imparts.

Fortunately I had the delight of reading Hudson's first book while I stayed in the city where its opening and closing scenes are laid; but that was after I had moved back from the Argentine shore of the River Plate to the Uruguayan. ' The Purple Land ' was Hudson's first book, and a curious book it must have seemed to the critics of 1885 when Messrs. Sampson Low sent its ' two slim volumes ' out for review bearing the title of ' The Purple Land that England Lost '. How was a reviewer to know that it was a romantic fiction, unless he read it? Hence the few perfunctory notices of it were printed under the heading of ' Travels and Geography '. This first edition I have not seen, as my copy is the reduced and revised version included in Duckworth's ' Readers Library ' and dated 1911.

When lately I read it through again by my study window, which looks upon that very different terrain, of which Hudson writes in ' Nature in Downland ', it did bring back something of the old joy with which I read it first in Montevideo. On my occasional visits to the old fort that crowned the Cerro, that low conical hill whence I loved to gaze across the

far undulating grasslands—the wonderful Tablada—
with their vast herds of cattle, I would try to imagine
that the scenes of the story were still being enacted
there: well-knowing that the Uruguay of which he
wrote was almost as much lost to the world as it was
lost to England. But I was more intent upon the
quality of the book itself at this latest reading, and
although I suspect from his friendly foreword to
'Far Away and Long Ago' that 'The Purple Land'
is a high favourite with Mr. John Galsworthy (one
of my literary heroes), I find it notably amateurish.
I am not surprised that the reviewers of 1885 were
unimpressed; that the public did not buy; that
Sampson Low were left with a large stock of unsold
copies to 'remainder'. Possibly these may yet be
worth their weight in gold. I know a living English
author copies of whose first editions each sell in
America for larger sums than he can get any English
publisher to pay him to write a new book!

'The Purple Land' is a romantic narrative of
actual experience in the country of Uruguay, inter-
woven with the imagined adventures of a soldier
of the Blancos (on whom I shall have a note or two
later) in one of the innumerable civil wars which,
until the early years of this century, were the com-
monest feature of political life in the Banda Oriental
(or the 'Eastern Strip') as the natives liked to call
their land whose official designation is La Republica
Oriental del Uruguay. But, in all the innocence of
the amateur, its author smothered the reader's interest
at the start by writing a long historical introduction,

which must effectively have disguised the true nature
of the book, and made a lively and thrilling tale
appear a mere tedious narrative of travel.

The supposed narrator is one Richard Lamb, an
Englishman, who has made a run-away match in
Argentina with a dark-eyed daughter of the pampas,
and has fled with his Paquita across the River Plate
to her aunt's home in Montevideo. The author had
probably been reading ' Gil Blas ' not long before,
and so he sets himself to the writing of a similarly
rambling yarn of adventure. It has the same incon-
sequence as ' a slice of life ', but it never fails to
hold the reader by the sheer interest of the moment,
without relation to what has gone before or what
may follow. Yet you can understand a reader who
at the outset encounters such a passage as I quote
below feeling that he has come in contact with a
beginner in the art of romance. Paquita is now in
Montevideo, but speaks as though she were still in
Argentina, whereupon Richard:

' Soul of my life,' said I, ' you have never left Buenos Ayres
in heart, even to keep your poor husband company! Yet I
know, Paquita, that corporeally you are here in Montevideo
conversing with me at this very moment.'

' True,' said Paquita; ' I had somehow forgotten that we
were in Montevideo. My thoughts were wandering—
perhaps it is sleepiness.'

' I swear to you, Paquita,' I replied, ' that you shall see
this aunt of yours to-morrow before set of sun; and I am
positive, sweetest, that she will be delighted to receive so near
and lovely a relation. How glad she will be of an opportunity
of relating that ancient quarrel with her sister and ventilating

her mouldy grievances! I know these old dames—they are
all alike.'

'Corporeally you are here in Montevideo conversing with me ' . . . oh, dear no! There never
was a Richard who so spake to his Paquita! Then
note the amateur describing his emotions in the
true Jane Porter style as he stood upon the Cerro
and looked across the purple land:

When I reached the old ruined fort which crowns the
summit, I got upon a wall and rested for half-an-hour, fanned
by a fresh breeze from the river and greatly enjoying the
prospect before me. I had not left out of sight the serious
object of my visit to that commanding spot, and only wished
that the malediction I was about to utter could be rolled down
in the shape of a stupendous rock, loosed from its hold, which
would go bounding down the mountain, and, leaping clear over
the bay, crash through the iniquitous city beyond, filling it
with ruin and amazement.

'Whichever way I turn,' I said, ' I see before me one of
the fairest habitations God has made for man: great plains
smiling with everlasting spring; ancient woods; swift beautiful
rivers; ranges of blue hills stretching away to the dim horizon.
And beyond those fair slopes, how many leagues of pleasant
wilderness are sleeping in the sunshine, where the wild flowers
waste their sweetness and no plough turns the fruitful soil,
where deer and ostrich roam fearless of the hunter, while over
all bends a blue sky without a cloud to stain its exquisite beauty?
And the people dwelling in yon city—the key to a continent—
they are the possessors of it all. It is theirs, since the world,
out of which the old spirit is fast dying, has suffered them to
keep it. What have they done with this their heritage?
What are they doing even now? They are sitting dejected
in their houses, or standing in their doorways with folded arms

and anxious, expectant faces.   For a change is coming: they
are on the eve of a tempest.   Not an atmospheric change;
no blighting simoon will sweep over their fields, nor will any
volcanic eruption darken their crystal heavens.   The earth-
quakes that shake the Andean cities to their foundations they
have never known and can never know.   The expected change
and tempest is a political one.   The plot is ripe, the daggers
sharpened, the contingent of assassins hired, the throne of
human skulls, styled in their ghastly facetiousness a Presidential
Chair, is about to be assaulted. . . .

'I swear that I, too, will become a conspirator if I remain
long on this soil.   Oh, for a thousand young men of Devon
and Somerset here with me, every one of them with a brain
on fire with thoughts like mine!   What a glorious deed would
be done for humanity!   What a mighty cheer we would raise
for the glory of the old England that is passing away!   Blood
would flow in yon streets as it never flowed before, or, I
should say, as it only flowed in them once, and that was
when they were swept clean by British bayonets.   And
afterwards there would be peace, and the grass would
be greener and the flowers brighter for that crimson
shower.'

And yet I like that 'purple' patch in spite of its
obvious crudities.   It has a charm for me, perhaps,
because I regard it (and indeed the whole book) as
the 'toddling' stage of one who became a master
of the most beautiful and vigorous English written
in our time.   Another and a special attraction which
'The Purple Land' has for me lies in the agreeable
memories it awakens at the mere mention of such
places as Durazno, Canalones, Yi, and many another,
for the streets of Montevideo where I was an untired
and ever interested wanderer for some six months

are named after the departamentos of the provincial
cities of the country and it is to the lovely places of
Montevideo and Santiago de Chile, of all the hundreds of towns I saw in South America, that I am
always readiest to be transported: to these only
have I any longing to return. But this is a peculiar
interest; an adventitious one, which a still more
amateurish book than 'The Purple Land' might
have been not less potent to vivify.

In my judgment Hudson was always best in
describing things seen, in sharing with us his rich
and abundant harvests of the quiet eye. That is
why I do not esteem his 'Green Mansions' as a
great romance, although it is immeasurably greater
as a piece of writing than 'The Purple Land'. His
Rima, so foully burlesqued on that stupid stone in
Hyde Park, was never a creature of flesh and blood;
she is a fairy phantom flitting through a scene of
vivid actuality and visible only to her author. You
will remember that her clothes were spun from cob-
webs. To endeavour to visualise in coarse stone
and with a blunt chisel so vaporous a figment of the
mind was a vain thing. Hudson had none of your
Conrad's superb command over imagined personages,
making them live out their lives in our minds with
the fullest measure of credibility. He was a lover
and an interpreter of nature: a lover of life—'What
soul in this wonderful various world,' he cries,
'would wish to depart before ninety!'—and in our
time he has had no rival in that most gracious office
of the pen. Here he is trying his hand at the

romantic: a Colorado rascal has him (in his character of Richard Lamb) in his power:

At length I made an appeal to him, for I began to despair of the Alcalde coming to deliver me. 'Friend,' I said, 'if you will allow me to speak, I can convince you that you are mistaken. I am a foreigner, and know nothing about Santa Coloma.'

'No, no,' he interrupted, pressing the knife-point warningly against my stomach, then suddenly withdrawing it as if about to plunge it into me. 'I know you are a rebel. If I thought the Alcalde were not coming I would run you through at once and cut your throat afterwards. It is a virtue to kill a Blanco traitor, and if you do not go bound hand and foot from here then here you must die. What, do you dare to say that I did not see you at San Paulo—that you are not an officer of Santa Coloma? Look, rebel, I will swear on this cross that I saw you there.'

Suiting the action to the word, he raised the hilt of the weapon to his lips to kiss the guard, which with the handle formed a cross. That pious action was the first slip he had made, and gave the first opportunity that had come to me during all that terrible interview. Before he had ceased speaking the conviction that my time had come flashed like lightning through my brain. Just as his slimy lips kissed the hilt, my right hand dropped to my side and grasped the handle of my revolver under my poncho. He saw the movement and very quickly recovered the handle of his knife. In another second of time he would have driven the blade through me; but that second was all I now required. Straight from my waist, and from under my poncho, I fired. His knife fell ringing on to the floor; he swerved, then fell back, coming to the ground with a heavy thud. Over his falling body I leaped, and almost before he had touched the ground was several yards away, then wheeling round, I found the other two men rushing out after me.

AN IMPRESSION OF MONTEVIDEO

facing p. 289

'Back!' I shouted, covering the foremost of the two with my revolver.

They instantly stood still.

'We are not following you, friend,' said one, 'but only wish to get out of the place.'

'Back, or I fire!' I repeated, and then they retreated into the porch. They had stood by unconcerned while their cut-throat comrade Gandara was threatening my life, so that I naturally felt angry with them.

I sprang upon my horse, but instead of riding away at once stood for some minutes by the gate watching the two men. They were kneeling by Gandara, one opening his clothes to look for the wound, the other holding a flaring candle over his ashen corpse-like face.

'Is he dead?' I asked.

One of the men looked up and answered, 'It appears so.'

'Then,' I returned, 'I make you a present of his carcass.'

Lively enough and much improved upon the level of the early parts of the book, but still nothing that any serial writer could not achieve, and a whole book of it worth far less than any one of his brief essays in 'A Traveller in Little Things'.

Hudson is buried in Broadwater Churchyard, Worthing, but I doubt not that he would have liked to have been laid in the rich black soil of his well-loved pampas and that the *gaucho* song he translates in 'The Purple Land' ends on the note he would willingly have ended on when end he must:

Then tell me not—then tell me not
'Tis sorrowful to dwell alone:
My heart within the city pent
Pines for the desert's liberty;

U

The streets are red with blood, and fear
Makes pale the mournful women's faces.

O bear me far—O bear me far,
On swift, sure feet, my trusty steed:
I do not love the burial-ground,
But I shall sleep upon the plain,
Where long green grass shall round me wave—
Over me graze wild herds of cattle.

And now, to turn from these things of the imagination to my impressions of that distant land which gave them birth, I would offer a modest sheaf of my own gleaning from later 'rambles in modern Troy' as (as it pleased Hudson's fancy to describe his opening chapter), a strangely different place from the quaint city known to Richard and Paquita fifty or sixty years before.

The people that pass in the street present certain points of contrast with the passers-by in Buenos Ayres. Clearly the writer, in a North-American encyclopedia, who stated that Montevideo was 'one of the most cosmopolitan towns in South America' was scarcely entitled to the editorial description of 'authority on Latin America'. I remember also that the same writer alleged there were no fewer than sixteen public squares in the city, which assertion, together with that already mentioned, leads me to suspect he never saw it with his own eyes. Cosmopolitanism is precisely the last impression one is likely to carry away from Montevideo. Italians are to be seen in considerable

numbers, but the appearance of the people as a whole
is essentially Spanish. The Iberian type has been
better preserved here than on the other side of
the river; Spanish character informs the life of the
people to a larger extent.

The women of Montevideo are celebrated throughout South America for their beauty and elegance of
manners. In this regard the town enjoys something
of the European fame of Buda-Pesth, and certainly
no Oriental ever talks to a Gringo about his capital
city without mentioning that it is celebrated for its
lindas mujeres. True enough, it deserves its reputation as a town of beautiful women, for most of the
Montevidean ladies have a beauty that is curiously
in keeping with the official name of the Republic—
Oriental. They are of the languorous, dark-eyed
type—beauty that has a touch of the Semitic in it—
and they are far more naturally graceful than the
ladies of Buenos Ayres, whom they make no effort
to imitate in the matter of elaborate dress, their
tastes running on simpler lines, with the exception,
perhaps, of a notable fondness for ornate coiffures.

Fresh from Buenos Ayres, it was particularly
pleasing to me to notice the marked respect which
the women of Montevideo received from the male
population. Nothing that I observed during my
wanderings about South America seemed to me to
present a greater contrast in manners than this.
Across the river, a few hours' journey, it was made
possible for the native women to walk unmolested
in the streets only by passing and strictly enforcing

an act against *falto de respeto á la mujer*. This instrument materially improved the liberty of women in Buenos Ayres, as all that a lady had to do when molested was to call a policeman, give the offender in charge, and walk away. The molester was then marched to the police station, fined substantially, and his name and address published in all the journals next morning, the lady suffering no further inconvenience than the momentary trouble of telling the policeman that the man had annoyed her.

No such law was ever necessary in Montevideo, where one was reminded of home by noting how women, unaccompanied, and young girls, could go freely about the streets at all hours of the day, even until midnight, it being not uncommon to see mothers with their children sitting in the plazas enjoying the cool, sea-borne breeze as late as eleven or twelve o'clock at night. In this alone I think there was evidence of a subtle difference of character between the peoples of the two cities.

The whole atmosphere of the town in its social life was to me infinitely more pleasing than that of Buenos Ayres. It was a friendly town—a town of homes. The ambition of the Montevidean is to secure a comfortable berth in the Government as quickly as he can, and build for his family a comfortable home in which he will take a genuine pride, so that there was an air of comfort, of leisure, and of life being pleasantly lived in Montevideo. The town boasted many theatres—more, proportionately, than any other South American city—several of

these, such as the Solis, the Politeama, and the
Urquiza being commodious and well-built. The
dramatic instinct is pronounced in the natives, and
there was quite a considerable band of literary enthu-
siasts in Montevideo working to create a body of
national dramatic literature—surely a remarkable
ambition for a nation whose total population was less
than that of the city of Buenos Ayres. Florencio
Sanchez and Samuel Blixen, both Montevidean drama-
tists of distinction (the first-named died at an early
age, after winning an international reputation), were
two of the chief forces in this modern movement
which has resulted in so keen an interest in the drama
that a local publisher has been able to issue a long
series of plays written by Uruguayan authors.

The literary activity was certainly remarkable
when we bear in mind the extremely limited public
to which Uruguayan authors can appeal. Two very
stout volumes of a critical survey of Uruguayan
literature were published during my stay, and these
were but the advance-guard of others to follow, the
work being designed to occupy several bulky tomes.
The roll of Uruguayan authors in poetry and prose
is truly a formidable one, though I doubt if more
than two names would be known in England, and
those of authors whose reputations, but not their
works, may be familiar to a small circle of English
critics. Juan Zorilla de San Martín is the great
poet of the country, and José Enrique Rodó, who
died in Europe during the Great War, was its leading
philosophic writer. Both are famous throughout

Latin-America and Spain, and both very remarkable
men, who had to look to politics as well as to
literature in their struggle for a living.

Rodó, who was one of the deputies for Montevideo,
had long been recognised as a master of Spanish
style, a great critic of literature, and a philosopher.
Different in all else, he had points of contact with Lord
Morley, as they belonged to the same liberal school of
thought. Withal, he was one of the last of the
Bohemians, so far as that implied absolute disregard for
sartorial display and businesslike ordering of one's
daily life. You would meet him at any strange hour
of the night wandering about the streets, lonely and
contemplative, and if you glanced at his shirt cuff
when shaking hands you would find it soiled and
scribbled over with many pencilled notes. He had
much of the old-world courtesy of the Spaniard, with
the wider outlook of the American mind, and, notably,
a profound admiration for English character and
Anglo-Saxon civilisation. His opinion was sought
on great public questions and on matters of literature
from all parts of South America, and I have often
thought it strange that this rather shabbily dressed
and retiring gentleman whom I used to meet wandering alone in the dusk up side-streets, and with whom
I would stop and gossip for five or ten minutes,
was the object of admiration of literary circles
wherever Spanish-American men of letters gathered
together—*el gran Rodó!*

Señor Zorilla de San Martín was of a different
type, shorter in stature and more pronouncedly

Spanish in appearance, with the darting fire and restlessness of the imaginative Oriental rather than the careless repose of his philosophic contemporary. He was essentially a poet, though his signature used to appear on all the bank notes of Uruguay by virtue of some official post he held. He had also represented his country in England and in Spain, and had been honoured in many ways by the nation which is justly proud of his poetic achievement, for in ' Tabaré ', his epic of early Spanish life in Uruguay, he has produced a classic. Neither of these eminent authors, by the way, though both owning indebtedness to our English literature, had acquired a vocal command of our language, French appealing to them, as it does to the great majority of the educated Latin-Americans, more readily than English.

Surely there never was such a town for newspapers. I believe you could not throw a stone down any street without hitting a journalist. An English city of the same size would probably possess not more than two daily newspapers; Montevideo had a dozen or more, and at least half of these would bear comparison with our best provincial dailies, while *La Razon*, the principal evening paper, was equal to any London penny evening journal, and probably superior as a literary production. Many of the journalists do not limit their activities to that profession, but are also engaged as lawyers, account-ants, and in other businesses, as it is very common to combine several occupations; the warehouse clerk may play in an orchestra in the evenings, and make up some tradesman's accounts on the Sundays.

In the older part of the town the pleasant custom, which used to be universal throughout Europe, of the merchant or tradesman residing on the premises where he plied his business, still lingers. The successful lawyer lives right in the heart of the business district, and has his office in his house. So, too, the doctor, while the printer, bookseller, and the importer often have their private residences on the floors above their business premises. One of the wealthiest families of bankers thus lived over the bank, not far from the docks, in a street so noisy that the unceasing rattle of its traffic still sounds disturbing in my memory of the busy days I spent there. But this old custom was rapidly giving way before the attractions of the beautiful suburbs that had opened up along the sandy shores of Pocitos and inland as far as the charming little town of Villa Colón, with its great avenues of trees, its rippling streams, and leafy, undulating landscapes.

Uruguay retains, in Europe at least, an unenviable reputation as a hotbed of revolutions, and we may not have seen the last of these. But forces are at work which will make the upheavals of the future more decorous than those of the past. During our summer in Montevideo all the elements of a first-class revolution were in existence, but they spent themselves in a wordy warfare among the newspapers, in public demonstrations and counter-demonstrations; not a shot was fired, though the President's suburban

retreat at Piedras Blancas, a few miles from the city,
was continually under strong military guard.

' You will still hear much talk of revolution among
our young men at the cafés,' said Rodó to me on
one of the many occasions when we discussed the
entertaining politics of his country. ' That is one
of their amusements, and will continue to be so for
some time yet, but every new batch of emigrants
that lands in the port of Montevideo helps to banish
further the revolutionary era, and if we could but
divert to Uruguay some portion of the great stream
of emigration that rolls past our shores each year
into the Argentine, nothing would be more effective
in producing a peaceful and prosperous Uruguay.'

In these words of Rodó we have the explanation
of the bellicose history of this charming little country.
Uruguay was left too much to itself; its people were
so long content to let the natural fruitfulness of their
land supply their simple needs that the only outlet
for their energies was to quarrel among themselves,
and thus grew up the two political camps, the *Blancos*
and the *Colorados*, concerning which I do not recall
any approximately accurate description in the writings
of any foreign author on Uruguayan politics. Even
so skilled an observer, so admirable a student of
political conditions, as the late Viscount Bryce would
appear to have fallen into absurd mis-statements of
facts when he wrote of Uruguayan affairs in his
' South America: Observations and Impressions '.

As I have not read Lord Bryce's well-known
work, and know it only through numerous extracts

translated into the native journals of the Argentine,
Uruguay, and Chile, it would be ungracious of me
to say anything in criticism of it beyond the passages
thus coming to my notice. Certainly his explanation
of the two parties into which Uruguay is divided is
no better than the nonsense one hears talked among
casual visitors on whom some local resident has been
performing the operation known as 'pulling his leg'.
Translating from one of several articles on the work
in question, which appeared in *La Tribuna Popular*,
of Montevideo, I find that Lord Bryce is alleged
to have written to this effect:

The children of Uruguay are born little Blancos or little
Colorados. It is the political heritage of the early days of
Independence. Scarcely any ever desert their colours. In
a White district it is dangerous to wear a red necktie, just as
it is in some parts of *Yolanda* (?Irlanda—Ireland) to show an
English badge.

This is described by the editor as 'a very pretty
paragraph', and here is another which he quotes
as 'a curious paragraph that might be regarded as
an example of Mr. Bryce's Yankee humour' (for
he was under the impression that the literary Viscount
was a 'Yankee Constitutionalist'):

General Oribe mounted on one occasion a spirited white
horse. On seeing this, all his sympathisers followed his
example by mounting themselves on beautiful white steeds.
Hence came the name of the White Party. General Rivera,
the irreconcilable enemy of Oribe, mounted himself in turn

on a superb horse of a reddish colour, in contrast to his terrible rival. The Riveraists then sought for coloured steeds, and mounted on these followed their chief. Henceforward, the Red Party disputed successfully for power with the White Party.

This, of course, is mere moonshine. It may possibly have originated in some fertile Uruguayan imagination, but I cannot understand so fine a historian as Lord Bryce accepting it. As a matter of fact Blancos and Colorados (the latter word, by the way, does not mean 'coloured', but signifies 'red', or 'ruddy') may live together in perfect amity. So incorrect is the statement that every child is born a Blanco or a Colorado, that there are innumerable families in the country divided in politics, and in my own short experience I met instances of brothers who adhered to different parties. I recall in particular two brothers who, in a perfectly friendly discussion, admitted that they took no real interest in the politics of the country, and were largely indifferent to the course of affairs so long as Uruguay continued to prosper, but who, before the evening had gone, were disputing so hotly the respective merits of the two parties that they almost came to blows, the one being clearly a pronounced Blanco and the other an equally tenacious Colorado.

What is inevitable to every Uruguayan is that he shall be a politician. Politics is the passion of the country, and at an age when young men in England would probably be at a loss to mention the name of our Prime Minister, or to state which party

was in power, young Uruguayans grow disputatious
with each other on affairs of state.

Another very curious mis-statement of fact is
cited from Bryce's book by the *Tribuna*, which
observes that the paragraph is a revelation of ' the
rich imagination of its author '. Our eminent publi-
cist wrote to this effect with reference to revolutions
in Uruguay :

> When a revolutionary movement is about to break out
> in Uruguay, the organisers make an appointment to meet,
> mounted, at a certain place and on a day agreed upon before-
> hand. The Government always knows well in advance of
> this, and is able to possess itself of all the horses in the country,
> keeping those in a safe place so that they may not fall into the
> power of the revolutionaries. The latter, therefore, remain
> perforce on foot. The horse is the soul of Uruguayan revolu-
> tionists. It is the heroic tradition of the glorious epoch of
> the gauchos. Without horses the rebels are lost.

The amusement of the Uruguayan editor over
these paragraphs and many others equally distant
from the truth was entirely justified, and I have
quoted them here (roughly retranslating them) out
of no desire to belittle the work of so able a writer,
for whom I have the greatest admiration, but merely
to show how erroneous one's impressions may be as
the result of a too brief visit, and the lack of opportunity to study at leisure the condition of a country,
together with its historical past, as these have been
expressed in its native language. Such miscon-
ceptions are familiar to us, and to be expected in

the writings of irresponsible globe-trotters, but
not in the well considered pages of him who gave
us a work so authoritative as 'The American
Commonwealth'.

It is no easy matter to furnish a satisfactory
explanation of the two political parties of Uruguay,
and when I find so competent an authority as C. E.
Akers, in his 'History of South America', affirming
that there are really no distinctions between them,
that each professes the same ideals of government
and seeks merely to wrest political power from the
other, I attempt an explanation only with trepidation.
Not that I propose a detailed account of their origins
and evolution, for that would involve an extremely
long disquisition, and would scarcely hold the
attention of an English reader, but that any attempt
to distinguish between them in a few words is
attended with difficulty and apt to be misleading.
Readers of 'The Purple Land' may take this as a
footnote to the story, whose author does not offer
any definition of Blanco or Colorado.

The root difference of the two parties can best
be described as Nationalist *versus* Progressive.
Broadly, the White Party is the Nationalist Party,
and the Colorado the Progressive. The colours
distinguish the Spanish Colonial origin of the one
party from the democratic origin of the other. That
is to say, the Blancos have always tended towards
exclusiveness and the assertion of the superiority
of the white race, whereas the Colorados, originally
sneered at by the Blancos as savages (*salvajes*), on

account of their more liberal ideas, which embraced
the aborigine and the emigrant alike, have always
stood for the wider conception of democracy. At
certain times in their history the Colorados have
even accepted the title of ' savages ' as a compliment
to their liberalism; to their maintenance of the
primal rights of man. Thus, and not otherwise,
have the colours of the two parties a real significance,
and the red of the Colorados is also a cry back to the
French Revolution, the influence of which on South
American democracy has been profound. The great
Garibaldi commanded a Brazilian regiment in support
of General Rivera when General Oribe was laying
siege to Montevideo, and the city was defended
principally by French, Italians, and Brazilians against
the onsets of the Blancos, until Oribe was eventually
crushed by the Argentine general, Urquiza. This
historical fact helps to elucidate the party origins.
In these later years, although the politics of the
country are still divided between Reds and Whites
it has become more common to refer to the latter
as Nationalists, they themselves having adopted
that title. Hence appears a distinct and appreciable
difference between the two political camps; almost
as much, indeed, as between the old Radicals and
Conservatives in Great Britain.

Blancos are strongest in the provinces, and draw
most of their support from the agricultural and
stock-raising classes, while the Colorados preponder-
ate in the capital and the larger towns, where modern
ideas of democracy find a more fertile soil. The

policy of the Blancos is exclusiveness—'Uruguay for the Uruguayans' might be their battle-cry, but, paradoxically, not for the original Uruguayans—while the Colorados are for encouraging immigration in every way, for the building up of a large and active population, without the slightest regard to racial origins, believing that, once radicated in the country, the whole would weld itself into a complex nationality, such as we see in the making in Argentina.

Meads,
  Eastbourne.

XVIII

OF FOREIGN LANGUAGES AND 'THE INTELLECTUAL LIFE'

To Henry D. Davray

I WONDER if you remember, my dear Davray, the kind things you said in the *Mercure de France* about a certain book of mine years before I had the pleasure of your acquaintance? *La façon dont l'auteur se tire de l'épreuve est digne de tous éloges* . . . these were grateful words concerning an undertaking which in your judgement *était grosse d'embarras et d'obstacles.* But they were more grateful than you could have supposed, for while they were appearing in your sympathetic review of my book, to which I had given, as you realised, *un labeur énorme,* a former colleague of mine, then, as now, and probably to the end of his days, an anonymous paragraphist on a London journal, was sneering and sniffing at it in a shabby review chiefly (as it seemed) because I had not made enough of certain writings and translations of yours. He was no doubt right in pointing to this weakness of my work; but it was merely a stick to beat a dog—a dog that had dared to succeed where the beater had notably failed. That sort of anonymous spite is unfamiliar to your men of letters because of the French custom of signed reviews. And you, who had the best right of complaint, wrote with enthusiasm and kindliest praise of the offender. In later years I trust I have made amends, and you will, I hope, find further assurance of my regard in the inscription of this paper, written in a Latin country geographically remote from France, but intellectually closer to the spirit of France than to that of its own motherland.

It was doubtless Mr. Chesterton who first observed that 'a thing worth doing is worth doing badly'. To learn a foreign language seems to me a thing worth doing, and if you cannot do it well, still it is worth attempting. But there are those who may not agree with me in this opinion.

I was introduced in Buenos Ayres to an American who had spent some three or four years in trying to master the Spanish tongue. So anxious was he to speak only 'the purest Castilian'—a perfect reading knowledge of which he was supposed already to have acquired—that he seldom attempted to utter a word, and preferred to use an interpreter, whose Spanish had no Castilian grace or purity. I later discovered that this gentleman was so indifferent a student and so extremely self-conscious (a synonym for conceited) that any effort of his to speak a simple phrase in Spanish brought great beads of sweat to his forehead and proclaimed him the incompetent he was. In my estimation his literary knowledge

v

of the language did not greatly excel his power of speech therein.

I confess to having but little patience with those who ' know it quite well, but cannot speak it '. One encounters many of this sort here in South America. How often have I been told ' *No puedo hablar inglés, pero lo entiendo muy bien* '. In every such case a perfectly polite reply would be ' *Que mentira !* ' Or, in our homely speech, the brief dialogue might run:

' I can't speak English; but I understand it quite well.'

' What a lie! '

For in Spanish it is not bad manners to tell a gentleman he is lying—and if the gentleman happens to be a South American you are very likely telling him the truth.

Nothing is easier than to persuade oneself that one knows something of a foreign language while remaining in profoundest ignorance of its simplest principles. I recall some ludicrous errors of a good friend who, being hopelessly deficient in the gift of tongues, had acquired a smattering of several. Wayfaring in your pleasant land of France, many a year ago, he enlivened our journey with numerous ' howlers '. For instance (in passing a tiny hamlet ' La Croix Verte '): ' Just fancy calling a place " The True Cross! " ' and (reading a roadside noticeboard which proclaimed ' Pêche reservée '): ' Oh, they grow peaches there! '

It seems to me, however, that even to make an ass of oneself in attempting to speak a foreign tongue

is better than not to try at all. My own method of
gaining confidence in early efforts at conversation
I venture to recommend. Little more than a year
after I began the earnest study of Spanish, I was able
to spend several hours of a memorable afternoon discussing in that tongue the literature of Latin America
with one who was admittedly its most eminent literary
celebrity, so that I may claim to have made more than
ordinary progress. Apart from a certain aptitude
for acquiring a working knowledge of any language
I care to tackle, my rapid progress in the speaking
of Spanish was due largely to a determination to
seize every chance of conversing in that tongue at
no matter what danger of saying ludicrous things.
In the experimental stage, when I had to engage
any native in speech, I began in English and if this
drew a blank ' no comprendo, señor,' I immediately
switched to Spanish, fortified by the knowledge that
I knew much more Spanish than he did English,
and that he, being unable to talk in my native tongue,
must needs be patient with me while I struggled to
explain myself in his. It is surprising what a sense
of self-confidence may thus be gained, whereas by
starting a serious conversation in the unfamiliar
tongue while still in the initial stages of its study,
one is suddenly conscious of degenerating into a worm.
    Moreover, my experience is that all cultured
foreigners take it as a compliment that a visitor to
their country should endeavour to speak to them,
however falteringly, in their own tongue. Nor do
any people in the world behave more politely, more

generously to the foreigner in this respect than those
of the British Isles. There is certainly no people
who more often witness the maltreatment of their
native language.

My thoughts have turned in this direction to-night,
as I chanced, while smoking my after-dinner cigar,
to pick up a copy of ' The Intellectual Life '—famous
work of a more worthy kinsman—which had been
given to my wife by a friend in Buenos Ayres.
Association of ideas probably made me think of you
as I thought of the author. A large part of his fine
literary achievement was to interpret the French to
the English, while you have been the brilliant interpreter of the English to the French. The years
are many since I first read ' The Intellectual Life ',
so that I turned its pages merely to glance through
the chapter headings. Presently I found myself
reading the letters ' To a Student of Modern
Languages ', and dissenting very strongly from the
opinions there set forth. The propositions laid
down in these letters seem to me unsound.

According to their author, an imperfect knowledge
of a language is quite useless as a factor in enriching
the intellectual life and ' a language cannot be learned
by an adult without five years' residence in the
country where it is spoken, and without habits of
close observation a residence of twenty years is
insufficient.' Here indeed is a cheering prospect for
the earnest student who would fain widen his mental
horizon by acquiring some first-hand knowledge of
foreign thinkers. So convinced was Philip Gilbert

Hamerton of the accuracy of his observations that he added: ' This is not encouraging, but it is the truth.'

That is precisely what I decline to admit. Although I have known and spoken French with some fluency since my early twenties, and have been an assiduous reader of French literature, I am far indeed from claiming a ' perfect ' knowledge of that language, and have no hope of approximating to your command of English. Yet I do claim that my knowledge of French has been to me an important instrument of mental culture. That command of any foreign tongue is an absolute essential to the intellectual life I am not so ready to assert, and on this point I may have a thought to set down farther on. Naturally a long-standing knowledge of French and the fact that I could read Italian a little falteringly, have recently proved of immense value in my study of Spanish, just as my school-day (long-since-evaporated) Latin was a help at the outset in the acquirement of French.

What a picturesque liar must George Borrow have appeared to the author of ' The Intellectual Life '! I confess that Borrow's claim to having learned Armenian by studying a New Testament in that language along with one in English has always been an indigestible lump to me. But what of Elihu Burritt and his twenty-nine languages? Burritt was an American; but I would put his sense of honesty higher than Borrow's; nor do I believe he suffered from ' the too common vanity ' of thinking he had come to understand a language which was still a puzzle to him.

The truth is that in this matter of language personal aptitude differs astonishingly. And it requires a much wider intercourse with men than Hamerton possessed in order to formulate conclusions which will stand close examination. For instance, a colleague of mine in Buenos Ayres is a living denial of everything set forth in these letters ' To a Student of Modern Languages '. He speaks English as perfectly as any well-educated Englishman, and without the least small suspicion of ' foreign accent '. He is equally fluent in Spanish and French to my certain knowledge, writing both these languages, as well as English, not merely with grammatical accuracy, but with literary distinction. I have been told by a German that this same linguist speaks German remarkably well; and he has written and corrected literary matter for me in Italian, which passed the test of publication satisfactorily. He can read Portuguese and speak it also, but with less accuracy; and altogether he has a good working knowledge of nine languages. There must necessarily have been exceptional circumstances contributing to such mastery of tongues. This person was born in Paris, where his father held a post in the Spanish embassy, and throughout his childhood he had an English nurse. He grew up with the three languages, speaking all naturally, and thus upsetting Hamerton's proposition that no child can learn more than one language at a time. I have known many other instances to the contrary.

An old colleague of mine on the London press— a countryman of yours, by the way—could speak twelve languages. Among these were included Chinese, Japanese and Persian, from which he made important translations for an encyclopedic work of which I was editor. He spoke English admirably, but not so well as my Buenos Ayres acquaintance, although he wrote nearly two columns of a famous London newspaper every day.

A very eminent Indian judge, who is an authority on Persian literature, assured me that a fortnight was ample time to get a grip of that language. I have a friend who watches England's interests in a far corner of Asia where there is such a babel of tongues that no fewer than fourteen different languages are spoken among his own domestic retinue, and he often sits as a judge in cases where evidence is given in twelve strange tongues, in all which he is sufficiently skilled to follow the story.

These are a few facts of personal knowledge set down merely to indicate what an overwhelming case one could make against the propositions of the author of ' The Intellectual Life ' if that were worth while.

I have met many men before whom, despite my speaking knowledge of three foreign tongues and my reading knowledge of as many more, I have felt a stammering incompetent in this matter of foreign languages, but I have also noticed that a mastery over many tongues does not usually carry with it certain far more precious qualities of mind. On the other hand, it appears to me that to be totally unable to acquire a foreign language, even after many years of opportunity, indicates a certain limitation of mind; at the very least a lack of application.

Among Englishmen there is also a deep-rooted notion that foreigners ought to learn English in order to speak with them. An English vice-consul at Tucumán, in the Argentine, told me he was once in the office there of a leading English merchant, who, having to give some instructions to one of his staff, did so in his own native tongue. The assistant misunderstood the instructions, and the merchant, nettled, turned to his visitor, saying: 'Here have I been for nearly seven years, and these blighters have not learned to speak English yet!'

But, to return to my subject, I submit that a knowledge of a foreign language which may fall very far short of 'perfect' is a most desirable attainment. Although I converse for hours some days in Spanish with complete understanding, I make frequent mistakes, but *I know my mistakes*, and with continued practice these would disappear. There is small likelihood that I shall ever be able to claim a 'perfect' knowledge of the language, in the sense that I might modestly claim to know my native tongue; but I have just finished the reading of 'Gil Blas' in Spanish, and when I think of the rare delight that has given me nearly every evening for two weeks past, I strongly resent the suggestion that my imperfect knowledge of this foreign language has not added to my intellectual pleasures. I have come into a new literary world: I read 'Don Quijote' without the aid of Urquhart, I can follow Calderon and Lopez de Vega in their own sonorous verse, I am making numerous new friends among the brilliant Spanish writers of to-day, and because, forsooth, I always keep an English-Spanish dictionary at my elbow to make clear the occasional cloudy phrase, am I to suppose that all this is not worth while, merely because I did not suck in the language with my mother's milk or marry a dark-eyed señorita from Valladolid?

The author of 'The Intellectual Life' gives some curious instances of persons who forgot languages they had originally known. He also asserts that with children a new language will completely push out an old one. This I do not doubt. There are probably more people in the world to-day who have forgotten Latin than remember it. In my youth I had a fair knowledge of Russian, deliberately and laboriously acquired: to-day I do not even recall the letters of the Russian alphabet.

Before taking up the study of Spanish, the foreign language in which I had most proficiency was French. In my preliminary lessons in Spanish I was continually 'thinking in French', and for a time I could not compose or speak a Spanish sentence which did not contain several French words. This was a surprise, as I had expected my lesser knowledge of Italian to assert itself owing to its closer affinity with Spanish. So it continued for some months, until, by sheer and persistent effort of will, I conquered the inclination to mix my old French with my new Spanish. But with what results? A few

days ago I was called upon to speak in French on
an affair of some importance, and what would have
been a matter of ease and pleasure to me a year ago
proved a task of some trial. Understanding every
word that was spoken to me, I found it impossible
to reply in decent French, as every second word
that came to my tongue was Spanish! The tables
have been turned—I now mix my new and daily more
familiar Spanish with my old, and daily less familiar,
French! I have not arrived at that enviable stage
of adroitness which enables one to change his thoughts
at will from one language into another. Before I
can hope to recapture my old, though inaccurate,
fluency in French I must be able to use the Spanish
absolutely without conscious effort. No doubt a
few weeks in France at any time would restore me
to some fair command of the language.

A peculiarity I have noticed among Englishmen
at home and abroad is the comic habit of reiterating
in a loud voice single words of English when they
have failed or perhaps never attempted to convey
to a foreigner any idea in his native tongue. I
recall an amusing scene at Ostend many years ago.
Two tourists of the 'Arry Belleville type, which
Keane used to satirise so deftly in *Punch*, entered a
café where I was lounging in a corner. One of
them attempted some French phrases which proved
mere gibberish to the waiter. The other, thereupon,
saying ' Let me have a go, Bill,' addressed the waiter.
Shouting in a voice that might have been heard a
street away, he said, with an inquiring look, ' Beer? '

The waiter answered ' *Oui, m'sieu.*' ' Two,' commanded 'Arry in tones of thunder, holding up two stubby fingers to make his meaning plainer. The waiter seemed to comprehend. Next he bellowed ' Bread? ' and made a pretence of eating. Again the waiter's dull foreign brain evidently received the impress of some thought wave. ' Cheese? ' now yelled the sturdy Briton, his face purpling with the effort. ' *Fromage?* ' ventured the waiter timidly, while the patron and several other waiters, who knew English excellently well, were collapsing with mirth in farther corners of the café. 'Arry got what he wanted, and I do not doubt that to this day he tells his friends: ' English is good enough to take you anywhere.'

It is a quaint trait, this of bellowing single words of your native speech to those who do not know it in the hope that excess of sound may in some mysterious way germinate understanding, and I have daily noticed it with quiet amusement in an Irish assistant of mine here in Buenos Ayres, who, with more favourable opportunity for practice than I have enjoyed, can speak Spanish, as a native colleague puts it, only in single words (*en palabras sueltas*).

So far as 'the intellectual life' is concerned, it is easy to over-value a knowledge of foreign languages. The intellectual level of life in the Athens of Socrates and Plato was higher than that of Port Said to-day and yet the current knowledge of alien tongues in Athens was contemptible by comparison. Victor Hugo, though knowing Spanish during his boyhood in Spain, found his native French sufficient to serve him throughout a life in which intellectual activity was maintained at a high pitch.   Anyone born to the heritage of a great European tongue can live a full and fruitful life of the mind without knowing any other language, dead or living; translation has made literature universal.   But a Finn, a Basque, just like an Afghan or an Ethiopian, must acquire a key to world literature by attaining proficiency in one of the great cultural languages of Europe.   No translation can ever carry from one tongue to another the delicate bloom which gave the last touch of beauty to an original masterpiece; but they are the merest coxcombs who love to tell us what we lose in reading a translation.   I know a journalist who is a pretentious liar about his travels.   Having asked you where you went in Algeria or Spain, in Portugal or Peru, he will surely tell you that you should have seen this or that place which was ' worth all the others ' you did see.   You know this type, of course; it is extremely common.   It is next of kin to the conceited literary person who swaggers his superior knowledge by pitying the poor wights who have to be content with translations where he can read in the original.   There is nothing vital in world literature; nothing essential to the fullest measure of intellectual life, that may not be found in English; though it is also true that where the value of the original consisted chiefly in charm of style there may be loss of pleasure in the translation unless this be the work of an equal genius, when—as in ' The Rubaiyat ', let us say—the translation becomes a new and original creation of art.

In Hamerton's book which has set me a-rambling there is not much that would pass for humour, though I think the page which I transcribe below is offered in humorous mood. He tells us that he knew a Frenchman to whom most of our great authors were known, ' even down to the close critical comparison of different readings ':

Aided by the most powerful memory I ever knew, he had amassed such stores that the acquisitions, even of cultivated Englishmen, would in many cases have appeared inconsiderable beside them. But he could not write or speak English in a manner tolerable to an Englishman; and although he knew nearly all the words in the language, it was dictionary knowledge, and so different from an Englishman's apprehension of the same words that it was only a sort of pseudo-English that he knew, and not our living tongue. His appreciation of our authors, especially of our poets, differed so widely from English criticism and English feeling that it was evident he did not understand them as we understand them. Two things especially proved this: he frequently mistook declamatory versification of the most mediocre quality for poetry of an elevated order; whilst, on the other hand, his ear failed to perceive the music of the musical poets, as Byron and Tennyson. How *could* he hear their music, he to whom our English sounds were all unknown? Here, for example, is the way he read ' Claribel ':

> ' At ev ze bittle bommess
>   Azvart ze zeeket lon
> At none ze veeld be ommess
>   Aboot ze most edston
> At meedneeg ze mon commess

An lokez dovn alon
Ere songg ze lintveet svelless
Ze clirvoic-ed mavi dvelless
    Ze fledgling srost lispess
Ze slombroos vav ootvelless
        Ze babblang ronnel creespess
Ze ollov grot replee-ess
Vere Claribel lovlee-ess.'

This will amuse you, my dear Davray, whose
knowledge of English literature is as profound as
Hamerton's of French, of which, by the way, he was
pardonably proud, but more apt to display it than
I have found you to parade your mastery of English.
I would ask you, however, to read aloud the burlesque
Claribel in the most exaggerated ' broken English '
manner and tell me whether the ' music ' of Tennyson
has been utterly lost.   Excluding all sense from the
verses, I find that they may be made quite pleasing
to the ear, as pleasing, indeed, as Russian, French,
or German poetry recited to an audience that knows
no word of it and applauds the reciter solely for the
pleasing nature of the sounds he utters.   Here, I
suggest, the critic has proved the reverse of what
was in his mind; for we have to remember that this
Frenchman knew the meaning of the original words,
and must have derived a high measure of pleasure
from their recital, however ludicrous they appear to
an English eye or sound to an English ear.

Once in Montevideo I had the good fortune to
spend an afternoon in his study with Don Juan
Zorrilla de San Martin, the national poet of Uruguay

and author of ' Tabaré ', an epic poem of the conquest of America, written in a Spanish measure curiously suggestive of ' Hiawatha '. We talked of books and authors. The poet, who had spent two years as Uruguayan Minister in London, was a great reader of English books, and Carlyle—a strange choice for a foreigner—was his favourite author. He was emphatic about the superiority of English to Spanish as an expressive tongue. And he quoted from Shakespeare an example of the splendid directness of our speech. It was the only English phrase used in our conversation and it sounded thus:

Fryltee tienime ees ooman

I looked incredulous and ventured the suggestion that I thought the Spanish would be quite as expressive, whereupon, to my relief, he put it into Spanish, but would not allow that it ran so well:

Fragilidad, tu nombre es mujer!

And thus I came by the English:

Frailty, thy name is woman!

of which the Spanish is a literal and, to my ear, an equally sonorous rendering. And the moral of this? Well, I think I have suggested it above in my comment upon Hamerton's Frenchman.

Concerning ' The Intellectual Life ' itself I would like to add a word or two, although probably that

work is better known to you than to the common
English reader of to-day.   It had a great and deserved
vogue in the later Victorian era, and must have been
a valuable source of self-culture to many thousands
throughout the English-reading world; but it is
strangely distant from the temper of these later
times.   The desire ' to be done good to ', the wish
for ' uplift ', has passed in England, though it is
still rampant in the United States, where every form
of ' improving ' literature has a ready sale.   That
attitude of mind is requisite to the right reading of
' The Intellectual Life '.   If we approach it in the
cynical spirit of our age we find it unconsciously
humorous.   ' To an Author in Mortal Disease ',
' To a Moralist who said that Intellectual Culture
was not conducive to Sexual Morality ', ' To a Country
Gentleman who regretted that his Son had the
Tendencies of a Dilettant ', ' To a Lady who lamented
that her Son had Intellectual Doubts concerning the
Dogmas of the Church ', ' To a Young Gentleman
of Intellectual Tastes, who, without having as yet
any Particular Lady in view, had expressed, in a
general way, his Determination to Get Married '—
these are a few characteristic titles of the seventy-one
' letters ' which the work comprises.   They raise a
smile to-day.   We are certainly more sophisticated
than in 1873, when they were written.

And yet I like the book and hope still to spend
some more profitable hours with it, as I find the
author so urbane, so unfailingly sincere, so leisured
and often so sensible, that I feel ' The Intellectual

Life' can go into the category of companionable books, despite its avowed intention, its *malice prepense* 'to do good' to its reader. There is no literary bore comparable with him who seeks to improve his readers, and that P. G. Hamerton can show the cloven hoof of the intellectual improver in every chapter heading and still remain readable implies a triumph of authorship.

'The Intellectual Life' also does a service to Victorianism. It is Victorian in the good sense of revealing a reflective mind that could take serious views of life, exhibiting a wise toleration and wide sympathy with one's fellows in their progress tomb-wards. In the trite phrase, these earnest Victorians, according to their lights, were intent on 'leaving the world better than they found it'. Perhaps, shorn of rhetoric, what they were really after was to acquire so much knowledge by the way that they would leave this world with such a store as would give them a better start in some unknown world whither they were journeying. The pursuit of knowledge for its own sake is something very different and more commendable than 'art for art's sake'.

I had laid these pages aside some weeks ago, intending to 'write in' a few words about one of the most remarkable linguists of my acquaintance: a strange little man of extraordinary gifts, my friend of twelve years in London. He was a Wesleyan minister, but dissenting on some points, never quite clear to me, from the beliefs of that body, lived an independent religious life for many years. Languages

x

were the passion of his life, and I believe he was proficient in French, German, Norwegian, Italian, Russian, Greek and Latin, and from all these he made translations for different editorial enterprises under my care. Nor did these represent the sum of his linguistic attainments; they were merely those in which I had occasion to call for his literary help. Most likely he knew Spanish also. He was in North America when I sailed from England, and I have often looked forward to talking over my South American experiences with him on my return; to discussing the very subject that occupies these pages. But yesterday was ' Mail Day ' and I got my *Times Weekly Edition*, in the obituary column of which I read with sorrow: ' The Rev. William Durban, B.A., a Wesleyan minister: sometime English editor of the *Homiletic Review*, aged 71.'

That was all to tell me that another friend of mine would not be in his old familiar haunts when I came back to Fleet Street. Durban was one of the quietest and least pretentious of literary men, endowed with great gifts, which, owing to his utter lack of ambition, were never pressed to full issue. With all his stores of learning he was accounted worthy of one line and a half of small type in the *Times*. Yet sometimes noisy nobodies, by the simple act of dying, attain to half a column or more in the Valhalla of its obituary columns.

Calle San Martin,
    Buenos Ayres.

XIX

OF CHRISTMAS AND DRAGON-FLIES

To T. Athol Joyce

IT is Christmas Day, in the afternoon. The fiery summer sun is contending with the cool sea-wind for the fate of the green plane trees that deck the plaza, upon which my turret window opens. The sea breeze is still match enough for the Christmas sun and keeps up a gentle stirring of the leaves so that they shimmer in white fleckings and promise to hold their freshness for some time yet, while myriads of glittering dragon-flies, like tiniest aeroplanes, dart on aimless wings athwart the sunny spaces.

It is the day of good will to all mankind, and I am saying to myself that I am a good hater. My dislikes have always endured in my memory—but indeed I have a memory so retentive that my difficulty has ever been to forget rather than to recall. By some odd chance to-day, looking out across the pleasant city of Montevideo to the oily, glistering waters of the River Plate, I find myself thinking of one of the least pleasing personages of modern times —the late Thomas de Witt Talmage.

I never saw that man, but his impudent, self-satisfied face has often stared at us all from some hoarding or newspaper when he used to go a-preaching for dollars, and even since he has gone where no dollars are; for he has left, like our own Spurgeon, enormous quantities of rubbishy philosophisings for posthumous exploitation. As a boy I used to read some of his sermons ' for fun ', and remember to-day how distinctly my youthful common sense was offended by a discourse of his on ' Christmas '.

He began by telling his dear hearers how, all his life, he had thought it a beautiful thing that Jesus was a Christ of the snow-time. That He had not been born in the golden days of summer when life was easier and most people were happy. That He had come to gladden the earth when the roads were miry and the snows lay thick and the gloom of winter had descended upon the land!

Ere I read that quaint comment on the first Christmas, I had seen many a fine ship sail away from Glasgow docks bound for South America, and with them all my thoughts sailed too. Just as Tennyson in boyhood was strongly affected by the mere repetition of the words ' Far, far away ', so I recall most vividly how, at Sunday School in the old Barony Church of Glasgow—where, in an earlier epoch, the great Norman Macleod lashed the follies of his times—I used to be stirred by the liveliest emotions when we sang together:

Had I the wings of a dove I would fly
Far, far away, far, far away,
Where never a cloud ever darkens the sky,
Far, far away.

And as we sang, my memory visualised clearer than in any photograph a full-rigged merchantman, seen by me when a boy of eight or nine, somewhere off the Kyles of Bute, heading out to sea, ' bound for South Ameriky ', as I was told by the kind old ' auntie ' who had taken me for a sail in the ' Hero ' —where, I wonder, are the worthy bones of that antique Clyde steamer resting now?

Of course I knew where South America was, as did any boy who had been taught his geography at the excellent school of Daniel Macmillan in the Duke Street of Glasgow, facing the grim old prison, where they had some wholesome hangings in my time —on which interesting occasions we boys were prohibited from being in the neighbourhood of the school until the solemn ceremony was over; a restriction the more keenly felt when the janitor confessed to some of us elder lads that he had gone up to the tower of the school, which commanded the inner courts of the prison, and had been able to see ' very nearly ' to the top of the scaffold, ' just as the black flag was run up '.

We knew that ' South Ameriky ' was away down there, beyond the Kyles of Bute and ever so much farther. We knew that Christmas there was the hottest season of the year, because it was on the other side of the equator—that ' menagerie lion that runs

all round the middle of the earth ', as the school girl
had once described it.   Hence, when I came to the
reading of ' the Christ of the snow-time ', I had a
proper contempt for the parochial mind that could
conceive so limited a notion of a world-event.

There is nobody so parochial as a certain type of
Yankee, unless it be the average South American.
It is curious that to cultivate a narrow, bigoted notion
of the earth, the ideal environment is a land of
mighty distances.   Down here in South America,
where one individual owns an estate more extensive
than an English county, the narrowness of the
native outlook is astounding.   Our small ' surge-
vexed ' islands in these northern seas have given
us Britons an outlook that is incomparably wider
than that of any people who dwell in the midst of
great spaces.   The endless plains of the Argentine
oppress and draw the minds of those whose lot it
is to dwell thereon; the mighty distances of North
America leave the inland native with the dim impression that on the selvedges of his land the world ends.
Before the penny postage was established between
Britain and the United States, many thousands of
letters were sent every year to England by Americans
who thought that an inland stamp would carry them.
That is true parochialism.   Surely no Englishman
ever deliberately posted a letter to America with a
penny stamp, in the tuppence ha'penny days!   He
knew that there were seas to be crossed, great distances to be traversed, to deliver his missive; and he
supposed the cost would be greater than sending it

from Balham to Birmingham. The sea enlarges the
mental vision; the land dwarfs it. The thoughts of
Englishmen are bosomed on the sea; and thus I
hold that ' insularism ' is one of the stupidest stigmas
ever fastened on the land I love. It took a Yankee's
parochial brain to conceive a universal Redeemer
being born ' in the snow-time '.

But it is Christmas Day; so I must endeavour to
forget that the name of Talmage is a peculiar irritant
to me. Here, in a land where all North Americans
—the good suffering for the bad—are objects of
some distrust, one need simply catalogue him
among his race and so dismiss him. Nay, one can
almost be charitable to him; for it is curious how
we are tempted to charity even against our better
judgment, when local opinion is adverse! At
home, where I lived alongside of Americans without
finding them better or worse than the average
humanity, there was always a tendency to look
upon them with suspicion; here, where the very
name ' Norte Americano ' carries something of contempt, and one might find cause to share that
contempt, I find myself more tolerant. I do not
think this is due to the bond of language, for the
speech of many ' Norte Americanos ' encountered in
these latitudes seems about as remote from English as
the Spanish. Doubtless it is mere perverseness.

I have also felt more charitable since I fared forth
into the glowing afternoon, and, wandering by the
docks, watched the crew of H.M.S. ' Glasgow '
diverting themselves on board that trim little cruiser,

whose presence in South American waters has touched
to new issues of patriotism the grey lives of the
exiles ' in these parts '. There is something very
comforting in standing among a crowd of foreigners
by the quayside, some seven thousand miles from
home, observing the movements of one's com-
patriots, and, above all, listening to the friendly
tongue.

To-day, however, there was a little touch of disappointment for me. In the speech of the Jack Tars
there was a painful paucity of ' h's ', and never a
hint of the real, right ' Glesca ' accent. To one who
once looked on Glasgow as his home, there is
something unnatural in a ship named ' Glasgow '
being manned by h-less Englishmen.

Another and greater disappointment was in store.
By an odd freak the winds of fate had blown that
fine old sailing ship ' Clyde ' across the far seas to
berth beside the ' Glasgow ' in this harbour of
Montevideo. I was rejoiced at the happy touch
which this gave to my Christmas stroll by the dock-
side. So straightway at home did I feel, in this
conjunction of names once dear to me, that I should
have been sorely tempted to engage some of the crew
of the ' Clyde ' in ' guid braid Scots ', had there been
any of them visible. But, figure my disillusionment
when, on looking at the stern of the wind-jammer
to see if she were registered at Glasgow or Greenock,
I found she hailed from Sarpsborg, and was flying
the Norwegian merchant flag, which, at a distance, I
had mistaken for the Union Jack. Her figure-head

was a Highland chief, probably none other than the bold Rob Roy!

'Ma Conscience!' as the Bailie might have said, 'it maun be unco hearing when they jabbering buddies frae Norroway gabble the name of their ship!' Is this, then, the fate of many a fine old clipper that has set sail out of Clyde for a generation or more—to be turned over to some Norwegian company who scratch out Glasgow or Greenock from the stern and paint thereon in crude letters of white the heathenish names of their outlandish ports of register? Other wind-jammers in the harbour made me think so. An ex-winner of the Derby in the shafts of a frowsy suburban cab were no more sorry sight.

I leave the quayside, having had once more the old lesson, that appearances are deceptive and things are not always what they seem.

Certainly, this does not seem like Christmas Day. Nowhere is there the least small sign of rejoicing. But that is to be expected, as these South Americans are the most joyless races I have ever studied. The heat of the day has given place to that cool evening breeze which makes Montevideo one of the most naturally healthy towns in the world; the dragon-flies no longer dart to and fro in the plaza; the night is falling quickly—ah! there is no gloaming here— and the town will presently be as dead as a little French village, save for the ceaseless rattle of the seemingly superfluous electric trams—many of them carrying no more than a solitary 'nigger'. Presently

my wife and I will go down to our lonely dinner in the
hotel, then back to our lonely sitting-room, to look out
once more from its turret windows on the little plaza;
but with eyes that will see nothing there, yet, for
to-night, will see seven thousand miles away as clear
as noonday, and will peep in on cosy hearths where
good British coal is glowing and touching with
heightened friendliness the dear faces of the folks
at home.

Try as one may—and I have tried with clenched
teeth—it is no easy matter for the British-born, far
from home, to bar the door against sentiment on
Christmas Day, even when the thermometer has
risen above ninety in the shade.

Plaza Matriz,
    Montevideo.

INDEX

331